Voices from the Delaware Big House Ceremony

THE CIVILIZATION OF THE AMERICAN INDIAN SERIES

Interior of the Big House. Oklahoma Delaware Annual Ceremony, 1912. Painting by Earnest Spybuck. Accession Number 3/2720. Courtesy National Museum of the American Indian.

Voices from the Delaware Big House Ceremony

Edited by ~ *Robert S. Grumet*

Volume Consultants   *John Bierhorst*
                      James A. Rementer

New Contributions   *Bruce L. Pearson*
                      Terry J. Prewitt

Commentaries   *Ruthe Blalock Jones*
                      Delaware, Shawnee, and Peoria tribes

                      Marlene Molly Miller
                      Stockbridge-Munsee Tribe of Mohican Indians

                      Michael Pace
                      Eastern Oklahoma Delaware Tribe

                      Darryl Stonefish
                      Moraviantown Band of Delaware Indians

University of Oklahoma Press : Norman

ALSO BY ROBERT S. GRUMET

Native Americans of the Northwest Coast: A Critical Bibliography (Bloomington, 1979)

Native American Place Names in New York City (New York, 1981)

The Lenapes (New York, 1989)

Historic Contact: Indian People and Colonists in Today's Northeastern United States in the Sixteenth Through Eighteenth Centuries (Norman, 1995)

Northeastern Indian Lives, 1632 to 1816 (editor) (Amherst, 1996)

Journey on the Forbidden Path: Chronicles of a Diplomatic Mission to the Allegheny Country, March–September, 1760 (editor) (Philadelphia, 1999)

Library of Congress Cataloging-in-Publication Data

Voices from the Delaware big house ceremony / edited by Robert S. Grumet ; volume consultants, John Bierhorst and James A. Rementer ; new contributions by Bruce L. Pearson . . . [et al.].
   p. cm.
   Includes bibliographical references and index.
   ISBN 978-0-8061-6312-3 (paper)
   1. Big House Ceremony (Delaware rite)   2. Delaware Indians—Rites and ceremonies.
   3. Delaware Indians—Religion.   4. Delaware mythology.   I. Grumet, Robert Steven.

E99.D2 V65 2002
299'.74—dc21

2001027570

Voices from the Delaware Big House Ceremony is Volume 239 in The Civilization of the American Indian Series.

The paper in this book meets the guidelines for permanence and durability of the Committee on Production Guidelines for Book Longevity of the Council on Library Resources, Inc. ∞

Copyright © 2001 by the University of Oklahoma Press, Norman, Publishing Division of the University. All rights reserved. Paperback published 2019. Manufactured in the U.S.A.

In Memory of Richard Snake

Contents

	List of Illustrations	ix
	Preface	xi
	Acknowledgments	xvii
	Pronunciation Guide, *Bruce L. Pearson*	xix
	Delaware Commentaries, *Ruthe Blalock Jones, Marlene Molly Miller, Michael Pace, and Darryl Stonefish*	xxi
INTRODUCTION	The Big House Described, *Terry J. Prewitt*	3
CHAPTER 1	The Earliest Accounts, 1655–1780	23
CHAPTER 2	Beate and the White River Revival, 1805–1806	38
CHAPTER 3	Mid-Nineteenth-Century Accounts	49
CHAPTER 4	Richard C. Adams's Accounts, 1890 and 1904	55
CHAPTER 5	Eastern Oklahoma Delaware Big House Ceremonies, 1907–1910	61
CHAPTER 6	Canadian Munsee Big House Ceremonies, 1907–1910	79
CHAPTER 7	Charlie Elkhair's Text, 1912	87
CHAPTER 8	The Charlie Webber [Wi.tapano'xwe] Text of the Oklahoma Delaware Big House Ceremony, 1928	95
CHAPTER 9	Additional Notes to the Big House Ceremony, 1937	116
CHAPTER 10	The Nicodemus Peters [Nekatcit] Account, 1945	126
CHAPTER 11	Lula Mae Gibson Gilliland's Account, 1947	147
CHAPTER 12	Eastern Oklahoma Delaware Reminiscences, 1972–1994	151
CHAPTER 13	Nora Thompson Dean's Accounts of the Eastern Oklahoma Unami Delaware Big House, 1973–1984	180
APPENDIX	Delaware and English Names of People Referred to in the Texts	195
	Glossary	197
	Bibliography	201
	Index	206

Illustrations

FIGURES

	Interior of the Copan Big House, Eastern Oklahoma Delaware Annual Ceremony, 1912	*frontispiece*
1.	Plan of the Big House and camp	9
2.	Dancing patterns associated with vision recitations	11
3.	Generational roles of the Big House Ceremony	15
4.	Ceremonial fire drill	63
5.	Box-turtle-shell rattle	66
6.	Eastern Oklahoma–style deerskin drum	66
7.	Sacred drumsticks, plain drumstick, and prayer stick	69
8.	Carved wooden Mïsi'ngwe mask	74
9.	Munsee-style deerskin drum	81
10.	Charlie Elkhair	88
11.	Charlie Webber	96
12.	Artist's conception of the Boston Creek Big House near Hagersville, Ontario, ca. 1850	129
13.	Floor plan of the Munsee-Mahican Big House	132
14.	Turtle-shell rattles and replica of a wooden hand rattle used by vision reciters	137
15.	Folded hide drum and beaters	139
16.	Nora Thompson Dean	181

MAPS

1.	The Delawares and Their Neighbors, ca. 1650	2
2.	Delaware Diaspora, 1600–2000	6
3.	Delawares on the Advancing Frontier, 1650–1850	7
4.	Kansas and Oklahoma Delaware Communities, 1829–2001	12

Preface

Spirituality suffused every aspect of the lives and cultures of the Delawares, Munsees, Mahicans, Conoys, and other Coastal Algonquian people whose homelands stretch across today's Middle Atlantic seaboard from New York Harbor to Chesapeake Bay. In this they were not unusual; all people have a sense of spiritual awe, an awareness of something intangible but more vast that lies beyond human understanding. These things give guidance and meaning to everyday life. Coastal Algonquians expressed their particular sense of this in ceremonies giving thanks to spirits for gifts of power and protection.

Attacked by missionaries and Native converts, suppressed by government agencies, and seemingly unable to halt the devastations of disease, dispossession, and the disappearance of deer, bears, and other game animals crucial to their continuation, traditional Coastal Algonquian religions gradually disappeared. Knowledge necessary for their preservation mostly died with elders. Some information on traditional rituals such as the Green Corn Ceremony and the Doll Dance has survived (Kraft 1986; Miller 1976; Speck 1937; Witthoft 1949). More is known about the ways Delawares and other Coastal Algonquians adopted and adapted new religions such as Christianity and the Native American Church (Newcomb 1956b; Petrullo 1934).

Today the Big House Religion, known to its adherents as the Gamwing, is the only intensively documented expression of traditional Delaware religious belief. Although both scholars and present-day Delaware people debate its origins, structure, and symbolic meanings, all concerned generally agree that the Big House Religion developed into its chronicled form only after the Delawares were forced from their homeland. And, although attempts to revive it continue, they also agree that the ceremony's last full traditional rites were, as its adherents say, "brought in" by the Eastern Oklahoma Delaware community in 1924. Much of what we know about the ceremony today survives only because the last knowledgeable elders chose to pass these traditions on to a few dedicated chroniclers in the belief that the knowledge would benefit future generations.

The vagaries of time and circumstance brought Big House elders together with young men such as Mark Raymond Harrington, Frank G. Speck, Truman Michelson, and other members of America's first generation of professional anthropologists. Unlike earlier chroniclers, who tended to view Delaware and other Indian traditions as savage customs or doomed curiosities, the anthropologists tried to document cultural knowledge dispassionately. Different goals motivated the elders and the ethnographers. The elders tried to preserve knowledge for their descendants. Anthropologists wanted information needed to develop vast cross-cultural data banks required to construct and test models capable of increasing scientific understanding of human behavior.

Anthropology is not only an exercise in scholarly detachment, however. Deeper intellectual understanding also leads to greater appreciation. University of Pennsylvania ethnographer Frank Speck, for example, was moved to write that the Delaware Indian Big House Ceremony possessed "riches of religious imagination, symbolism, art in music and dance" (Speck and Moses 1945: viii). He and succeeding generations of scholars affirmed what Delaware elders and traditionalists have always known: that the Big House, by combining moral lessons with expressions of thanksgiving and prayer, is a defining ritual affirmation of a people's beliefs, concerns, and values. As the ceremonial embodiment of a unique Northeastern Indian way of life, the Gamwing ranks in significance with the Iroquois Longhouse Religion and the Midewiwin of the Great Lakes Indian nations.[1]

This book brings most of the Big House texts, narratives, and accounts together in a single volume for the first time. Some of these sources—such as Charlie Elkhair's account, recorded by Truman Michelson in 1912; Lula Mae Gibson Gilliland's history of the Big House Church, submitted to the Smithsonian Institution in 1947; and Ruthe Blalock Jones's 1972 and 1973 interviews of Eastern Oklahoma Delaware Big House elders—are unpublished manuscripts printed here for the first time. Others are published sources issued in limited runs, printed by scholarly presses, or published in difficult-to-find scholarly journals or monographs. Almost all are entirely out of print and only readily available in large research libraries or collections not easily accessible to most readers.

Many voices speak from these pages. The book begins with commentaries by Delaware traditionalists from communities in Oklahoma, Wisconsin, and Ontario, where most descendants of the members of the Delaware Big House Church live today. They are followed by the writing of a major scholar of the Big House, University of West Florida anthropologist Terry J. Prewitt, who presents a detailed ethnographic description of the ceremony based upon his own fieldwork in Oklahoma and his analysis of many of the earlier texts, notes, and other accounts published there. The earliest of these texts, dating from the seventeenth

---

1. See Tooker (1979) for a comprehensive overview of Eastern Woodland Indian spirituality. Particularly useful descriptions of the Iroquois Longhouse Religion can be found in Tooker (1970) and A. F. C. Wallace (1969: 3–18). Classic accounts of the Midewiwin include Hoffman (1891) and Landes (1968).

and eighteenth centuries, give voice to the impressions of Europeans unfamiliar with or unsympathetic to Delaware culture and religion. Later, during the nineteenth century, voices of highly acculturated, literate Delawares such as Richard C. Adams and pioneer ethnographers such as Lewis Henry Morgan join in. These are followed by the voices of Charlie Elkhair, George Tom Anderson, Nicodemus Peters, and other elders speaking through the anthropologists who recorded their knowledge during the early decades of the twentieth century. The book ends with the nostalgic voices of people who were young when the last full Big House Ceremony was "brought in" in 1924.

The many voices brought together in this book produce something more akin to a chorus than a chant. Certain elements, such as visions, songs and dances of the visionaries, and prayers of thanksgiving, emerge as major themes, lending unity and continuity to the whole. Differing personal perspectives, changes over time, and contrasts among rites in different places—such as variations in the number of days devoted to observances and the salient spiritual role of deer in the Oklahoma rite and bear in Ontario—provide sharp contrasts.

Continuity and change can be viewed in two ways. On one hand, stability can be seen as stagnation and change can be regarded as evidence of chaotic disintegration. On the other, stability can be seen as the persistence of core values and differences, even as dynamic responses to changing conditions. Instead of searching for, and decrying, contradictions and inconsistencies, I believe it makes more sense to try to understand differences, similarities, and changes in Big House practices as parts of a long path of evolutionary adaptation that has formed, informed, and enriched Delaware spirituality.

Such issues spark current debates centering upon the ceremony's origins and antiquity. More than half a century ago, anthropologist W. Vernon Kinietz suggested that the Big House was a syncretic religion deeply influenced by Christianity (Kinietz 1940). In a widely cited article published nearly twenty years later, University of Pennsylvania anthropologist Anthony F. C. Wallace, a student of Frank Speck, identified the Big House as a revitalization of existing Delaware beliefs (Wallace 1956). Affirming the ceremony's syncretic nature, Wallace proposed that the Big House, as practiced by nineteenth-century Delaware and Munsee communities in Ontario and Oklahoma, represented a revised version of traditional Delaware beliefs and ceremonies developed by a Munsee prophet in 1805. Known only by her Moravian German name Beate ("beatific"), a relic of the time she spent as a convert in the Susquehanna Valley mission town of Friedenshüetten, Pennsylvania, the prophet was living among other exiled Delawares in Indiana at the time she began preaching about the wisdom received in her vision.

Most recently, anthropologist Jay Miller (1997) has challenged this widely accepted interpretation of the origins of the Big House. One of the most active scholars presently studying Delaware Indian belief systems,[2] Miller approaches the

---

2. See Miller (1979) and (1980).

issue from a structural perspective in which religions and other cultural institutions represent a unique gestalt, or mix, whose identity is altered when constituent elements change. Miller begins by disputing the validity of Kinietz's interpretation. Then, asserting that the stability of major thematic elements suggests great antiquity, he criticizes Wallace for suggesting that the Big House Beate "invented" (a term never used by Wallace) replaced the earlier Green Corn Ceremony. Whether or not the Big House replaced an earlier rite, it is clear that Wallace does not regard structural changes in the Big House as the invention of a completely new religion supplanting old beliefs. His identification of the Big House as what he calls a "New" religion instead reflects his view that it was an innovative adaptation of existing traditional beliefs to new and difficult circumstances.

Big houses are mentioned in some of the earliest extant written records documenting Delaware Indian life. Perhaps the first pictorial representation of such a structure was drawn at the time of a raid on the Delaware town of Kittanning in the modern city of the same name on the eastern banks of the Allegheny River in western Pennsylvania. The drawing was probably made by Col. John Armstrong, who led the force of three hundred Pennsylvania militia that attacked and burned Kittanning on September 8, 1756, at the height of the Seven Years' War in America (1754–62). A note on the map states that the drawing was based on information provided by John Baker, a soldier who had escaped captivity at Kittanning several months earlier.

A "Long House," located in the center of the drawing, is noted as being thirty feet in length. A caption below it states that it is the place "where the frolicke and War Dances are held." C. A. Weslager, who published a photograph of the sketch in his book, *The Delaware Indian Westward Migration* (Weslager 1978: 6–7), suggests that the building may have been a Big House. Whatever it was called, the "Long House" in the sketch was a big Delaware building specifically devoted to frolics and war dances after the collapse of Pennsylvania's Quaker peace policy.

Other big Delaware houses, sometimes decorated with carved images, had been mentioned in earlier records. As Jay Miller (1997: 121) points out, in 1650, Adriaen van der Donck noted the presence of "rough carvings of faces and images ... in the houses of chiefs."[3] Neither this account, Jasper Danckaerts's 1679 description of the longhouse at Nayack in present-day Brooklyn (in James and Jameson 1913: 54–57), nor any other known contemporary archival material or archaeological evidence specifically documents center poles, ritually cleared oval dance floors, or other unequivocally identifiable features uniquely associated with the historically chronicled Big House.

Old or new, most of the evidence of the Big House Religion lies in the written records, and much of this material is gathered here. The presentation of the material in this book is straightforward. The introduction, a new and updated version of an earlier published general description of the Oklahoma Delaware Big

---

3. From the "Representation of New Netherland, 1650," published in Jameson (1909: 302).

House (see Prewitt 1981: 48–71) written for this volume by Terry J. Prewitt, serves two functions. First, it briefly describes the Big House and some of the major issues involving its origins, functions, and structure that are debated by scholars. Second, it introduces and describes the historical and social context of each of the accounts presented in the book. The introduction is followed by thirteen chapters presenting key Delaware Big House texts in chronological order. These are followed by a glossary containing all Delaware words and a list of personal names mentioned in the accounts published here. All citations are keyed to a bibliography at the end of the book.

However one views the accounts documenting the Big House, few today will disagree with John Bierhorst's eloquent assessment of Delaware traditions: "Looking back over the entire record, spanning 337 years from 1655 to 1992, a vibrant, persistent tradition emerges, obscured in part by faulty transmission and long silences, yet rich in textual detail and eminently worthy of future study" (Bierhorst 1995: 17). It is this tradition that is documented in the chronicles gathered in this book. Echoing Bierhorst, I can only hope that the knowledge preserved in these pages will stimulate future study by both Delawares intent upon recovering ancient traditions and others interested in better understanding human spirituality.

EDITORIAL NOTE

All texts are presented as they appear in their original forms. Vision songs and personal prayers considered sacred by Delaware people are not reproduced in this book. A new notation system has been prepared. Footnotes in the original sources have been updated, abridged, or otherwise revised and appear as footnotes. Proper nouns appear as they were recorded. Minor punctuation errors have been corrected and added words inserted within brackets. Paragraph breaks have been inserted to separate particularly long passages, and orthographic infelicities such as "accross," "pardner," and "the" in place of "they" have been changed to conform to current usage.

Acknowledgments

Many people generously gave their time and energy to make this book happen. Foremost among these is University of Oklahoma Press director, John Drayton, who has seen the project through from its beginning. Thanks are also due to the Press's Native American Studies acquisitions editor, Jeff Burnham, and his assistant, Shelia L. Buckley. Special thanks go to Darryl Stonefish, who suggested the potential usefulness of an accessible collection of Big House texts. Thanks also to Darryl and other Delaware traditionalists who were kind enough to provide needed guidance and write accounts describing what the Big House means to their communities today.

Volume consultants John Bierhorst, Bruce L. Pearson, Terry J. Prewitt, and James A. Rementer provided text, data, and critical comments. John gave me excellent advice and pointed out important sources. Jim sent photocopies and computerized text files of unpublished materials and checked up on the renderings and translations of the Delaware words and names appearing in the texts. Bruce provided transcriptions and wrote the pronunciation guide for Delaware words. Terry went the extra mile, granting permission to revise and print his excellent ethnographic description of the Big House, first published in 1981. Mary Davis, formerly of the Huntington Memorial Library, Cecile Gantaume of the National Museum of the American Indian, and Robert Leopold of the National Anthropological Archives provided assistance. The three scholars who provided critical readings of the manuscript for the University of Oklahoma Press gave me useful guidance.

The National Park Service provided the block of time in which to complete this book as a partnership project with the Delaware people. Special thanks go to Bonnie Halda, Chief, Stewardship and Partnerships Branch of the Philadelphia Support Office. Thanks are also due to the following individuals and institutions kind enough to grant permission to publish materials in the book: Charles A. Bello, Editor, Bulletin of the Archaeological Society of New Jersey; Pamela Bennett, Director, Indiana Historical Bureau; Ellen Goodman, Syracuse University Press; George Hanlin, Assistant Editor, Indiana Historical Society; Chris Herbert, Rights and Permissions Assistant, University of Michigan Press; Ann Kawasaki,

National Museum of the American Indian; the late Herbert C. Kraft, Director, Seton Hall University Museum; Carole Lefaivre-Rochester, Editor, American Philosophical Society (retired); Diana Peirsel, Paulist Press; Diane B. Reed, Chief of Publications, Pennsylvania Historical and Museum Commission; R. Michael Stewart, Editor, Pennsylvania Archaeologist; Kim Wahl, Office Manager, William and Mary Quarterly; and Deborah Winkler, Reading Public Museum.

The texts presented here only survive because Delaware people and a few interested scholars were determined to preserve them. Like the Delaware elders and their scholarly amanuenses past and present, I hope the wisdom preserved through these texts will continue to inform, inspire, and inspirit future generations.

Pronunciation Guide

Bruce L. Pearson

The Delaware language has survived into modern times, with a Munsee variety spoken in Ontario and a Unami variety in Oklahoma. Speakers of both dialects refer to their language as Delaware (in English) or Lenape (pronounced as a three-syllable word with an accent on the second syllable in their own language).

Several challenges confront those involved in transcribing and translating Delaware words. Although Delaware remained the sole language of the Big House up to its last full observance in 1924, many surviving speakers have forgotten older terms. Pronunciations of Delaware words in texts and narratives must often be inferred from imperfect or inaccurate spellings.

Although chroniclers over the years have used several spelling systems to represent Delaware words, no single standardized writing system has been adopted by all Delaware people. Early commentators, most of whom had difficulty expressing certain sounds in the Delaware language, used their own language's spelling systems to represent Delaware words. More recently, linguists using the International Phonetic Alphabet to transcribe the Delaware language have not always agreed upon precise word sounds or forms. These difficulties can partly be traced to differences between the Munsee and Unami dialects. While closely related, the two dialects could be considered separate languages, differing from one another much as Spanish differs from Portuguese.

Working together, linguists and Eastern Oklahoma Delaware speakers have experimented with three schemes for writing the language. Each approach provides a way to distinguish the language's thirteen vowels (including two dipthongs) and thirteen consonants.

The first of these, used in tribal language classes, utilizes a combination of familiar English alphabetic symbols modified by less readily understood diacritic marks to represent Delaware vowels:

i	ì			ë			ù	u
e	è	ay	à	a	aw	ò	o	

The second approach utilizes International Phonetic Alphabet symbols familiar to linguists but unclear to anyone else:

i	ì					ʊ	u
e	ɛ	ay	ʌ	a	aw	ɔ	o

The third system, influenced by a scheme developed by Munsee people in Ontario, uses multiple English alphabet vowel symbols (with the exception of _, for which no satisfactory equivalent has yet been found) to indicate the longer duration of many vowel sounds in the Delaware language:

ii	i					u	uu
ee	e	ay	a	aa	aw	o	oo

The tribe uses the following system to represent consonants:

p	t	č	k
m	n		
	s	š	x	h
	l		
w		y	

Each of the familiar symbols matches its equivalent English phonetic value. č represents the ch sound as in church, š the sh sound as in shoe, and x the sound of ch as in German Buch or Bach. Seven of the consonants (p, t, č, k, s, š, and x) are voiced following the sound n.

Delaware Commentaries

Ruthe Blalock Jones   Delaware, Shawnee, and Peoria tribes

I had heard of the Delaware Big House Ceremony all of my life from my mother, Lucy Parks Blalock, my aunts, and others. I enjoyed listening to the grownups talk about the traditions, the events of the old days, and the Big House people, all now deceased. I was always interested in the old Indian ways and, as an artist, particularly in how they could be recorded and preserved through drawing and painting.

Most of the interviews published in this book are from texts I gathered in 1972 and 1973 through a research grant awarded to me while I was a graduate student in anthropology, under the direction of Professor Garrick Bailey, at the University of Tulsa. The full report, entitled *Hi'ngwikan: Delaware Big House Ceremony*, preserves transcribed oral accounts from many of the last of the living traditionalists who attended the final full meeting of the Delaware Big House near Copan, Oklahoma, in 1924. Some of these speakers also told of attending an abbreviated six-day-long meeting held in 1945, during World War II, in a tent at Mrs. Minnie Fouts's Post Oak home, just north of Dewey, Oklahoma.

Most of the traditionalists I interviewed were full-blood Lenapes who spoke the language. At the time of the interviews, they lived in and around the Washington County locales of Dewey and Bartlesville, and in Tulsa. My mother, a devoted Lenape traditionalist, lived in Quapaw in nearby Ottawa County. She and the other interviewees were tribal members descended from Lenape people who had been compelled to remove from Kansas to Indian Territory in 1866. All of the people I interviewed were descendants of leaders or active members in the last meetings of the Big House.

Each of these men and women were familiar with the writings of anthropologists Frank G. Speck and Mark Raymond Harrington, and many of them knew one or both of these scholars personally. At that time, they were the younger generation. Most were students in boarding or residential schools, and all had to take the time from their studies and household chores to attend Big House Ceremonies with their elders.

Everyone I interviewed spoke with me about their memories of the Big House Ceremony while I was a guest in their homes, and all of them also graciously allowed me to take their photographs. All were well known to me and my family, and many were relatives.

I was deeply moved by the faith and trust these elders showed in passing their legacy on to me. Filled with emotion, I found it difficult to be objective, and I put the resulting monograph aside for a later day. Since then, my mother and almost all of the other elders who shared their memories of the Big house Ceremony with me have passed on. With the passing of so many elders, I now feel the time has come to honor their memory and fulfill the trust they placed in me to carry on the history and traditions of my Lenape ancestors by publishing their accounts. Some of these accounts appear in this book. I plan to place all of the texts gathered from my elders within their broader cultural and historical contexts and offer them in a single published volume sometime soon.

Until then, I am pleased to share extracts from selected interviews in this book, whose proceeds will benefit not only the Delawares of Eastern Oklahoma, but my Stockbridge-Munsee and Moraviantown brethren as well. *Wanishi.*

Marlene Molly Miller — MOHICAN NATION, STOCKBRIDGE-MUNSEE HISTORICAL COMMITTEE

It was exciting to read the compilation of Big House Ceremony stories from the past and from all who remember "how it was." In Wisconsin the Stockbridge-Munsees had a copy of Nekatcit's account as told to Speck, and we have a copy of the Oklahoma Delaware Ceremonies book. Grumet's account of "oral" tradition is a treasure, because I tend to give the oral tradition more respect.

It appears that during our time at Stockbridge, Massachusetts, almost all of our Indian spiritual ways or beliefs (at least our ceremony) were weaned from us. We embraced the Christian Church wholeheartedly. At least this is what is written and has been evident over the years. However, a yearning for the Indian ways has never left all of the Stockbridge-Munsee Mohican people, and today there is renewed interest.

In 1993, in need of community healing and unity, a small group of members met and decided to do some type of community ceremony. Utilizing Nekatcit's account of the Big House Ceremony, we very loosely based a ceremony on that. We included the twelve-day prayer fire. We had talking circles, feasts, potlucks, prayers, sweat lodge, and Lenape football. Today we continue the new tradition and add events to it. This year (1998) we will have a powwow, Lenape football, elders' teachings, contemporary music, prayers, women's retreat, sweat lodge, and, as always, the prayer fire, which is pure fire. Through this ceremony W'Chindin (feasting together), we are creating a new tradition—based somewhat on the old, yet nonetheless a tradition.

The ceremonial stories obviously changed in the telling, but the remembering, the time gone by, will help us to continue to bring tradition—our tradition—back to a community where the church no longer can attract its young people. Culture-based youth programs are popular and seem to have healing power for our young people.

In reading the accounts in this book, I could see the outside influence of what I presume to be Christianity, or Christian ideas, as the elders began to change a ceremony of prayer and thanksgiving into something associated with "devils" and "witches." This happened to many of the Indian ways. Now that it is in rebirth, there is a better understanding of what our spirituality really is.

Michael Pace — Eastern Oklahoma Tribe of Delaware Indians

In the recorded history of our world, every culture, past and present, has a unique way of celebrating its existence. All the cultures have developed ways of showing thankfulness for their lives, of showing their appreciation for the bounties of our Earth. Over the millennia the Lenape have created the Big House Ceremony to offer thanks to Kishalameeng, the Creator, and to the Mesingw, who is the Guardian of the Animals. The ceremony is a gift of appreciation to the Mesingw.

The Big House Ceremony, which was a fall ceremony, has undergone some changes as the Lenape were forced from their homelands in New Jersey and found themselves pushed halfway across the continent to northeastern Oklahoma, where the main body of the Lenape people live. The ceremony altered only slightly as the Lenape people changed from a Woodland tribe to a Plains tribe, and was followed faithfully over time until it was put to sleep in the 1920s.

Although I am too young to remember, my mother, Thelma Elkhair, and my aunt, Anna Anderson Davis, often referred to those times with great fondness, recalling their experiences of sharing in the ceremony or of listening from the outside and hearing the songs and dance going on inside the Big House and of taking part in the tribal events during the twelve days it took to complete the ceremony. In sharing stories with other tribal members, they tell stories of their relatives who participated, and in all of them there is a great deal of pride and sadness at the demise of the Big House.

Because of the transition of tribal members into white society, the separation of the tribe, the scattering of allotments, and a concerted effort by the U.S. government to weaken the tribes, splits occurred in the tribe that could not be reversed. The commitment needed to carry on the Big House slowly weakened to the point that the leaders of the Big House finally and reluctantly put the ceremony to sleep. In the late 1920s the last Big House, just west of Copan, Oklahoma, was left to fall in and all the items used were left inside the building, with the proviso that the Big House was never to be used again and the items left were not to be recreated again. That was the end of a long and rich heritage for the Lenape people. Although a small, shortened version of the Big House was used again just after the start of World War II for the young men who went to serve their country, the Big House has never been and never will be reopened again.

My great-grandfather Charlie Elkhair, despite efforts to christianize him when he attended the Baptist Mission School in Kansas in the 1860s, always kept to his language and heritage and refused to give up his traditional ways. I believe that he was rewarded in mind and spirit for the rest of his life and was a stalwart Lenape to his final breath. I often wish I could have met him. I have always wished I could have lived as he did, and I wish I could be just a tenth of the person he was. He was greatly revered in his time and is still greatly admired today.

I appreciate the efforts of Dr. Grumet for his compilation of this book. I have found many references in it to my relatives and friends, now gone.

It is a great source of pride to the present-day Lenape to hold onto the legacy of the Lenape people and to remember those who practiced the Lenape Way and contributed to it. The Lenape people are alive and well today and are still practicing the Lenape Way. We are a proud people. Long may the Lenape live, and long may their Way serve as an example of the Native American legacy. *Wanishi Ta.*

Darryl Stonefish   Moraviantown Band of Delaware Indians

Voices from the Delaware Big House Ceremony gives the most thorough description of what went on in Lenni Lenape (Delaware) religion and spirituality. The gathering of so many accounts under one cover gives readers a full view of the way of life of the ancient Lenni Lenape peoples.

The Lenni Lenape were some of the first Native people to encounter the Europeans, and what the European strangers saw and what goes on today in old ways are not as different as one might think. The writers and the storytellers have captured enough of the past to be able to share some important messages with their people today. With the help of written accounts left by their ancestors, the Lenni Lenape people have been able to practice some of the Delaware Big House ceremonies in their communities. With the sources contained in this book, much more can be done to help in the healing of our Nation. We have suffered much in the past five hundred years or so.

Our ancestors were ridiculed and scorned by the Europeans for doing their ceremonies. They were made to feel ashamed and had to stop their old ways. In later years sometimes their own people made them feel ashamed of their own culture. Some even criticized the Native oral historians for taking part in the printing of the sacred parts of the ceremonies, but these oral historians and keepers of the past prevailed, for they feared all would be lost. They had to share what they knew before their own suns set.

Today we are proud to say, yes—this book, *Voices from the Delaware Big House Ceremony*, is about our people, the Lenni Lenape. Read it and please listen to what it says. There is a great message in it for you. There is a great message in it for all the peoples of the world. May peace and friendship be with you.

Voices from the Delaware Big House Ceremony

Map 1. The Delawares and Their Neighbors, ca. 1650

INTRODUCTION
The Big House Described

Terry J. Prewitt

THE DELAWARE BIG HOUSE CHURCH AND RELIGION

The last active Delaware Big House Church, Xingwikáon, was located on Delaware land in northeastern Oklahoma near the banks of the Copan Lake Reservoir in the Little Caney River Valley in Washington County. Last used in 1924, it was located about one-quarter of a mile north of an earlier structure it replaced sometime around 1908. Most of the elders who officiated at the services had been young men and women at the time the Delawares first came to Oklahoma from Kansas in 1867. They gained their experience in the conduct of the twelve-day observances by growing up in the earlier church established by their own elders. Most of the records documenting construction details of the Copan Big Houses suggest that the structures were substantially similar to one another. Both were large log structures enclosing hard-packed dirt floors. Each had a two-pitch roof covered with shingles. Thick end-post poles supported a single ridge pole running the length of the building. Additional support was provided by a center post. Horizontally laid log walls were supported by internally and externally placed posts. There was a door on each end of the east-west oriented building, and fireplaces were located between the center post and each of the doors on the midline of the structure. Smoke holes were cut through the roof above each fireplace.

Xingwikáon wall logs were rough hewn and set with overlapping double-notched corners. Fresh mud was placed between the logs before the ceremonies each year. Above the level of the door the gable ends of the house were sheathed with vertical planking extending to a maximum height of fifteen feet from the floor.

Twelve carvings of faces representing Məsingw, the "Spirit of the Game Animals," adorned the tops of posts in the building's interior. Ten of these, three on each long wall and two on both side walls, were located near the tops of interior building-support posts. The other two were carved high atop the eastern and western sides of the center pole. Delaware people believed the faces observed the ceremonies of the people. All were painted red on the right half and black on the left. Red paint was applied to the cheek on the black part of each face during the observances of the purification night of the ceremony. Red paint was also applied to the right cheek of each participant in the ceremony on the same evening. Similar paint is used today as part of dance dress and at burials among traditional Delaware people. Some have suggested that the color red represents life and black symbolizes death. Others associate the colors with different principles deeply embedded in Delaware culture, red representing female attributes or light and black representing maleness or darkness.

The Məsingw is only one among many spiritual beings believed to inhabit the twelve levels of the traditional Delaware cosmos. Paramount among these figures is Kišelamúkɔng, "He Who Created Everything With His Thoughts," or the Creator, to whom the ceremonies of the Big House were ultimately directed. Kišelamúkɔng resides in the twelfth level of heaven, and the prayers of the people reached successive levels in the heavens as the ceremony progressed through its twelve days. Other spirits reside on different levels. The most important ones are addressed by terms of kinship.

Different spirit beings are believed to possess various characteristics. Delawares believe the Grandfather in the North, for example, is easily angered. He is thought to send fierce snowstorms if people dance in the winter or break the icicles he uses for canes. Directional spirits are never encountered in person, although they are thought to have form. They are offered water and tobacco on special occasions such as naming ceremonies. Another type of spirit, the Thunderers, is not only offered tobacco but is also presented with burnt deer-tail-hair offerings to forestall any harm the Thunderers might do. These beings are regarded as "Winged-People," whose sound is thought to reveal their age. Thunderers possessing sharp, crackling voices are believed to be young, and older spirits speak in low, rumbling tones.

Məsingw is said to live in the woods and ride upon the backs of deer. He figured prominently in daytime activities on the Big House grounds. An impersonator of the Məsingw, called Məsinghɔlíkʌn, would appear periodically in the camp and on occasion participate in the dance associated with the ceremonial hunt. He was offered tobacco by those he encountered, especially children, who were both mystified and terrified by him. The association of the term Məsingw with the faces on the posts in the Big House may indicate that he was an earthbound spirit formerly considered one of many similar beings occupying the different heavenly realms.

Traditional Delawares address intermediary spirits believed to carry messages to the Creator as "Sky-Keepers." Today, Thunderers are thought of as such beings. Big House adherents also evidently believed Məsingw fulfilled similar functions. Oriented to the four cardinal directions with its floor representing the earth, its roof the heavens, the visionary path the Milky Way leading to the heavens, and its center pole adorned with Məsingw—a sort of *axis mundi* linking heaven and earth—the Big House itself physically represented and reflected Delaware cosmology.

The spiritually purified fires maintained during the ceremony and the prominently used traditional ground corn-meal dishes such as hominy during the twelve days of the ceremony invoked other spirit forces during observances. Opening prayers in the Big House gave direct thanks to the Creator for all of the spirit forces and general provisions of the earth. These references and symbolic associations affirm the significance of spirit beings in past and present traditional Delaware religious life.

THE BIG HOUSE CEREMONY

The following reconstruction of Big House ceremonialism traces, describes, and analyzes aspects of continuity and change in the Big House Religion as it was practiced by Eastern Oklahoma Delaware people during the late nineteenth and early twentieth centuries and described in the accounts of Harrington, Miller, Dean, Speck, and others reprinted in this book. Hosted by one of the three Delaware phratries, the ceremony was held during a twelve-consecutive-night period in October. The rites progressed through several stages of symbolic transformation, building toward a final culmination, Təmahəma, on the morning after the twelfth night of observances. Although most Big House ceremonies were conducted after nightfall, all accounts refer to activities as conducted on particular days. Thus, informants occasionally said that the final ceremony occurred on the thirteenth morning, evidently exceeding the ritually significant number twelve. This is preserved, however, when ceremonial days are regarded as beginning at sunset rather than sundown. In so doing, the closing ceremony occurs at the end of the twelfth day of the rites.

The most fundamental activity of the Big House Religion was the vision or experience recitation known as Wənjikanéi. This consisted of a recitation in narrative form of an experience through which spirit forces had given guidance or promised support to an individual. Boys normally acquired such experiences when sent alone into the uninhabited countryside upon reaching puberty. Many years would pass, however, before they could recite their vision as a respected elder in the Big House. Such a person was known as a Wənjikanéit, "Person of Vision." Only those who had such experiences while they were young could attain this position, and public opinion assessing the validity of one's Wənjikanéi experience often determined whether an individual was accepted as a true person of vision. Vision men delivered their songs on every night of the ceremony.

Women only recited their vision songs on the twelfth night in a part of the ceremony known as Ahtehumwi. Like their male counterparts, women who sang vision songs in the Big House were elders regarded as possessors of extraordinary power. Unlike men, blessed women did not formally seek visions but were instead granted power by sympathetic spirits. Participants in the women's night ceremony wore more elaborate dress than that worn on other nights.

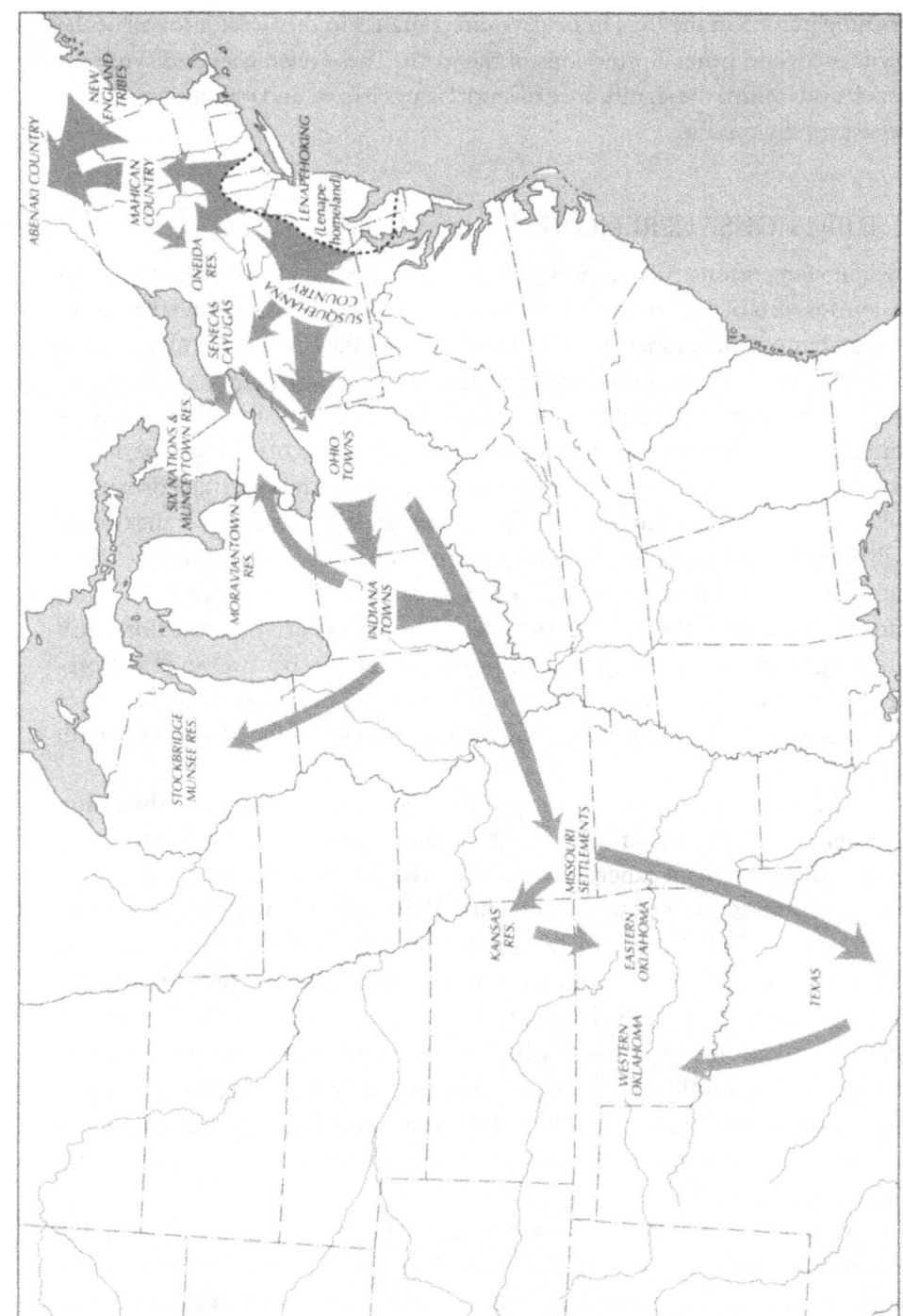

Map 2. Delaware Diaspora, 1600–2000

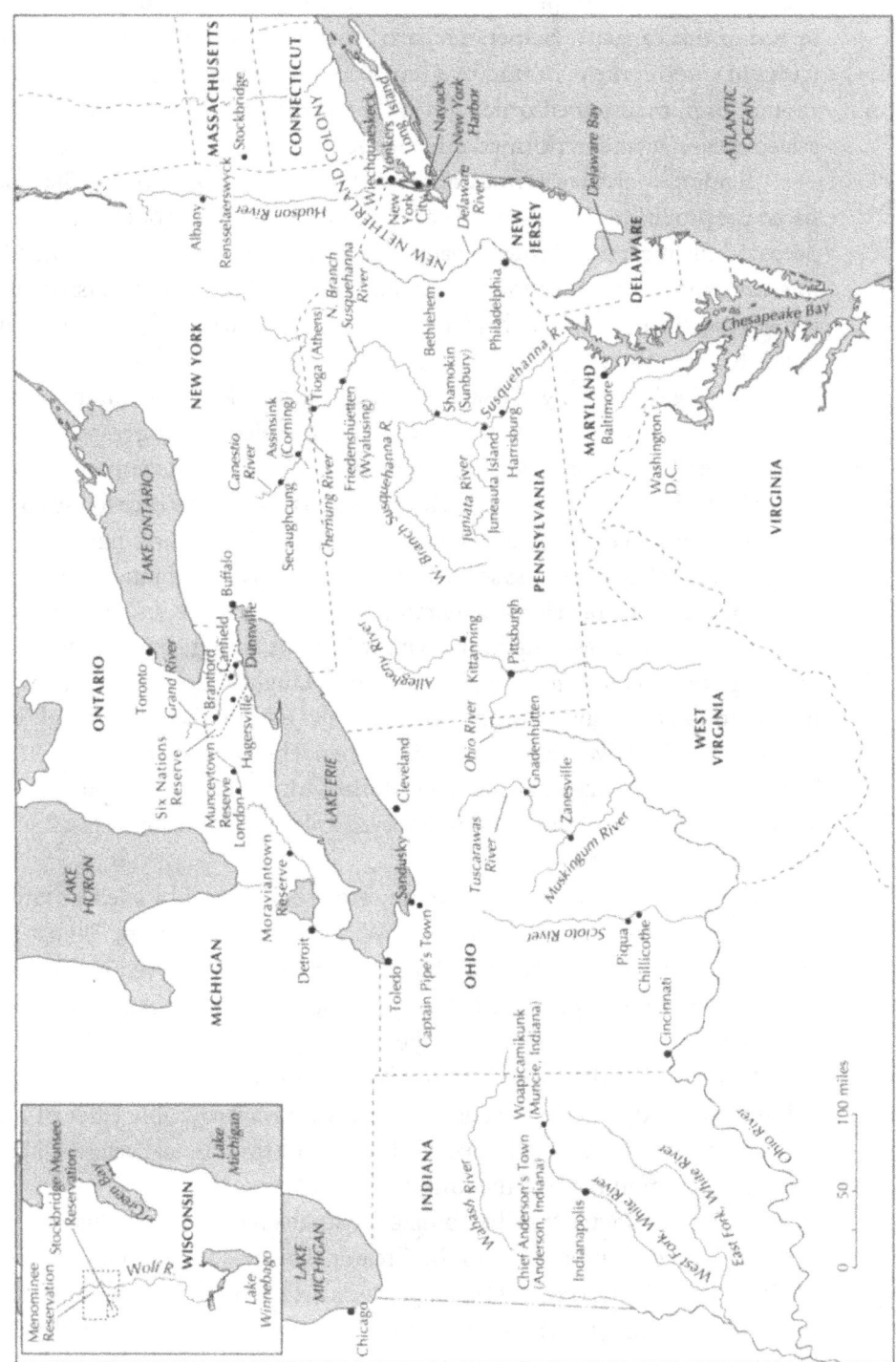

Map 3. Delawares on the Advancing Frontier, 1650–1850

Men and women known as ʌškásʌk, "Helpers," played major roles in the ceremony. Two ʌškásʌk, a man and a woman, were specially appointed every year from each of the three phratries. In later years particular individuals regularly served in this capacity. Helpers prepared special ceremonial meals, used turkey wings to smooth the path trod by visionaries in the Big House, tended the ceremonial fires, maintained order during the ceremony, wakened those who fell asleep during it, and performed other duties.

Tending cook fires in front of the east door of the Big House, ʌškásʌk prepared the provisions carried by ritual hunters who were sent out the first day and prepared the meat they brought back to the Big House. They also pounded corn into meal in large wooden mortars called Kohókʌn located just outside the eastern door of the Big House. This meal was then boiled with meat and other ingredients to make Sapan.

Two Təlekáok, "Singers," sat beside a folded deerskin drum on the south side of the church directly across from the center pole. Təlekáok sang responsively with vision singers as they danced. Often translated as "Cranes," the term is more properly linked with the Delaware word for goose, Mələk, in reference to the gooselike echo effect produced by Təlekáok when accompanying vision singers.

Təlekáok had to possess special knowledge, skills, and abilities. A good singer had to be a devoted Big House adherent, have a strong voice, and be familiar with the many vision songs sung in the Xingwikáon. A young singer might learn by working with an older man, just as singing is taught today among many Oklahoma groups, but only established singers could take on the role of a Təléka. Jake Parks, Mɛčpahkúxwe, "He Who Walks When The Leaves Are Worn Out," and Willie Longbone, Pwɛthɛkkʌmən, "He Pushes, Moves, Kicks, Or Rolls Something This Way," were two of the best remembered Təlekáok active in the last Big House between 1908 and 1924.

Ceremonies in the last Big House were presided over by a leader known as a Təmikɛt, "Enterer." Ben Hill and Frank Wilson (Pɛmataekʌmən, "Things Bloom Where He Steps"), both Túkwsit, Wolf phratry members, served in this capacity during the final years of the Oklahoma Big House. The Təmikɛt was assisted by the headman of the phratry hosting the services. Charlie Elkhair, Kokwəlupuxwe, "He Walks Backwards," generally served as the headman for ceremonies held before 1924. Widely acknowledged as the most knowledgeable elder of his era, Elkhair was one of the most respected elders of the traditional Eastern Oklahoma Delaware community up to the time of his death in 1935.

All accounts agree that the Təmikɛt began the ceremonies at dusk of the first day with a speech and prayers to the Creator. This was followed by a succession of vision singers. The order of the singers was determined by the seating arrangement of the people (fig. 1). In ceremonies brought in by the Túkwsit phratry, the women of the clan sat on the north side of the house to the east of the Təmikɛt; Túkwsit men sat on the same side to the west. The six ʌškásʌk sat at the east end of the church, the three women on the north, and the three men on the south.

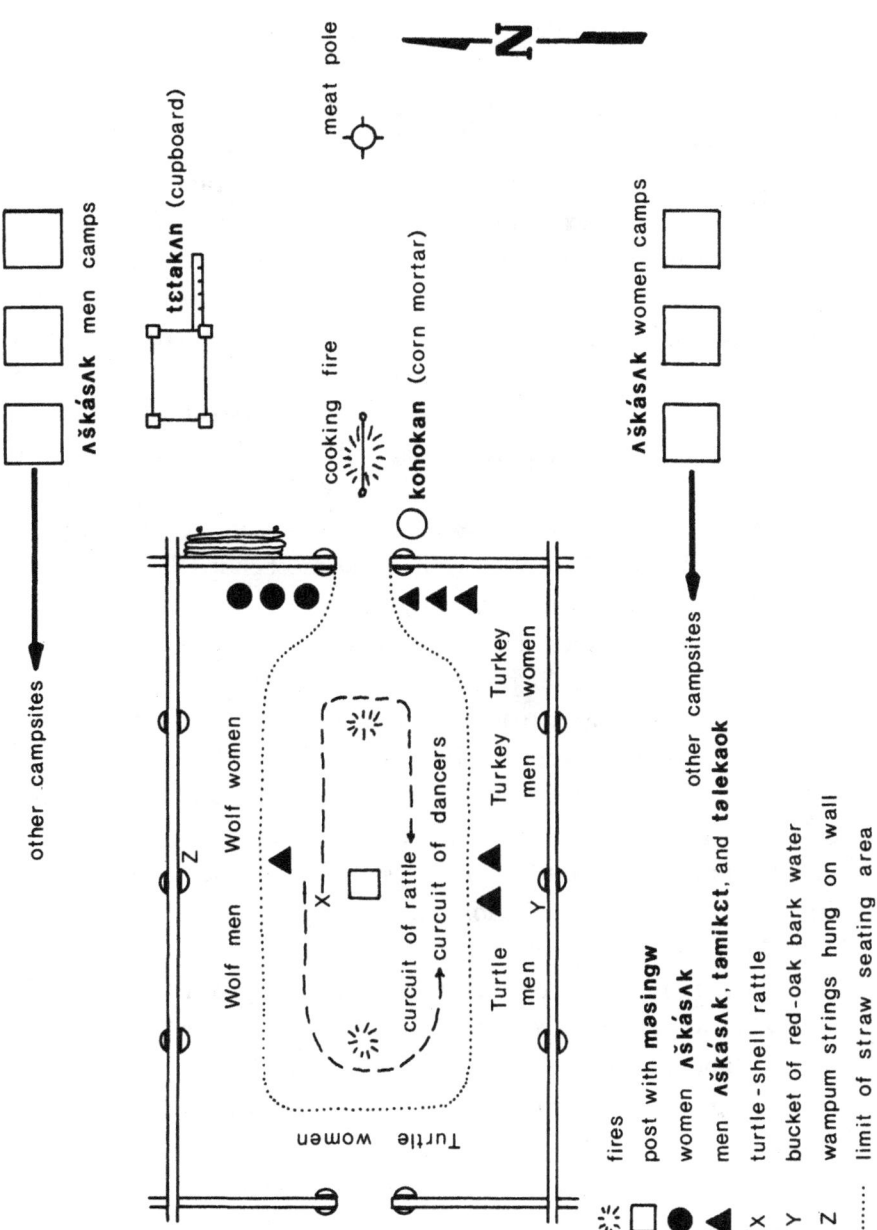

Fig. 1. Plan of the Big House and exterior camp locations (fig. 16, Prewitt 1981: 56). Courtesy Terry J. Prewitt.

The two Təlekáok sat on the south side of the church facing the Təmikɛt. Pele, Turkey phratry people, sat along the south wall on to the east of the Təlekáok; Pukwango, Turtle phratry people, sat on the west side of the south wall. Pele women sat between the male ʌškásʌk and the Pele men along the eastern wall of the Big House; Pukwango women sat at the west end of the structure. Although seating arrangements evidently varied when different phratries hosted the ceremonies, such arrangements are not fully known since neither the Pukwango nor the Pele phratry is known to have "Brought In" a ceremony at the last Big House.

Ceremonies held in the last Big House began when Chief Elkhair sang the first vision recitation. Sitting in the place of the headman at the center of the north side of the Big House next to the Təmikɛt, he started the service by taking up and shaking a Šuhənikʌn, turtle-shell rattle. The Təlekáok would respond with beats on the deer-hide drum. Chief Elkhair would then begin his recitation with a speech followed by the singing of his vision song to the accompaniment of the Təlekáok. He danced as he sang in a counterclockwise direction followed by a line of men; women also followed in a line set slightly to the side behind the men (fig. 2). The dancers circumnavigated the dance floor, tracing a route around the fires and the center post. The line would stop periodically as the Wənjikanéit sang more verses of his vision recitation. Although some Wənjikanéit continued to sing until they reached the north side of the center post, most ended their song upon arriving at the place where their recitation began.

All of the dancers returned to their seats at the conclusion of the song. Spectators who had been standing during the Wənjikanéi would also sit down at this time. Two of the ʌškásʌk, a man and a woman, then swept the path of the dancers using turkey wings as brooms. The turtle rattle was then passed to the left by "Walking It" from person to person around the room until another vision man took it up and shook it to signal the beginning of the next recitation. People were careful not to allow the rattle to make a sound unless they intended to sing their vision song, because the Təlekáok immediately beat their drum as soon as they heard the rattle shake.

The rattle followed a route that passed along the north side of the Big House to the ʌškásʌk women, across the doorway to the ʌškásʌk men, and from them along the lines of people sitting on south, west, and north sides of the building until it returned to its starting point. The return of the rattle in its clockwise circuit of the room to its point of beginning signaled the end of the evening's observances. It is said that the large numbers of vision singers caused the ceremony to continue through the night when the Delawares first came to Oklahoma. In later years the rattle tended to complete its journey by 2:00 A.M. on all but the final nights of the service.

Things were organized in a slightly different manner when women sang their vision songs. The women stood in a line starting by the east door. Men stood beside them in a parallel line closer to the center of the house. Each of the men

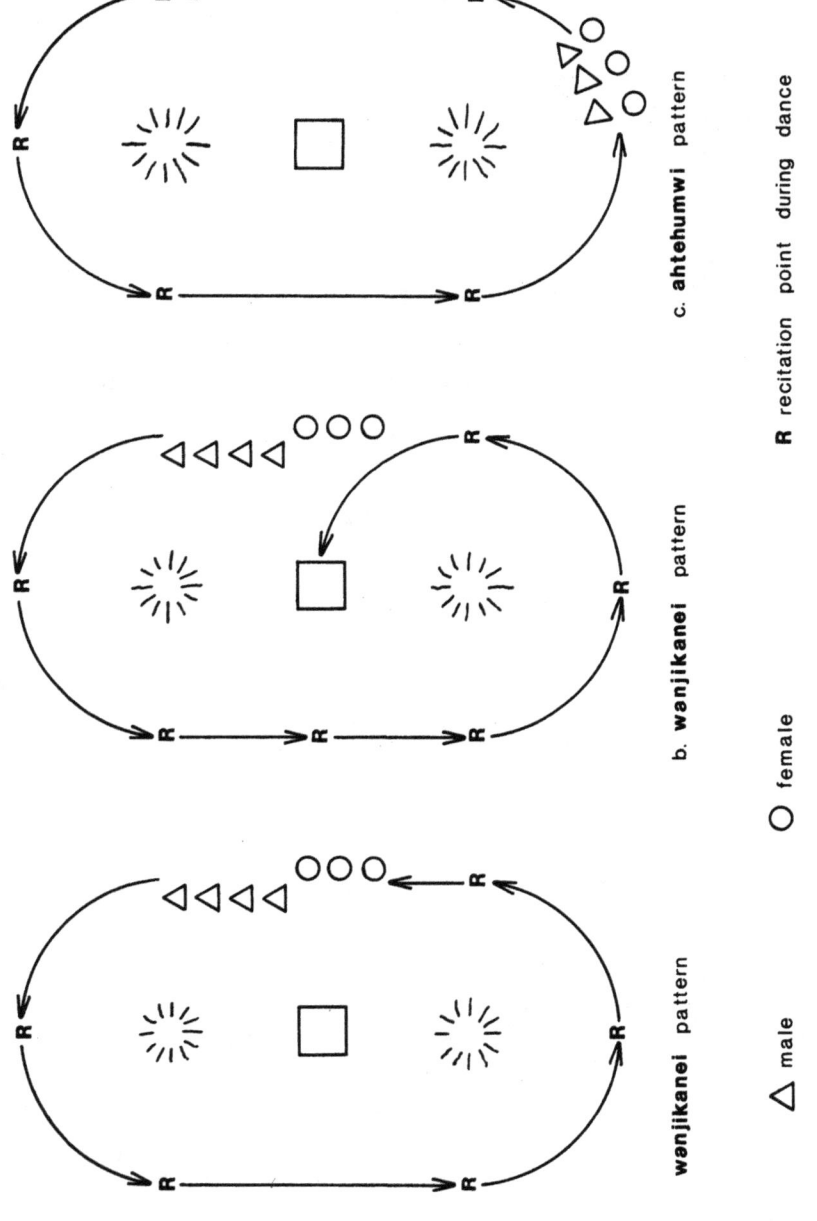

Fig. 2. Plans of dancing patterns associated with the men's and women's vision recitations (fig. 17, Prewitt 1981: 57). Courtesy Terry J. Prewitt.

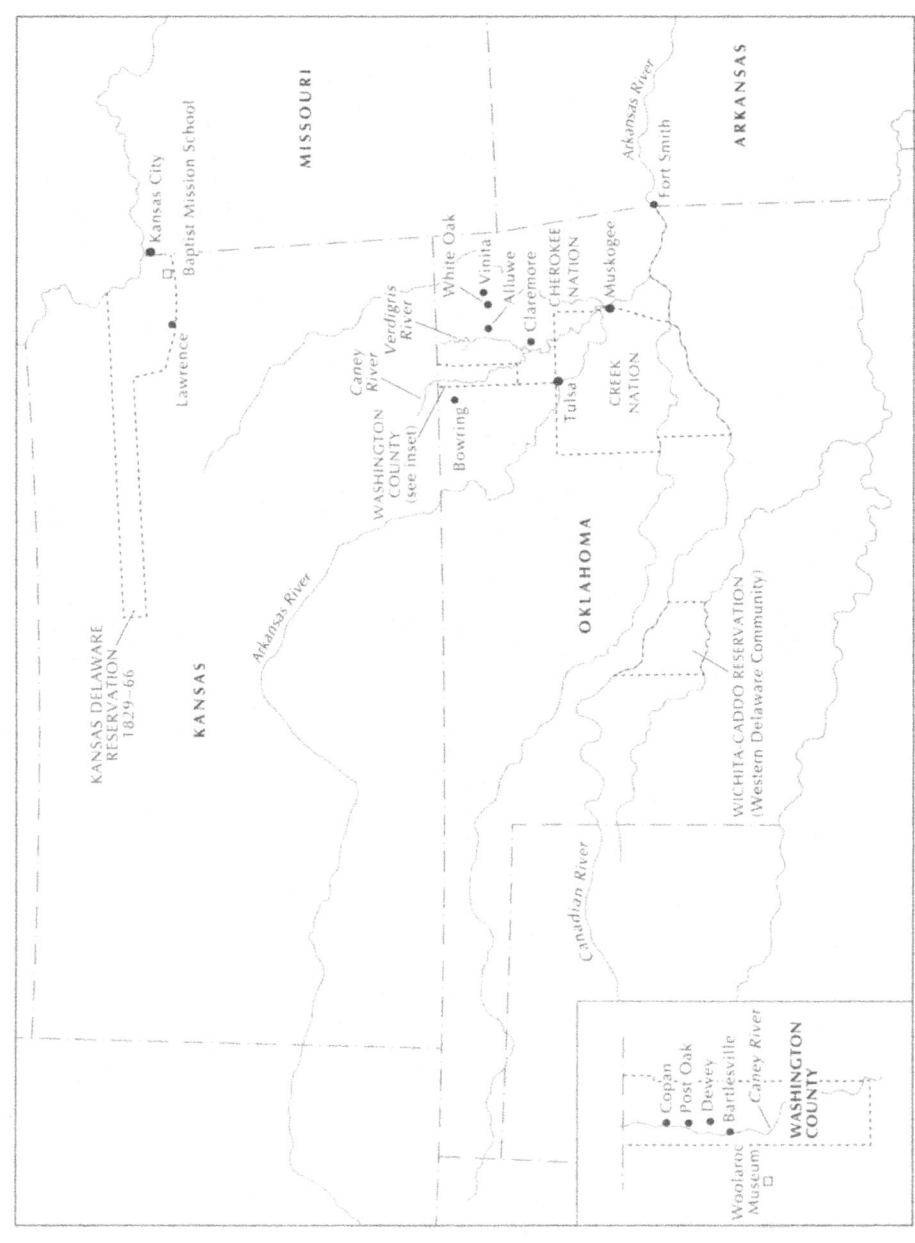

Map 4. Kansas and Oklahoma Delaware Communities, 1829–2001

held a turtle-shell rattle. The files proceeded side by side, the men accompanying and shaking the rattle in time with the song sung by the leading woman. The line stopped as the woman recited further parts of her song, and the recitation ended when the dancers completed their circuit of the room at the eastern doorway.

Sources differ on which night the women sang their vision songs. Harrington states that the Ahtehumwi was preceded by the burning of cedar, Pilhlksutin. Both Nora Thompson Dean and Charlie Webber recollect that the Pilhlksutin ritual was performed on the ninth night. Charlie Elkhair's account places the cedar purification rite on the seventh and twelfth nights. The replacement of plain with specially decorated drumsticks and the painting of people and Məsingw representations that were also identified by Elkhair as the seventh-night activities, however, are identified as ninth-night activities by other sources. The ninth night marked the part of the ceremony when everything was purified and "Made New" to bring the people and the Creator closer together during the climactic final days of the ceremony.

Different informants reported the occurrence of at least two other rituals, the Mawêsi and the Wiltin, on different nights. In the Mawêsi, ʌškásʌk filled their mouths with wampum beads, Kakw, that had been scattered on the dance floor. In the Wiltin, ʌškásʌk summoned men to the Big House by calling out their Delaware names. These men would divide a string of wampum among themselves, file outside, and pray while facing toward the east. Earlier sources state that these rituals were performed on the fourth and ninth nights, while sources documenting activities at the last Big House state that the activities occurred on other nights. The earlier pattern, closely coordinated with rituals associated with the hunt and the Məsinghɔ́líkʌn, may reflect a time when the hunt was a central focus of the Big House observances. The performance of the Wiltin and Mawêsi on other nights in the last Big House, by contrast, may reflect ritual reorientations brought on by the diminishing importance of the hunt and the cessation of the Məsinghɔ́líkʌn performance.

Indeed, the key differences between earlier and later Big House rites center mainly on the association of hunting activities with the earlier ones. Harrington developed a scheme relating the Big House ceremony into the following four three-day sunset-to-sunset periods integrating hunting, meat distributions, and other exchanges of goods (especially wampum) to the overall structure of the ceremony:[1]

---

1. The account of Charlie Elkhair collected by Michelson in 1912 places the departure of the hunters on the morning after the fourth ceremony and their return on the seventh day. Chief Elkhair also placed the introduction of new equipment and associated activities on the seventh night, but Harrington adjusted the chronology of events to include all of these activities except the meat distribution on the ninth night. Additionally, Harrington's placement of the Pilhaksutin on the twelfth night before the Ahtehumwi is based on Chief Elkhair's description. Elkhair also indicated that a meat distribution occurred on both the seventh night and the twelfth day, but Harrington only lists the final distribution, placing it after the Ahtehumwi on the twelfth night. Since the Harrington study is based upon broader contact with Chief Elkhair and other informants, it probably represents a more accurate understanding of the ceremonies than that of the Michelson document. If the Harrington material is accepted, then the four divisions

- During the three days beginning at sunset of the first night and continuing through the departure of the hunters on the third day after commencing the rites, the ʌškásʌk aided the hunters in preparing for the hunt, the selection of the hunters and chief hunter was accomplished, and the Məsinghɔlíkʌn appeared in the camp and aided in setting the hunters to their task.
- This was followed by the three-day period of the hunt, marked by the introduction of the Wiltin and Mawêsi on the fourth evening and ending with the return of the hunters on the sixth day. When the hunters returned they were taken into the Big House, blessed, and released from their hunting obligation.
- With the release of the hunters, the ʌškásʌk took on the responsibility for preparing the deer and distributing their meat, hides, and other usable parts. This period was terminated on the ninth night with the purification, renewal ceremonies, and, according to Chief Elkhair, a meat distribution.
- During the final three nights and days of the ceremony, the activities intensified through further observances of the Wiltin and the use of the new equipment introduced on the ninth night. Loose wampum beads were distributed, the Ahtehumwi was held, and the final ceremony was conducted on the final morning.

Big House ceremonial participants can be divided into four generational divisions: Elders, Adults, Young Adults, and Children. Elders included those who were advanced in years and were established visionaries. Wənjikanéi recitation or Ahtehumwi participation signaled assumption of this status. Married people with established families and those in their age group were regarded as Adults. Young Adults were either unmarried or only beginning to have children. Persons not yet of marriageable age comprised the children's generation.

Elders and Adults carried out the most important roles of the Big House ceremony. Elders provided spiritual guidance for the whole congregation and the prayers and vision recitations needed to implore the Creator and other spirit forces to help and protect the people through the coming year. Adults served as ʌškásʌk and assisted in the Wiltin and other activities. Young Adults were responsible for carrying out the hunt. Children helped gather firewood, carried ashes, and performed other chores.

The hunt was a metaphor for intergenerational cooperation. Supported by provisions given by the ʌškásʌk, Young Adult hunters in turn gave all deer and other game obtained in the hunt to them. The ʌškásʌk prepared and distributed game from the hunt to all participants, reserving the choicest pieces for the Elders.

---

of three sunset-to-sunset periods are consistent with pre-1908 ceremonies. Moreover, the divisions serve to identify important elements of reciprocity between generations during the activities of the Big House rites.

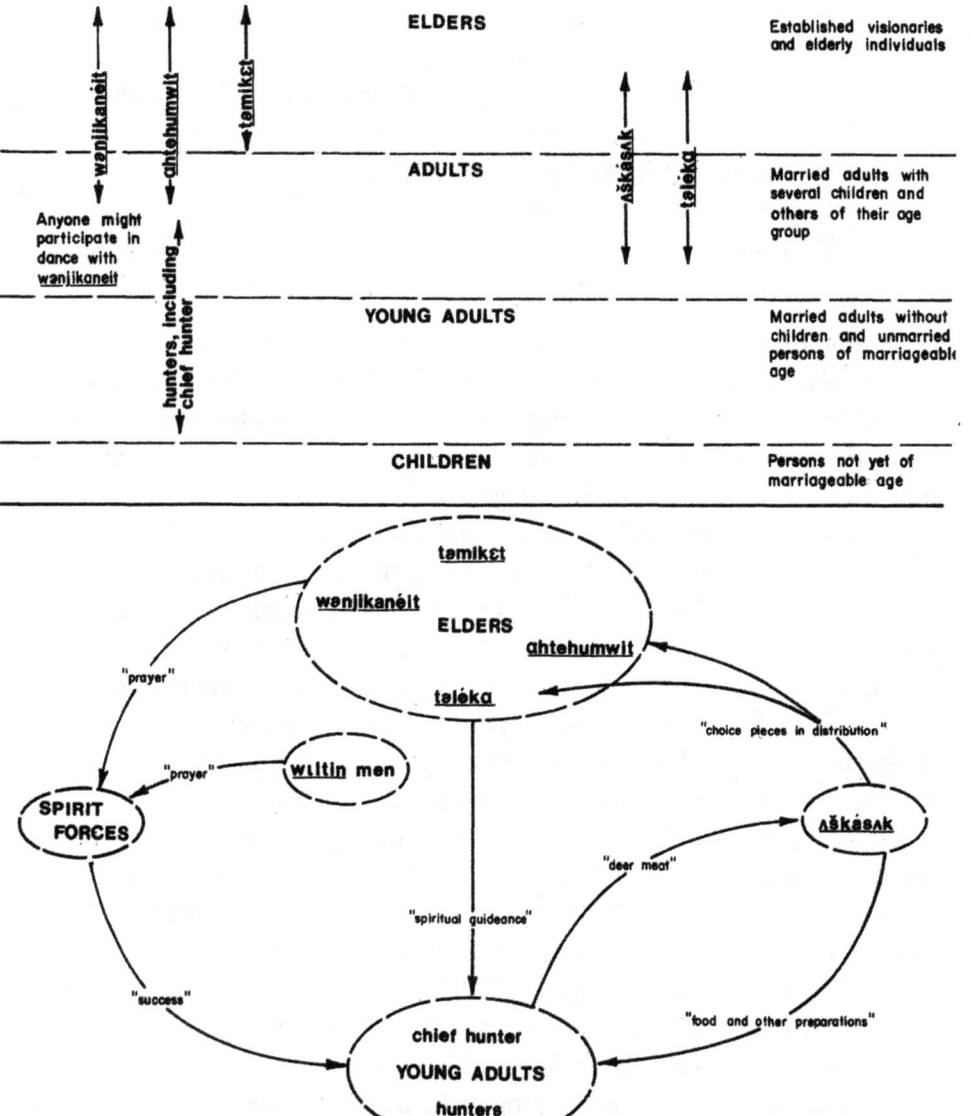

Fig. 3. Generational associations, roles, and spiritual associations of the Big House Ceremony (fig. 19, Prewitt 1981: 62). Courtesy Terry J. Prewitt.

Figure 3 summarizes these generational role associations and shows the relationships linking the spiritual activities of the Xingwikáon to the hunt. In this way the diverse segments of the population and the spirit world were linked in common activity promoting the welfare of the people.

The contributions of the generations were organized in the four periods of the ceremony as follows:

- Days 1–3: Elders and Adults helped prepare the Young Adults for the hunt.

- Days 4–6: Young Adults carried out the hunt and turned over all game to the ʌškásʌk Adults.
- Days 7–9: Adults, ʌškásʌk, prepared the meat for general distribution. Elders received gifts of meat and wampum, the beads being measured in lengths on personal turtle rattles.
- Days 10–12: All generations participated in Church ceremonies. Deerhides and food were distributed. The ʌškásʌk, Təmikɛt, and Təlekáok received wampum strings for their services.

The ceremony entered its most intensive spiritual phase between the sixth and seventh days. During the first six days the people thanked the spirit forces and prayed for help and support. During the final six days, they intensified their efforts through prayer and the special participation of all generations in ceremonial activities as the observances reached their conclusion.

Distributions of symbolically powerful substances such as meat from game animals taken by Young Adult ceremonial hunters, corn and other traditional foods prepared by ʌškásʌk, and wampum linked the people to one another, the earth, and the spirit world. The disappearance on game animals during the last decades of the ceremony evidently led to an increased emphasis of wampum as a gift acknowledging the efforts of people who provided important services. Harrington's data indicate that all families participating in the Big House ceremonies contributed wampum to establish a general fund for use during the twelve days. Chief Elkhair observed that participants extending thanks to the Creator during the Ləntkən, "Common Dance," for example, received gifts of a few beads for their participation. The bulk of the fund of wampum, however, went to repay the primary participants in the rites. On the final day, payments in lengths of wampum were made to all of the key people, including the Chief Hunter and the men who closed the ceremony. These payments supplemented prior payments to ʌškásʌk made during the Mawêsi. The ʌškásʌk also obtained beads as payment for meals they prepared for the people camping at the Big House during the twelve days. Not all key participants received wampum on the last day. Wiltin men, for example, were not given additional payments.

Gifts of wampum and other spiritually powerful substances simultaneously recognized and empowered crucial intermediaries, maintaining crucial links that joined the Delaware people with the material and spiritual realm. Although meat continued to serve as a metaphor for the hunt and the good things it could bring, later rites placed increasing emphasis on giving thanks for the blessings of the past and on prayers for continued blessings and protection.

THE LATE BIG HOUSE COMMUNITY

As the sources published in this book demonstrate, much of what we know about the Big House and the traditional Washington County Delaware community comes from people who participated in or witnessed ceremonies held in the last Xingwikáon after 1908. For this reason I will now turn to a consideration of the people who continued the Big House Religion through 1924 and who have maintained a strong respect for the values of the religion to the present day. It would be impossible to construct a complete list of the individuals who participated in every aspect of worship, nor would such a treatment be entirely appropriate. However, the following commentary identifies many of the people who were primary carriers of the traditional beliefs and attempts to show how the roles of the Big House worship integrated families in a unified social world. Through understanding the lives of these families, it may also be possible to gain some insight into the reasons for the end of the ceremonies and the failure of the attempts to revive Big House practices in the 1940s. I will also consider cultural factors that contributed to the rise of other religious participation, including the Peyote Religion, among some former Big House adherents.

The traditional Delaware community of the settlement era was relatively small. It is apparent that there might have been a broader participation in the ceremony had there been a tighter concentration of families of Delaware background in the Washington County area, although the fact that other groups did not construct their own meeting houses indicates that persons of traditional orientation were more thinly scattered in other parts of the Delaware region, especially in Nowata and Rogers Counties. By 1900 the traditional group north of Bartlesville, Oklahoma, was established as a social unit through marriages forming several very large family networks. This represented a continuity from the Kansas population, in which the "traditionals" had become differentiated from the "modernists" over both religious issues and general cultural concerns centering on education and entry into white society (see Weslager 1978: 419–21).

But also, by 1900, the Delawares represented a small minority of the population in Washington County and the last set of households comprised mainly of full-blood tribal members (see Roark-Calnek 1977). Indeed, several of the primary participants of the late Big House meetings were married to outsiders, including Shawnees, Cherokees, and whites. These outsiders generally did not participate directly in the Big House ceremony, although some camped with their families and aided in the outside work of the twelve days. Whites were specifically excluded from the rites. The presence of a non-Indian in the ceremony, if noted, was sufficient to prompt some elders to leave the meeting in protest. At any rate the entire service was conducted in the Lenape language, and general knowledge of the meeting was sent out within the traditional community. Indians, including Christian Delawares, who were unsympathetic to the religion or who violated the sanctity of the services were asked to leave. On some occasions the meetings drew individuals who attempted to disclaim the activities as heathen, but these persons were tolerated only if they did not actually disrupt the services or other daily camp routine.

Broad family networks participated in the ceremony yearly. The primary network included representatives of all the primary roles of the services and seventeen of the families that camped at the Xingwikáon site. There were at least two other such large family networks, including other campers, and there were also other families who did not camp but who attended the services regularly. Those who camped in later years were major participants and families who lived at some distance from the meeting site. In a conversation with her when I conducted fieldwork in the 1970s, Lucy Parks Blalock remembered the wagon trip to the Big House each evening from Copan and the long return that was made to town each night so that she could attend school during the day. Many individuals pursued their jobs throughout the period of the observances. Although the campers generally remained at the site throughout the ceremony, many gained release from school for their children for the entire period.

It is clear from documented clan associations that the Tŭkwsit and Pele clans were most prominent in this network. Other networks had somewhat different clan associations, but the Tŭkwsit clan dominated the community numerically and was most prepared to host the ceremony each year. Plural marriages were common in the Kansas Delaware community, but most of the multiple marriages of the elder generations were sequential. In earlier times the clans had been subdivided into smaller units that were possibly related to locations in the original homeland of the Delaware. It is for this reason that Harrington (1921) referred to the units as phratries (see Morgan 1976: 171–73). In Oklahoma the basic unit associations did not function to regulate marriages or geographic associations. One could marry a member of any of the matrilineal groups, including one's own. Children who went into the Big House sat with their matrilineal relatives in the section appropriate to their sex. Thus, girls sat with their mothers, while boys sat with maternal uncles. The children of the early twentieth century represent the last fluent Lenape speakers in northeast Oklahoma, among whom there remain only a very few today.

THE SIGNIFICANCE OF NAMES IN A RELIGIOUS CONTEXT

All the people who attended the Big House had Delaware names. Formal names were of religious significance, for it is by those names that individuals became known to the spirit world. The tradition of name-giving continues today, although formerly it was more widely practiced by elders (see Weslager 1971 and 1974). There are certain standard elements of names, such as the suffix -xkwe, "Woman," on many women's names. Formal names also referred to people's special attributes or marked them as having certain qualities of personality.

The names of some prominent people of the last Big House demonstrate the subtlety and significance of the naming process. Among the Wənjikanéit were John Anderson, Wítanahkúxwe, "He Walks With The Trees." The names of Joe Washington and Frank Wilson show similarities of construction with Anderson and Falleaf. Joe Washington was called Nikanipahkúxwe, "He Walks Ahead Of

Leaves." Frank Wilson, also one of the two men who usually served as Təmikɛt, was named Pɛmataɛkʌmen, "Things Bloom Where He Steps." Like many people of the era, Wilson had a nickname, ɛma:. Nicknames generally were abbreviated forms of Lenape names.

Two of the Ahtehumwéitcik were Liza Falleaf, Tatkowínau (translation unknown), and Sarah Wilson Thompson, ɛhɛlináoxkwe, "Two Women That Look Alike Woman." Minnie Fouts, who often served as an ʌškásʌk during the late years of the ceremonies, was called Wɛmeehəlɛxkwe, "Reverberates Everywhere Woman." Among the men ʌškásʌk were George Thomas Anderson, Kwəčkipahkíkʌmən, "He Makes The Leaves Move As He Steps," and Fred Washington, ɛnxinund, "You See A Bit Of Him." Fred Washington was one of three younger men who served as an ʌškásʌk during one of the last meetings at the Big House.

Among the older generation the names were sometimes developed into English equivalents, either as family names or as nicknames designating the individual. Thus, Captain Curley-Head, one of the major traditional figures of the settlement era, had the Lenape name Cəpəlʌntpas, "Curley-Headed One."[2] Similarly, Furgeson Longbone had the name Mɛtɛxin, "Where He Landed When He Jumped," and was also known as "Jumper." The attributes noted in names were sometimes determined in part by the name-giver. Some name-givers might provide many names having to do with trees, blooms, or leaves, while others might often relate names to appearance or sound. Names could also be very similar for men and women, such as Anna Anderson Davis's Lenape name, ɛnxinau, "That's All You See Of Her," which is essentially a feminine form of the name given to Fred Washington.

Calling the name of an individual was and is a sensitive matter to many Delawares, since the name has always been considered a special part of the person. Therefore, the names of individuals were known only in the limited social circle of the Big House community, and often they were used so little that they were not widely known at all. When an individual died, his or her name passed from use. To speak the name of a deceased person at night or in the late afternoon is still considered to be a dangerous act. During the settlement era as well as later, people were known by their English names or nicknames or were directly referred to by kinship terms. The Delawares did not give names to their children until they were beyond infancy, sometimes as late as the third or fourth year. Acquiring a name from a parent was also not as common as acquiring it from some older individual, a grandparent, or another elder, because names were given by people with status as visionaries. As the number of visionaries was reduced in the population, name-giving became less common in all Delaware circles, though a few names are still being given today within the traditional community. Whether a child had a regular name or not, an incident might result in his or her being dubbed with a

---

2. His photograph appears in Weslager (1972: 409).

nickname. Nora Thompson Dean related such a story from her childhood to me during a visit I made to her home while I was conducting fieldwork in the area in the 1970s:

> One time—I must have been about three or four—we were all up to the Xingwikáon. All the Delawares camped up there, that is, the traditional Delawares, and my mother had a purse that she had made, a buckskin purse with fringes. So she was known for her pie making ability, so the ʌškásʌk always had her to come and make pies for the people who ate inside the Xingwikáon. So she said, "You must stay with your dad now, because I'll be busy." Well, I didn't want to stay with him. I wanted to go with her. I said, "I want to go too," but she said, "No! You'll bother me . . . you stay with your dad." So I stayed at the camp with him, and my father went to mission school, so he could read, and while he was reading his newspaper there by the campfire, I saw my mother's purse. It was a very precious thing to her at that time, but I was . . . about three . . . I didn't know what precious things were. So I got this purse and I drug it over the high weeds outside of the camp area, and I just loved to see those fringes go over those weeds. And so, my mother got back and she saw me dragging her purse around over the weeds, and she took the purse away from me and shook me around a little bit—Delawares never punish their kids very much. And that scolding hurt me worse than the punishment. Well, I must have screamed out and I just really threw a tantrum I guess, and all the old ladies ran up there to see if I had got burnt or something in the fire. And they said, "No, she's just mad cause I took the purse away from her." And I kept saying èmsitunai, an improper pronunciation of èmsinutay, which means "the bag." And after that, the old ladies called me "The Bag" and said, "This bag here is sure growing a lot!" So I was glad when they finally quit calling me that.

This account reveals many elements of Delaware tradition. For example, parents and older siblings rarely displayed open emotion to children. They were neither severely punished nor given strong expressions of affection. This was tied to the belief that either emotional display would lead to the sickness or even the death of a child. However, adults in general were watchful of the safety and needs of children, and elders especially felt strong ties to the young. The children were also brought into the Big House, where they learned the proper rules of conduct in life and the many particular rules of the ceremony. All the accounts in Ruthe Blalock Jones's taped interviews with people who had been children in the last Big House affirm that the young regarded the ceremony with the sense of awe and responsibility (see chapter 12).

AFTER 1924

By 1924 there were very few visionaries, either men or women, through whom the main rites of the twelve days could be continued. Most Delawares reaching adulthood at this time were products of boarding-school educations that had removed them far from family and friends during the critical years when young folk obtained visions. And without visions, there could be no recitations in the Big House. The area had been so thickly settled that there were few deer to hunt, so the important hunting activities of the pioneer era had long since been discontinued. The suit worn by the Məsingw impersonator, along with other items used in the settlement-era church, were taken to museums in the East. Younger people increasingly married non-Delawares or moved away, removing opportunities for their children to learn the Delaware language through which the ceremonies were conducted. The Big House itself was nearly fifteen years old by 1924, and it rapidly deteriorated after it fell into disuse. The remains of the Xingwikáon were finally removed from the location, some parts finding their way into museums and homes. The ceremonial objects kept by its caretakers eventually passed out of the hands of Delaware families.

Furthermore, other religious forces held more appeal for some younger Delawares or were adopted by people of the old religion because the Big House ceremonies could no longer be maintained. The Peyote Religion, having been introduced in the late nineteenth century by John Wilson, a relative of Big House Təmikɛt Frank Wilson, became increasingly important among younger adults who had been deprived of the nineteenth-century traditional Delaware upbringing by conditions of the post-pioneer era (see Harrington 1921; Newcomb 1956b; Petrullo 1934). But among its adherents were also visionaries of the old days, and so a major division of the Big House community came in the wake of rising interest in the Native American Church. Many older people simply rejected the Peyote Way, and now most contemporary Delaware families know little of its practice or its former importance in the Delaware community. Thus, traditionalism among the Delawares is not totally tied to the shift of religious emphasis toward Peyote Spirit, even though it was among the most traditional Delawares that Peyote became an established focus of spiritual activity.

The Big House Religion was distinctively Delaware, however, and it ended because outside pressures prevented elders from passing on the knowledge and experience necessary to its observance. Today, Delaware traditionalism might best be expressed as the orientation possessed by those who remember and appreciate the Big House for what it was, a comprehensive knowledge of spirit forces acting on behalf of all people. The gifts of the Creator are still with the traditional Delawares in the absence of the Big House Church, and the heritage of prayer to the Creator is the heritage of all Delaware people at some point of genealogical connection. For those people descended from the Washington County family networks the genealogical connection is close, but for other Oklahoma Delawares it is not too much more distant. For a six-year-old Delaware boy dancing in a powwow today, detached and totally self controlled in his art, the act of a handshake from an elder extends a formal blessing to the new focus on traditional life, and a great cultural distance of five generations is bridged. This is the greatest significance of the Big House for the contemporary Delaware community—the significance of a still-living tradition that continues to enrich and enlarge the lives of the Delaware people.

CHAPTER ONE

The Earliest Accounts, 1655 to 1780

ADRIAEN CORNELISSEN VAN DER DONCK'S ACCOUNT, 1655

Dutch lawyer and colonist Adriaen Cornelissen van der Donck (ca. 1618–55) penned the earliest known descriptions of Indian spirituality in the Hudson River Valley homeland of the Mahican and Munsee people. Van der Donck first arrived in the New Netherland colony in 1641. He initially held the position of schout (a combination sheriff and prosecutor) for Kiliaen van Rensselaer's manorial estate (known as a patroonship) in and around present-day Albany. Van der Donck worked for van Rensselaer for five years before acquiring an estate of his own in today's city of Yonkers, in Westchester County, New York (the name preserves the memory of van der Donck as a "Jonkheer," or young gentlemen).

Van der Donck first published the following material in his "Description of New Netherland" in 1655. Impressionistic and ethnocentric, his account nevertheless preserves information available nowhere else. Although he does not precisely identify the subjects or sources of his Indian information, he refers to several conversations with Indian people in and around the Hudson Valley. Other records suggest more specific sources. A January 26, 1656, document, for example, states that an English-speaking Munsee Delaware Indian from Wiechquaeskeck (in present-day Westchester County, New York), known among the colonists as Joseph, was a good friend to the young patroon and tended his cows for awhile (O'Callaghan and Fernow 1853–87[13]: 59–60).

Van der Donck's book was published in at least two editions in Holland between 1655 and 1656. Sadly, like many seventeenth-century books, his original manuscript has disappeared. Nearly two centuries passed before Jeremiah Johnson translated and published an English version of the volume (Johnson 1841). Another 125 years passed before English professor Thomas F. O'Donnell produced the first fully annotated version of Johnson's translation (O'Donnell 1968).

Although linguists have long recognized serious deficiencies in the Johnson translation, an accurate modern revision only appeared in 1996, when Diederick Goedhuys produced the translations of the first three accounts, "Their Festivities and

Special Gatherings" (Goedhuys 1996: 116–17), "Of Their Knowledge of God and the Fear of Devils" (Goedhuys 1996: 128–29), and "Their Thoughts on the Creation and the Propagation of Mankind and Animals in the World" (Goedhuys 1996: 129–30), which are reproduced in this book.

Working independently, literature professor Ada van Gastel published translations of four chapters dealing with Indian life that were neglected by Johnson (van Gastel 1990). One of these, the section entitled "Of Their Presents and Veneration Ceremonies," appears following the Goedhuys translation extracts that follow (van Gastel 1990: 419–20).

Their Festivities and Special Gatherings

Feasts and big meetings are not regular events among them, but are sometimes held to deliberate concerning peace, war, contracts, alliances, and agreements. Also, to consult the devil on some future matter or outcome,[1] or on the crops and productiveness of the season; or else to rejoice over a success with dancing, and merriment. Peace or war with neighbors and surrounding nations are not decided in haste. But debated in all their councils. There, persons of some authority are free to state their opinions at such length and as amply as they please without anyone interrupting them, no matter how long the speech or whether it goes against the mood of many. But if they fully approve of what is said they voice their acclamation towards the end of the address. The councils always meet before noon and do not normally continue beyond noon. If no conclusion is reached by then they resume in good time in the morning. When they plan to practice witchcraft, however, and conjure the devil to reveal the future, as is their way, the meeting takes place in the afternoon towards evening. Some of their number are wonderfully able to consort with the devil and perform great magic, or so they make the common people believe. They begin by jumping, shouting, ranting, and raving as though they were mad and possessed, light big fires and dance around, beside, and right through them. They tumble and roll head over heels, beat themselves, and perform such queer pranks that they break out all over in a sweat that trickles down their bodies. With such sickening behavior and grimaces they seem to become devils themselves, so that it is horrible to see for someone not used to it. When properly in a trance, the devil charmers start a dismal jabbering and howling, and scream at one another as if demon-possessed. After this has gone on for a while the devil appears to them, so they say, in the shape of an animal; if a ferocious animal, it is a bad omen; a harmless animal is better. The apparition

---

1. I.e., to consult a spirit. In another section, van der Donck states that Indians compare wise, brave, or otherwise notable people "with the devil, the master of evil arts, and name them Manitto or Ottico" (O'Donnell 1968: 98). The former usage parallels that of Jasper Danckaerts, whose marginal notations identified manitous as devils in the manuscript of the journal (Gehring and Grumet 1987: 105).

tells them strange things in reply to their questions, but seldom so clear and detailed that they can rely on it or fully comprehend it. They learn or appear to learn something from it and grope for the meaning, like a blind man reaching for an egg. If the matter turns out differently it is their fault not to have understood. Sometimes they read more into the message than it contains. Any Christians who may be present can observe the hub-bub, but while they are there the devil will not make an appearance. The sorcerers can cast a spell on some of the common folk so that the subject foams at the mouth as if possessed, in a way not otherwise seen, for he throws himself into the glowing hot fire without feeling it. After a while someone whispers in his ear and he is once again as quiet and meek as a lamb. To celebrate some or other success or to dance they assemble in the afternoon. First a spokesman explains the matter, then food is served, as may also be done following a council meeting. They are hearty eaters and everyone consumes so much that it ought to last them for three days. Nothing must be left over; food not eaten there is to be taken home or fed to the dogs. When they have gorged themselves so fully they can only move their flushed heads, the old and staid have a smoke to round off the feast, while the young and not-so-young take to singing, skipping, and dancing, often the whole night through (Goedhuys 1996: 116–17).

Of Their Knowledge of God and the Fear of Devils

Although the original natives of New Netherland are heathens and unbelievers they all know and confess that there is a God in heaven, eternal and almighty. Since God is in the highest degree good and merciful, they aver, and unwilling to hurt or punish any human being He does not concern himself with the ordinary affairs of the world. The devil takes advantage of the scope thus given him, and all that happens to man here below, they believe, the devil disposes, guides, and governs at will. God, or the supreme chief, who dwells in heaven is no doubt much greater and higher than the devil and also has dominion over him, but declines to become involved in all those troubles. When we respond to this by saying that the devil is evil, cunning, and wicked, they frankly admit that to be true and also that he takes great pleasure in directing all matters in as baneful a way as he can. They further maintain that every misfortune, scourge, calamity, and infirmity is inflicted on them by the devil. They express by the general appellation of devil all accidents and illnesses they suffer, for example, in case of an internal disorder they say there is a devil within my body, and if something ails them in an arm, leg, foot, hand, shoulder, or head they say, pointing to the affected part, there is a devil inside. Since the devil is so malicious and merciless towards them they have no choice but to fear and yet keep on friendly terms with him and sometimes throw a morsel into the fire to please him, as stated above. When we refute those absurdities easily we do so by saying to them that God is omniscient and omnipotent; knows the nature of devils exactly; quietly observes their doings; and will not permit a puffed-up and faithless servant to tyrannize man, who is the most glorious creature of all and made in God's image, provided he duly puts his trust in God and does not forsake His commandments in favor of evil. To this they respond with a weird and fantastical argument; You Dutch say so, and seen superficially it may seem to be as you maintain, but you do not understand the matter aright. This God, who is supremely good, almighty, and beneficent, Lord of all heaven and earth, and all its host, is not alone up there in heaven without any company or diversion, but has with him a goddess or woman who is the fairest the eye has ever seen or can see. With this goddess or beauty He passes and forgets the time, being deeply attached to her, and meanwhile the devil lords it on earth and does whatever he wishes. That conviction is firmly inculcated in them and no matter how far one pursues the argument and reasons with them, whatever abominable absurdities they resort to, and whether one checkmates them in debate, in the end they return to the view, like the dog that licks up its own vomit, that the devil must be served because he has the power to harm them (Goedhuys 1996: 128–29).

Their Thoughts on the Creation and the Propagation of Mankind and Animals in the World

From the younger Indians or those leading an unsettled life and often met with our people no certainty or reply concerning this subject is to be had. One must await a suitable opportunity to discuss it with riper and wiser persons if one is to get some indication of it. It may happen during serious discourse that they themselves inquire after our views on the origin of mankind. When we relate the creation of Adam, in broken language and to the best of our ability, that cannot or will not understand it in regard to their own nation or the Negroes, on account of the difference in skin color. As they see it the world was not created the way we believe it was and as told in Genesis 1 and 2. They say that before the world and the mountains, humans, and animals had come into existence God was with the woman who dwells with him, and no one knows when that was or where they had come from. Water was all there was or at any rate water covered and overran everything. Even if an eye had existed at that time it could not have seen anything but water wherever it might have been, for all was water or covered by water. What then happened, they say, was that the aforementioned beautiful woman or idol descended from heaven into the water. She was gross, big like a woman who is pregnant with more than one child. Touching down gently, she did not sink deep, for at once a patch of land began to emerge under her at the spot where she had come down, and there she came to rest and remained. The land waxed greater so that some areas became visible around the place where she sat, like someone standing on a sandbar in three or four feet of water while it ebbs away and eventually recedes so far that it leaves him entirely on dry land. That is how it went with the descended goddess, they say and believe, the land ever widening around her until its edge disappeared from view. Gradually grass and other vegetation sprang up and in time also fruit-bearing and other trees, and from this, in brief, the whole globe came into being such as it appears to this day. Now whether the world you speak of and originally came from was then created as well, we are unable to say. At the time when all that had been accomplished the high personage went into labor and, being confined, gave birth to three different creatures; the first was in every respect like a deer as they are today, the second resembled a bear, and the third a wolf. The woman suckled those creatures to maturity and remained on earth for a considerable time during which she cohabited with each of the said animals and was delivered a number of times of various creatures in multiple births. Thus were bred all humans and animals of several kinds and species that can still be seen in our day. In due course they began to segregate according to the families and species still existing, both from an innate urge and for the sake of propriety. When all those things had thus been disposed and made self-perpetuating the universal mother ascended again to heaven rejoicing at having accomplished her task. There she continues to dwell forever, finding her entire happiness and delight in keeping and fostering the supreme Lord's love for her. To that she is devoted and from it derives her complete enjoyment and satisfaction; therefore, God vouchsafes her his fondest love and highest esteem. Here below meanwhile humans and animals of all the various species that were the result of miscegenation increase and multiply, as does all creation the way we find it still. That is why human beings of whatever condition still exhibit the innate characters of one or other of the three animals mentioned, for they are either timid and harmless in the nature of deer, or vindictive, cruel, bold, and direct in the nature of bears, or bloodthirsty, greedy, subtle, and treacherous like wolves. That all this has changed somewhat now and is no longer obvious or implicit, they attribute to the times and people's guile in disguising it. This, they say, is all we have heard on the subject from our ancestors, and believe to be true; had they been able to write like yourselves they might have left us a more complete account, but they could not (Goedhuys 1996: 129–30).

Of Their Presents and Veneration Ceremonies

All their treaties, agreements, peace negotiations, reconciliations, proposals, requests, alliances, and promises are sealed and given force with gifts or veneration ceremonies. Without these, their doing something or promising something is not worth much. However, those [treaties] that have been preceded or followed by gifts and veneration ceremonies are considered as fully sealed *quasi interveni-enti testimonio*, because usually all the points that they separately request or decide upon are presented and remembered by them with some little sticks (which they carry with them for this purpose and which each stand for one point). During a veneration ceremony, when a point is stipulated, decided upon, or recapitulated for the last time, the person who submits the request has the stick either in front of him or in his hand, and at the end of the talk he will put down the stick in front of the person whom he is addressing. Everything that is decided in this way with them or amongst them they will very precisely and exactly remember, and they will obey it and esteem it in all kinds of ways. The veneration gifts used usually consist of Zeewant [wampum], furs, duffel cloth,[2] or ammunition for wars, and seldom of grain. They are very much inclined to have veneration ceremonies for persons individually amongst themselves and also for our people; but because they like to have rather much in return, which (if one does not give it to them of one's own accord) they very well know how to demand, our nation does not make much use of their veneration ceremonies. When one wants to make a request to an individual or to them in general, one should send veneration presents to the person or to the place where one wants to make the request. The presents are then displayed there, and the request is brought forward and examined. And the person or persons to whom the request is presented will very seriously consider the request. If they accept the presents, the request has been accepted and approved in the form in which it was formulated; if the presents are still on display after the third day, that means that this time the request is not honored and the requesting party must revise the conditions or augment the veneration, or sometimes do both.

DANIEL DENTON'S ACCOUNT, 1670

The following brief account was first published in a volume written by an English colonist named Daniel Denton. Little is known about Denton beyond the fact that he settled on western Long Island and wrote a promotional pamphlet encouraging immigration to the colony, "A Brief Description of New York," in 1670. The extract reproduced below (Denton 1966: 8–9, 11) combines expressions of religious intolerance and condescension with descriptions of hallowing (perhaps the prayer call, Hoooo), black and red face painting, the use of sticks while dancing (perhaps reminiscent of Big House prayer sticks), and other aspects of Delaware spirituality and ceremonialism documented in later accounts of Delaware religious observances.

For their worship, which is diabolical, it is performed usually but once or twice a year, unless upon some extraordinary occasion, as upon making war or the like; their usual time is about *Michaelmass*, when their corn is first ripe, the day being appointed by their chief priest or Pawaw; most of them go a hunting for venison: When they are all congregated, their priest tells them if he want money, their God will accept no other offering, which the people believing, everyone gives money according to their ability. The priest takes the money, and putting it in some dishes, sets them upon the top of their low-roofed houses, and falls to invoking their God to come and receive it, which with many loud hallows and outcries, knocking the ground with sticks, and beating themselves, is performed by the priest, and seconded by the people.

---

2. Coarse woolen cloth of a type originally produced in the city of Duffel in present-day Belgium.

After they have thus a while wearied themselves, the priest by his conjuration brings in a devil amongst them, in the shape sometimes of a fowl, sometimes of a beast, and sometimes of a man, at which the people being amazed, not daring to stir, he improves the opportunity, steps out, and makes sure of the money, and then returns to lay [appease or banish] the spirit, who in the meantime is sometimes gone, and takes some of the company along with him; but if any English at such times do come amongst them, it puts a period to their proceeding, and they will desire their absence, telling them their God will not come whilst they are there.

At their Canticos or dancing matches, where all persons that come are freely entertained, it being a festival time: Their custom is when they dance, every one but the dancers to have a short stick in their hand, and to knock the ground and sing altogether, whilst they that dance sometimes act war-like postures, and then they come in painted for war with their faces painted black and red, or some all black, some all red, with some streaks of white under their eyes, and to jump and leap up and down without any order, uttering many expressions of their intended valor. For other dances they only show what antic tricks their ignorance will lead them to, wringing of their bodies and faces after a strange manner, sometimes jumping into the fire, sometimes catching up a fire-brand, and biting off a live coal, with many such tricks, that will affright, if not please an English man to look upon them, resembling rather a company of infernal furies than men.

WILLIAM PENN'S ACCOUNT, 1683

The following text is a comparatively well-known account written by William Penn (1644–1718). Penn was the founder, proprietor, and first governor of Pennsylvania ("Penn's Woods"), a vast province granted by English King Charles II. The eastern border of this domain ran along the Delaware River, the heart of the traditional Delaware homeland. A pacifist by religious conviction (he is perhaps the most famous Quaker in history), Penn stressed the use of love and respect rather than force in dealings with Indian people.

This attitude is clearly evident in the brief extract on Delaware religion printed in this book. Reprinted from Albert Cook Myers's definitive 1937 edition (Pomfret 1970: 34–35, 42), it is from a larger promotional pamphlet, "A Letter from William Penn, Proprietary and Governour of Pennsylvania in America, to the Committee of the Free Society of Traders . . . ," written in 1683. Penn's text, completed just ten months after he first arrived in his new colony, is now curated in the Library of the Historical Society of Pennsylvania in Philadelphia. The account contains perhaps the earliest known descriptions of a drumming board (thought to be a reference to the flat deer-hide drum used in the Big House).

Their worship consists of two parts, sacrifice and Cantico. Their sacrifice is their first fruits; the first and fattest buck they kill, goeth to the fire, where he is all burnt with a mournful ditty of him that performeth the ceremony, but with such marvelous fervency and labor of body, that he will even sweat to a foam. The other part is by Cantico, performed by round-dances, sometimes words, sometimes Songs, then shouts, two being in the middle that begin, and by singing and drumming on a board direct the chorus: Their postures in the dance are very antick and differing, but all keep measure. This is done with equal earnestness and labor, but with great appearance of joy.

In the fall, when the harvest cometh in, they begin to feast one another; there have been two great festivals already, to which all come that will: I was at one myself; their entertainment was a green seat by a spring, under some shady trees, and twenty bucks, with hot cakes of new corn, both wheat[3] and beans, which they make up in a square form, in the leaves of the stem, and bake them in the ashes: And after that they fell to dance, but they that go, must carry a small present in their Money, it may be six pence, which is made of the bone of a fish;[4] the black is with them as gold, the white, silver; they call it all Wampum . . . In Rites, they reckon by moons; they offer their first fruits; they have a kind of feast of Tabernacles; they are said to lay their Altar upon twelve stones . . .

DAVID BRAINERD'S ACCOUNT, 1745

The next account was written by David Brainerd (1718–47), a particularly zealous Connecticut-born Presbyterian minister. Inspired by the fervor of the "Great Awakening," a Protestant religious revival that swept the middle colonies during the mid-eighteenth century, Brainerd worked as a missionary among Delawares and other Indians in the provinces of New York, New Jersey, and Pennsylvania from 1744 until his death in 1747. Edited by his mentor, the prominent "New Light" cleric Jonathan Edwards, and first published by him in 1749, Brainerd's journals have been frequently reprinted as both historical documents and inspirational literature.

Among the many descriptions of Indian life in the region recorded in Brainerd's journals is an account of ceremonies he witnessed and a masked reformer he encountered during a visit to the central Pennsylvanian Susquehanna Valley Indian town of Juneauta between September 19 and 23, 1745 (Dwight 1822: 237–38, 344, 347, 349). Juneauta town, located on an island where the Juniata River flows into the Susquehanna, was occupied by displaced Nanticoke and Conoy people from Maryland between the 1740s and the 1750s (P. A. W. Wallace 1981: 112–13). The striking similarities of the Conoy ceremonies and ceremonial paraphernalia documented at Juneauta by Brainerd to Delaware practices suggest common origins or close connections between the rituals of the two peoples.[5]

---

3. Europeans frequently referred to corn as wheat during the seventeenth century.
4. Penn evidently refers to shellfish here.
5. I am indebted to University of Notre Dame historian Gregory Evans Dowd for pointing out the Conoy connection to Juneauta (Dowd 1998: personal communication).

Twentieth-century American anthropologist Mark Raymond Harrington regarded Brainerd's account as an early documented example of Delaware ritual life. Focusing upon the masked figure, Harrington noted that Brainerd's colonial-era description of the figure's characteristics closely matched later Oklahoma Delaware accounts of the Məsinghɔlíkʌn impersonator in all but one respect—the extravagant mouth was more reminiscent of an Iroquois false face than of Mesingw (Harrington 1922: 41–42).

Reflecting his "New Light" beliefs, Brainerd wrote with passion, conviction, and deep introspection. He suffered from tuberculosis and was in declining health throughout his ministry, and his observations are intertwined with extended reflections upon his spiritual and physical states. These reflections have been deleted from the extract reprinted here.

September 20. Visited the Indians again at Juneauta island, and found them almost universally very busy in making preparations for a great sacrifice and dance. . . . In the evening they met together, near a hundred of them, and danced around a large fire, having prepared ten fat deer for the sacrifice. The fat of the innards they burnt in the fire while they were dancing, and sometimes raised the flame to a prodigious height, at the same time yelling and shouting in such a manner that they might easily have been heard two miles or more. They continued their sacred dance all night, or near the matter; after which they ate the flesh of the sacrifice, and so retired each one to his lodging.

Lord's Day, September 22 . . . Near noon they gathered together all their powows (or conjurers), and set about half a dozen of them to play their juggling tricks, and act their frantic distracted postures, in order to find out why they were then so sickly upon the island, numbers of them at that time being disordered with a fever, and bloody flux.

In this exercise they were engaged for several hours, making all the wild, ridiculous, and distracted motions imaginable; sometimes singing; sometimes howling; sometimes extending their hands to the utmost stretch, spreading all their fingers; and they seemed to push with them, as if they designed to fright something away, or at least keep it off at arm's-end; sometimes stroking their faces with their hands, then spurting water fine as mist; sometimes sitting flat on the earth, then bowing down their faces to the ground; wringing their sides, as if in pain and anguish; twisting their faces, turning up their eyes, grunting, and puffing.

Their monstrous action tended to excite ideas of horror, and seem to have something in them, as I thought, peculiarly suited to raise the Devil, if he could be raised by anything odd, ridiculous, and frightful. Some of them, I could observe, were much more fervent and devout in the business than others, and seemed to chant, peep, and mutter with a great degree of warmth and vigor, as if determined to awaken and engage the powers below. I sat at a small distance, not more than thirty feet from them (though undiscovered), with my Bible in my hand, resolving, if possible, to spoil their sport, and prevent their receiving any answers from the infernal world, and there viewed the whole scene. They continued their hideous charms and incantations for more than three hours, until they had all wearied themselves out, although they had in that space of time taken sundry intervals of rest; and at length broke up, I apprehended, without receiving any answer at all . . .

The Indians of this island can many of them understand the English language considerably well, having formerly lived in some part of Maryland among or near the white people, but are very vicious, drunken, and profane, although not so savage as those who have less acquaintance with the English. Their customs in diverse respects differ from those of other Indians upon this river. They do not bury their dead in a common form, but let their flesh consume above ground in close cribs made for that purpose; and at the end of a year, or sometimes a longer space of time, they take the bones, when the flesh is all consumed, and wash and scrape them, and afterwards bury them with some ceremony.

Their method of charming or conjuring over the sick seems somewhat different from that of other Indians, though for substance the same. The whole of it, among these and others, perhaps is an imitation of what seems, by Naaman's expression, II Kings 5:11, to have been the custom of the ancient heathens. For it seems to chiefly consist in their "striking their hands over the diseased," repeatedly stroking them, "and calling upon their gods," excepting the spurting of water like a mist, and some other frantic ceremonies, common to other conjurations I have already mentioned.

When I was in these parts in May last, I had a opportunity of learning many of the notions and customs of the Indians, as well as of observing many of their practices. I then traveled more than one hundred and thirty miles upon the river above the English settlements. Had in that journey a view of some persons of seven or eight distinct tribes, speaking so many different languages.

But of all the sights I saw among them, or indeed anywhere else, none appeared so frightful, or so near akin to what is usually imagined of infernal powers—none ever excited such images of terror in my mind—as the appearance of one who was a devout and zealous Reformer, or rather, restorer of what he supposed was the ancient religion of the Indians. He made his appearance in his pontifical garb, which was a coat of bear skins, dressed with the hair on, and hanging down to his toes; a pair of bear skin stockings; and a great wooden face painted, the one half black, the other half tawny, about the color of an Indian's skin, with an extravagant mouth, cut very much awry; the face fastened to a bear skin cap, which was drawn over his head. He advanced toward me with the instrument in his hand, which he used for music, in his idolatrous worship, which was a dry tortoise shell with some corn in it, and the neck of it drawn on to a piece of wood, which made a very convenient handle.

As he came forward, he beat his tune with his rattle, and danced with all his might, but he did not suffer any part of his body, not so much as his fingers, to be seen; and no man would have guessed by his appearance and actions, that he could have been a human creature, if they had not had some intimation of it otherwise. When he came near to me, I could not but shrink away from him, although it was then noonday, and I knew who it was, his appearance and gestures were so prodigiously frightful. He had a house consecrated to religious uses, with diverse images cut out upon the several parts of it; I went in and found the ground beaten almost as hard as a rock with their frequent dancing in it.

I discoursed with him about Christianity, and some of my discourse he seemed to like, but some of it he disliked entirely. He told me that God had taught him his religion and that he would never turn from it, but wanted to find some that would join heartily with him in it; for the Indians, he said, were grown very degenerate and corrupt. He had thought, he said, of leaving all his friends, and traveling abroad, in order to find some that would join with him; for he believed God had some good people somewhere that felt as he did. He had not always, he said, felt as he now did, but had formerly been like the rest of the Indians, until about four or five years before that time: then he said, his heart was very much distressed, so that he could not live among the Indians, but got away into the woods, and lived alone for some months.

At length, he says, God comforted his heart, and showed him what he should do. Since that time he had known God, and tried to serve Him; he loved all men, be they who they would, so as he never did before. He treated me with uncommon courtesy, and seemed to be hearty in it. I was told by the Indians that he opposed their drinking strong liquor with all his power; and if at any time he could not dissuade them from it, by all he could say, he would leave them, and go crying into the woods. It was manifest he had a set of religious notions that he looked into for himself, and not taken for granted upon bare tradition; and he relished or disrelished whatever was spoken of a religious nature according as it either agreed or disagreed with his standard. And while I was discoursing he would sometimes say, "now that I like; so God has taught me," and so on. And some of his sentiments seemed very just. Yet he utterly denied the being of a Devil, and declared there was no such creature known among the Indians of old times, whose religion he supposed he was attempting to revive.

He likewise told me that departed souls all went southward, and the difference between the good and bad was this, that the former were admitted into a beautiful town with spiritual walls, or walls agreeable to the nature of souls; and that the latter would forever hover around those walls, and in a vain attempt to get in. He seemed to be sincere, honest, and conscientious in his own way, and according to his own religious notions, which was more than I ever saw in any other pagan. I perceived he was looked upon and derided among most of the Indians as a precise zealot, that made a needless noise about religious matters; but I must say, there was something in his temper and disposition that looked more like true religion than anything I ever observed among other heathens.

CHRISTIAN FREDERICK POST'S ACCOUNT, 1760

Moravian lay missionary Christian Frederick Post penned the following account of Delaware Indian religion in May 23–25, 1760, entries in his journal of an abortive peace mission undertaken on behalf of the Pennsylvania government as the worst of the fighting brought on by the Seven Years' War (1754–62) wound down in America. He had been charged with orders to invite the still-hostile Allegheny Valley tribes to a peace conference in Philadelphia.[6] Post's party, which included his traveling companion, provincial militia officer John Hays, Delaware diplomat Teedyuscung, and Christian Delaware interpreters Moses Tunda Tatamy and Isaac Still, got as far as the Delaware town of Secaughcung (also called Passigachkunk) on the Canestio River above Corning, New York, before receiving word from the Senecas that they refused Post and Hays permission to travel further.

Post's account contains some of the earliest known references to a house of worship, the revival of lapsed observances, the response-recitation of what appears to be a vision song, dance movement in a line, specifically repetitive words and actions, the giving of what appears to be the Hoooo prayer call (referred to by Post as "hallowing"), and an all-night prayer service.

The degree of detail in this account can best be appreciated by comparing it with entries for the same days in Hays's journal from the same expedition.[7] On the 24th, for example, a day well described in a paragraph by Post, Hays wrote a single sentence stating that "the Indians began to sacrifice to their Gods and spent the day howling and dancing raveling like wolves and painted frightfull as devils." The next day, he even more tersely noted that "the Indians went on in the same manner as yesterday" (Grumet 1999: 58, 60).

23rd. . . . there were a great Number of Indians together at Atsingnetsing[8] to revive an Old quarterly Meeting which had been many years laid aside, in which they related to each other their Dreams and Revelations every one had had from his Infancy, & what Strength & Power they had received thereby . . .

24th. It was a very fine day, and about nine o'clock they began their grand festival, which afforded us an opportunity of seeing their stupid and tragical way of worship. Their priests or conjurers, with about ten women, went first into the woods to paint themselves according to their different characters, their whole bodies were painted all over with various colors, some with the addition of rattlesnakes, some with squirrels, others with trees, birds, etc. Thus adorned, or rather disfigured, they came all in a row into the town singing as they went. One of them began

---

6. Original drafts of the Post journal are presently curated in the library of the Historical Society of Pennsylvania. The journal was transcribed by William A. Hunter, who passed away before he could see it through publication. James Rementer brought the manuscript to my attention and helped see it to publication.
7. The Hays account, originally published in Hunter (1954: 68), is reprinted in Grumet (1999: 59, 61).
8. Assinsink, "Stony Place," a mixed Delaware and Munsee expatriate community at or near present-day Corning in south-central New York State.

singing: "I saw two English birds flying together in love," which all repeated again four times, after which they went in procession four times round the meeting house and then turning their faces toward sunrise, hallowing all together as long as they had any breath; Then they shook hands with one another and called all the people to enter the house with them, where they continued walking, singing, and hallowing the whole day and night until six o'clock in the morning, when a certain spirit came over them and many wept bitterly.

25th. In the morning the whole company came out and stood in a row towards sun rise lifting up their hands towards heaven and hallowing six times with all their force, shook hands with one another and then went to every house to wish them a joyful good morning. They came to us also, wished us the same, gave us their hands in love and friendship, and invited us to their dinner.

DAVID ZEISBERGER'S ACCOUNT, 1779–1780

The final entry in this chapter presents the observations of Moravian missionary David Zeisberger, who lived and worked among the Delawares and other Indians along the moving frontier from Pennsylvania to Ohio from 1745 until his death in 1808. Zeisberger was fluent in the region's several Indian languages, a sympathetic observer, and a witness to nearly every aspect of Delaware life. This account was curated in the Moravian Archives in Bethlehem, Pennsylvania, for nearly a century before Ohio historians Archer Butler Hulbert and William Nathaniel Schwarze first published it in Zeisberger's History of the North American Indians *in 1910. Unlike his colleague and co-religionist John Heckewelder, whose own* History *was first published in 1818, Zeisberger described Delaware religious beliefs and practices. Zeisberger's account, written in an archaic German script between 1779 and 1780 and untranslated and unpublished for more than a century, is the earliest known detailed description of Delaware religious observances (Hulbert and Schwarze 1910: 136–39, 141).*

Worship and sacrifices have obtained among them from the earliest times, being usages handed down from their ancestors. Though in the detail of ceremony there has been change, as the Indians are more divided now than at that time, worship and sacrifice have continued as practiced in the early days, for the Indians believe that they would draw all manner of disease and misfortune upon themselves if they omitted to observe the ancestral rites.

In the matter of sacrifice, relationship, even though distant, is of significance, legitimate or illegitimate relationship being regarded without distinction. A sacrifice is offered by a family, with its entire relationship, once in two years. Others, even the inhabitants of other towns, are invited. Such sacrifices are commonly held in autumn, rarely in winter. As their connections are large, each Indian will have opportunity to attend more than one family sacrifice a year. The head of the family knows the time and he must provide for everything. When the head of such a family is converted [to Christianity], he gets into difficulty because his friends will not give him peace until he has designated some one to take his place in the arrangement of sacrificial feasts.

Preparations for such a sacrificial feast extend through several days. The requisite number of deer and bears is calculated and the young people are sent into the woods to procure them together with the leader whose care it is to see that everything needful is provided. These hunters do not return until they have secured the amount of booty counted upon. On their return they fire a volley when near the town, march in solemn procession and deposit the flesh in the house of sacrifice. Meantime, the house has been cleared and prepared. The women have prepared firewood and brought in long dry reed grass, which has been strewn the entire length of the house, on both sides, for the guests to sit upon. Such a feast may continue for three or four nights, the separate sessions beginning in the afternoon and lasting until the next morning. Great kettles full of meat are boiled and bread is baked. These are served to the guests by four servants especially appointed for this service. The rule is that whatever is thus brought as a sacrifice must be eaten altogether and nothing left. A small quantity of melted fat only is poured into the fire. The bones are burnt, so that the dogs may not get any of them. After the meal the men and women dance, every rule of decency being observed. It is not a dance for pleasure or exercise, as is the ordinary dance engaged in by the Indians. One singer only performs during the dance, walking up and down rattling a small tortoise shell filled with pebbles. He sings of the dreams the Indians have had, naming all the animals, elements, and plants they hold to be spirits. None of the spirits of things that are useful to the Indians may be omitted. By worshiping all the spirits named they consider themselves to be worshiping God, who has revealed his will to them in dreams. When the first singer has finished he is followed by another. Between dances the guests may stop to eat again. There are four or five kinds of feasts, the ceremonies of which differ much from one another.

In another kind of feast the men dance clad only in their Breech-clout, their bodies daubed all over with white clay. At a third kind of feast ten or more tanned deer-skins are given to as many old men or women, who wrap themselves in them and stand before the house with their faces turned toward the east, praying God with a loud voice to reward their benefactors. They turn toward the east because they believe that God dwells beyond the rising of the sun. At the same time much wampum is given away. This is thrown on the ground and the young people scramble for it. Afterward it is ascertained who secured the most. This feast is called 'ngammuin, the meaning of which they themselves are unable to give.

A fourth kind of feast is held in honor of a certain voracious spirit, who, according to their opinions, is never satisfied. The guests are, therefore, obliged to eat all the bear's flesh and drink the melted fat. Though indigestion and vomiting may result they must continue and not leave anything.

A fifth kind of festival is held in honor of fire which the Indians regard as being their grandfather, and call Machtuzin, meaning "to perspire." A sweating-oven is built in the midst of the house of sacrifice, consisting of twelve poles each of a different species of wood. These twelve poles represent twelve Manittos, some of these being creatures, others plants. These they run into the ground, tie together at the top, bending them toward each other; these are covered entirely with blankets, joined closely together, each person being very ready to lend his blanket, so that the whole appears like a baker's oven, high enough nearly to admit a man standing upright. After the meal of sacrifice, fire is made at the entrance of the oven and twelve large stones, about the size of human heads, are heated and placed in the oven. Then twelve Indians creep into it and remain there as long as they can bear the heat. While they are inside twelve pipes full of tobacco are thrown, one after another, upon the hot stones, which occasions a smoke almost powerful enough to suffocate those confined inside. Some one may also walk around the stones singing and offering tobacco, for tobacco is offered to fire. Usually, when the twelve men emerge from the oven, they fall down in a swoon. During this feast a whole buckskin with the head and antlers is raised upon a pole, head and antlers resting on the pole, before which the Indians sing and pray. They deny that they pay any adoration to the buck, declaring that God alone is worshiped through this medium and is so worshiped at his will.

At these feasts there are never less than four servants, to each of whom a fathom of wampum is given that they may care for all necessary things. During the three or four days they have enough to do by day and by night. They have leave, also, to secure the best of provisions, such as sugar, bilberries, molasses, eggs, butter and to sell these things at a profit to the guests and spectators . . .

The only idol which the Indians have, and which may properly be called an idol, is their Wsinkhoalican, that is image. It is an image cut in wood, representing a human head, in miniature, which they always carry about them either on a string around the neck or in a bag. They often bring offerings to it. In their houses of sacrifice they have a head of this idol as large as life put upon a pole in the middle of the room. . . . The Wsinkhoalican they like also to hang about their children to preserve them from illness and insure them success.

CHAPTER TWO

Beate and the White River Revival, 1805–1806

The following chapter presents Moravian accounts of Beate's prophetic mission in Indiana between 1805 and 1806. As shown by Anthony F. C. Wallace (1956) and, more recently, by Gregory Evans Dowd (1992: 128), Beate was one of a long line of prophets who emerged among the Delawares during the stressful decades of war, dispossession, and exile between 1745 and 1815. The accounts appearing here have been drawn from the German-language writings of Moravian missionaries Abraham Luckenbach (1777–1854) and John Peter Kluge (1768–1849). Working with Kluge's wife, Anna Maria Ranck, both men proselytized among the Delawares along the White River in central Indiana between May, 1801 and September, 1806. The missionaries conducted their work at Goshen, a small town near the major White River Valley Delaware community of Chief Anderson's Town in present-day Anderson, Indiana, at which the Delaware grand council had invited the Christian Indians in Fairfield, Ontario (but not their missionaries) to settle in 1800.

The following accounts, preserved in manuscripts curated in the Moravian Archives in Bethlehem, Pennsylvania, and published by historian Lawrence H. Gipson in 1938, are drawn from Luckenbach's autobiography and diary entries and letters written by Luckenbach and his colleague Kluge. They contain the earliest known detailed documentary descriptions of Delaware traditional worship and religious philosophy and also include reports describing the role of the Munsee prophet Beate in the Delaware revival and firsthand observations of Delaware observances at the town of Woapicamikunk in present-day Muncie, Indiana. In addition they document the travails of communities living in exile on strange land, riven by disease, alcohol abuse, and witchcraft fears and stirred by the messages of Beate and the Shawnee Prophet (Miller 1994). Periodically giving way to self-righteous pontifications whose youthful enthusiasm did little to endear them to the Delawares and contributed to the ultimate failure of their mission, the authors of these accounts nevertheless show that Beate and many other Delawares refused to take part in the witchcraft persecutions sanctioned by the Shawnee Prophet that resulted in the deaths of several Delaware chiefs and converts in 1806.

ABRAHAM LUCKENBACH'S AUTOBIOGRAPHY

In every Indian town there was a so-called long-house, about forty feet in length and twenty feet wide, in which the savages held their sacrifices and dances. It also served as a Council House. These houses were built of split logs set together between dug-in posts, and were provided with a roof, consisting of tree bark or clap-boards, resting on strong pillars dug into the earth. The entrance was at both gable-ends and there was neither floor nor ceiling. Near both ends and in the middle, there were three fires over which hung large kettles in which corn and meat were boiled for the guests and always kept in readiness for them to eat, when finished with the dance. In the roof there were openings over every fire, so that the smoke could escape. Along the inside of the house there were seats or elevations from the ground about a foot high and five feet wide. These were first covered with the bark of trees and then with long grass. On them the guests sat, or if they felt like it, lay down and smoked their pipes, while the others were engaged in dancing.

The dances of the Indians are generally held in honor of their protecting deities, concerning whom they declared that they once upon a time appeared unto them in a dream, in one or another form, for example, in that of a large bird; that they talked with them, told them their future fate for better or for worse; that they either would be great Chiefs or Warriors who would do great deeds, great witch-doctors who would deal in supernatural things, or that they would possess great riches and many relatives, or the contrary. If the latter was the case, however, they did not sing their dreams, but sadly related them. Those who had the former dreams, on such occasions step forward, holding the shell of a land-turtle containing a number of beans or kernels of corn. Then the one who is to lead the dance, in honor of the protecting deity, advances. After he has rattled the turtle-shell with his hand amid many grimaces, he stops, and, speaking in a loud tone of voice, he relates, by fits and starts, the contents of his dream, or the manner in which his god appeared and what he told him. When he is finished with it, he turns about and faces those who want to join him in the dance. These are arranged in a row and equipped with bells fastened to their legs and arms. The bells consist of deer-hoofs and all sorts of silver trinkets in the shape of crescents, scrapers, and bracelets. These are so fastened to the body that a jarring sound is produced, at every step taken. Two Indians, sitting at the side, beat time with sticks, on a dried deer-skin made for the occasion, while the whole crowd moves forward with short, regular steps, which all take at the same time at certain abrupt intervals. Meanwhile the leader relates his dream in lines, which are repeated during the dance and drum-beating. The leader cuts many capers and jumps up and down. This is all in harmony with the time, and brings to light the skill of the dance. In this manner, the whole mass, the men first and the women following them, moves around in the house until they come again to the place from which they started, whereupon all gather around the post or pillar standing in the middle and upon which the roof rests. Upon both sides of this pillar are cut men's faces, provided with hair and painted, making a hideous appearance. In conclusion, all stretch out their hands toward the totem, and with a terribly shrill yell the dance comes to an end, whereupon all take their places again. After a short pause, another steps forward, when the same performance is repeated. These dances are held only at night and are often continued for weeks at a time. At the conclusion a sacrificial feast is held, for which the deer and bear-meat is provided by all joining in a common hunt, the women furnishing a store of corn-bread. All is prepared, in common, in the house of sacrifice, and there partaken of amid certain ceremonies. For example, the bread is arbitrarily thrown among the guests, and each one catches as much as he can. In conclusion, two beautiful tanned deer-skins are turned over to two old men appointed beforehand, who hold them toward the sunrise, in front of the house of sacrifice, and spread them out, while murmuring something. In this way, they imagine they are praying to their god. They thank him for long life and health. For this service the old men afterwards receive the skins as their property. Before I could understand the language very well, I had the opportunity of attending such a dance for half a night, and that at Woapicamikunk.[1] There were present a large number of Indians, besides chiefs.

John Conner[2] the trader mentioned above, who had a Delaware Indian for a wife and with whom I stayed over night, invited me to the dance and introduced me. He himself appeared to be very much taken with it. He said that the Indians in this way sought to serve their god, and that he had learned to know many of them whose dreams had been fulfilled; in fact, their dreams, with few exceptions, generally came true. He himself danced with them and had not gotten much farther in knowledge than the heathen. On such occasions, the Chiefs addressed their people, both the men and the women, and, although they themselves did not abstain, strictly prohibited the use of strong drink, fornication, adultery, stealing, lying, cheating, murder and urged hospitality, love, unity, as things well-pleasing to God, which is proof that even the heathen is not without knowledge of good and evil and therefore has a conscience which accuses or excuses him, and which will also judge him. It was customary among them on these occasions to erect tents around the outside of the Council House. After the ceremonies were over, they went, in companies, from one tent to the other to visit and to greet one another with a mutual handshake. In connection with this, they assumed a solemn mien and used courtly language according to the age or circumstances of the family addressed. All this makes a good outward show to one who does not know them

---

1. "White River," the major Delaware town on the White River in and around Muncie, Indiana, at the time. Also known as Buckongahelas's Town, after the important Delaware war leader who lived there (Weslager 1972: 333).
2. Sons of Ohio English trader Richard Conner, and his wife (who was an adopted colonial captive raised by the Shawnees), John Conner and his brother William became important culture brokers in the Midwest during the first quarter of the nineteenth century. One of William Conner's sons, also named John Conner, became a principal chief of the Kansas Delawares at mid-century (Weslager 1972: 334, 362).

or their circumstances. But, after one has made a closer acquaintance with them, one learns, unfortunately, how they distrust one another, even their nearest relatives, because of poisoning, witchcraft and the black art, so that really not one confides in another. When one of their relatives dies, whether old or young it is not unusual for one or the other of the relatives, or even some one else, to be suspected of having brought about the death either by poisoning or witchcraft.[3] The fellowship of love is therefore unknown among them, and on such occasions they merely make a pretense, because they are really afraid of one another. One sees from this how far imagination, stimulated by fear, causes such people, who are still in the grip of superstition, to go. Because their hearts are evil they cannot think well of one another.

Their useless worship of God is based on sensual enjoyment and preferences and applies itself to the desire of long life, wealth, honor, and good fortune, and not infrequently supernatural powers and communion with the protecting deities, who are to grant them respect and dignity. Such as pretend to have this privilege generally succeed in gaining certain advantages over others, but at the same time, they also run the great risk of being looked upon as evil persons, who put others out of the way by means of this art and supernatural power. Of such things the minds of the Indians of both sexes are full and so deeply rooted are they that even those who have accepted Christianity and believe that through Jesus' death they are delivered from the power of sin and of Satan, still insist that such evil powers exist among the heathen, and that they can kill each other by means of secret poison and the black art, and therefore easily give room to suspicion that such things do happen.

Special grace is therefore needed for such as have been converted from heathenism to Christianity, especially under certain circumstances as, for example, sickness, that they may be kept from seeking help from the sorcerers who claim that, by means of their art, they can cure or drive out disease, and rather resolve to die in faith in the Saviour and to inherit eternal life than by means of an evil power to become physically well and then be eternally lost.[4]

If one tell the heathen of the world's Saviour or Son of God, that He became man to deliver us from the power of sin and of Satan, that He was by wicked men nailed to the cross and put to death and again arose from the dead and ascended into Heaven, they usually turn off the matter by saying that they had no part in the death of the Son of God, since it did not happen in their country nor at the hands of their Nation. On the other hand, they relate that God, their Protector, had also appeared unto them from Heaven once upon a time, and that in winter, in the midst of a snow-storm, and that He had large snow-shoes on His feet; that He had stayed with them for a long time and prescribed to them their mode of life

---

3. References to poisoning and juggling here and elsewhere in the White River manuscripts refer to actual and suspected acts of shamans and sorcerers.
4. In this passage Luckenbach both affirms and condemns the efficacy of Indian healers and healing.

and sacrificial feasts, which they had followed strictly ever since. They had not dealt so wickedly with their God, but had reverently dismissed Him again, and therefore did not have to reproach themselves on account of it like the white people, who said of themselves that they had crucified the Son of God.

Others declared that God had indeed given the Bible or written book to the white people who could read it, but to the Indians or children of the forest He had given the hunting-grounds, sacrificial feasts, and had shown them another mode of life; the former could therefore seek to live up to what God had commanded them, while they felt it their duty to hold fast to that which He had appointed for them. Others again are of the opinion, which is not generally held among them, however, that the Indians did not come from the same source as the white people, but had been created separately, for which reason they were not allowed to adopt the customs of the white people and to regulate themselves according to their religion. Such declare that because of the acceptance of the white man's religion on the part of some, their gods had become angry and sought their destruction; that their deities wanted to take away from them their land and all customs and liberties, including the use of whiskey, which was the discovery of whites, as well as their silver and their gold, and the practice of usury among them, all of which they regarded as an evil in the world, and as originally unknown among their race, and something that had been brought upon them by the white people.

Others who were unfriendly to the preaching of the gospel were not ashamed to declare that we came among them for political reasons; that our object was to preach to them in order that they might be made tame and afterwards delivered over to the white people, as was the case in the war on the Muskingum (Gipson 1938... 611–17).[5]

WHITE RIVER MISSION DIARY ENTRIES AND LETTERS

Diary Entry, February 13, 1805

Our two Indian brethren Joshua and Jacob ... related that the Chief[6] had told them that an Indian woman, who had been baptized with the name of Beade in Friedenshüetten,[7] and who now lived near Woapicamikunk in Moncy Town, had had a vision. There had appeared unto her one evening while she was alone in front of her house, two men, whom she could not recognize, and whose voice

---

5. This is a reference to the massacre of ninety Moravian Indian converts at Gnadenhütten, Ohio, by American militiamen on March 8, 1782 (Weslager 1972: 315–17).
6. Buckongahelas, chief of Woapicamikunk.
7. Beate, "Beatific." Her Indian name, as well as much else about her life, is not known. Friedenshüetten was a major Susquehanna Valley Moravian Indian mission town in present-day Wyalsing, Pennsylvania, occupied between 1763 and 1772 (Kent, Rice, and Ota 1981: 9).

she alone could hear. These told her "Stand still, because we have something to tell you." And when she stood still, the two spoke unto her and said: "We came to tell you that God is not satisfied with you Indians, because at your sacrifices you do so many strange things with wampum and all sorts of juggling, and also do not keep separate spoons with which to stir the sacrificial meal and to dip it out." Having said this, they threw down several wooden spoons, and continued: "You Indians will have to live again as in olden times, and love one another sincerely. If you do not do this, a terrible storm will arise and break down all the trees in the woods, and all Indians shall lose their lives in it. As a sign that our words are true, a child will be born that shall speak in the very beginning, and tell you everything, exactly how you shall live." According to the woman, the two spirits disagreed in regard to the latter point, and disputed with each other. As said, the one desired that a child should tell them everything, but the other one said: "No! They will not believe the child. An old Indian who lived in former times shall arise and he shall tell them." Thereupon the first spirit answered: "No! That shall not happen, for if one who died in olden times shall arise, the Indians of the present time will not know him, and they will not believe him. Therefore, a recently departed captain by the name of Schaponque shall come to life again; this one all the Indians know, and he shall tell them," etc. This foolish fable and gossip of the woman meets with the utmost approval of the chiefs, for which reason that had all the Indians come together these last days, in order to make it known to them, and to admonish them by all means to do what the woman said. And now everyone expects the captain mentioned to rise from the dead (Gipson 1938... 332–34).

Diary Entry, March 4–5, 1805

4th. A large number of heathen, who had attended the sacrificial feast and the new appearance, of which mention was made in the preceding month, in Woapicamikunk, returned and passed through our village. One saw with astonishment that no weather or way was too unfavorable to keep the poor, blind heathen away from their abominations and customs, for they came on foot, men and women in one stream, and with heavy burdens on their backs, in the midst of a pouring rain, and not one showed signs of a feeling that all this might be a hardship in spite of the fact that their journey was about twenty miles in length. On the other hand, the shortest way is too burdensome or not worth the effort to hear the saving Word of God. We often notice with sorrowful hearts that even the visiting heathen seldom attend the services.

5th. We heard that the heathen, in connection with the sacrificial feast which they attended from near and far, practiced all their abominations and customs again. The day before they had a great spree, which was preparatory to the sacrifice, and afterwards it came to an end after nightly revelries and dancing. According to their statement, this was directly the opposite of what they wanted to do, for in connection with the new appearance, in which they declared Manitto or their God had told them how they should live, among other things, they were expressly told not to have any jugglery and dancing, but only sacrifices and prayers.

Because this was not done, some of the heathen were not at all satisfied, and they told some of our people that they would not go so far any more, upon invitation of the chiefs, because they had hoped to see something new and things were just as they always had been. Nevertheless the chiefs had said: "Although nothing came of our intention this time, let us not forget what Manitto told us and do what we can; perhaps we can fulfill it another time" (Gipson 1938: 336–37).

Diary Entry, March 14 and 16, 1805

14th. Ten Indians passed through our village again on their way to Woapicamikunk, whither they had been called to hear about another vision. This vision appeared to a woman again and consisted of the following: "A man of enormous stature appeared unto her and told the woman: 'You Indians heard recently how you should live and sacrifice, and you came together for that purpose, too, but you after all offered your sacrifices according to your old customs, and did not observe that which had been told you. Now I want to tell you who I am: I am a Devil who speaks with you. I too was present at the sacrifice, and I confused you, so that you could not think properly. Because you always do according to my will, it will go badly with you, unless you turn about at once and do even as the first two spirits told you,'" etc. This babbling of the old woman made the chiefs active at once. They immediately sent messengers to all Indians for the purpose of inviting them in the most solemn manner to the new lie, with the resolution to spend many days and nights in sacrificing this time. Never, in all the time that we are here, have the Indians been in such a state of revolution as they are at present. Time will tell what the result of this unrest among the Indians will be. For the present they do not want to hear anything at all except what they learn through the extravagant visions.

Br. Luckenbach told an Indian woman in a heathen town, who related to him this vision in a very sad manner, that all their appearances were the deception of the Devil, but if they would hear and accept the Word of God which we proclaim, that God in love for us poor people had become man, and had allowed Himself to be tortured for the sins of mankind, and had died on the cross, so that all who would believe in Him might receive the forgiveness of their sins and eternal life,—then all the Indians would soon learn that this is the right way to God, whereupon the woman, in a most indifferent way, said: "So!"

16th. A large number of heathen women passed through our village on their way to the sacrificial feast repeated at Woapicamikunk (Gipson 1938: 339–40).

Diary Entry, April 5, 1805

Late in the evening the Indians were called together by the loud cry of two servants appointed for the purpose. Upon this signal those of the Indians present gathered in their large house newly built for the sacrifice. Here two fires were built. Along the sides the servants had thrown straw on which the congregated Indian men and women seated themselves or if it pleased them, stretched themselves full length. One after the other—with a loud voice—began to relate his dream, only a few words at a time, which those Indians present then repeated with a loud voice while he rattled a turtle shell in which there were a few small stones. This song they sang while dancing about, the leader making all sorts of gestures and jumping up and down, which those following him then imitated as best they could. In the middle of the house they had erected a post on which was cut, on both sides, a human face painted Indian fashion. Whenever a dream was related in full, they gathered about this post, stretched out their hands toward it, and sang a song which they closed with a howl wherewith, as they say, they thanked God that the dream had begun its fulfillment (Gipson 1938: 350).

Letter, April 28, 1805

Recently, the heathen teachers began to come to the forefront, to confuse the poor, blind heathen still more and to keep them in the power of Satan. They clothe their teaching in all sorts of pretended virtues and most strongly recommend heathen sacrifices. They say that their teaching came directly from the Great Spirit, who had recently appeared to a woman and told her that the Indians must live after their ancient manner, keep the sacrifices, and by no means believe anything else. This teaching makes a great impression on the Indians, at the present time. They often resort to the heathen teachers in great numbers for the purpose of hearing the narration of the old woman's foolish fable, in which connection they spend eight days and nights in sacrificing and dancing and drinking. They live in constant fear, because the old woman told them that they would all perish, if they would not live up to the letter in everything that she had said. (Gipson 1938: 531).

Diary Entry, May 14, 1805

14th. Toward evening 5 Indians came into our village, and on account of the lateness of the hour, they remained overnight. Very late in the evening they came to the house of Br. and Sr. Kluge. One of their number is a noted sorcerer among the Indians. He told us that he had been with the Indian woman, the teacher, who had recently had a vision, and he had heard her words; that she also forbade all evil, drinking, fornication, stealing, murder, and the like. She had also told him everything about himself, what he was and what he thought as he came to her, and that she had been right in everything she told him; that she knew everything the Indians do and think even though she does not see it. He thought to himself: "This is strange! We hear that all evil is forbidden us and also believe that this woman received her words through an appearance of God; we sacrifice and worship for a long time in accordance with her words, and still I notice that the Indians continue to do what they are commanded not to do, and are unable to give up what she forbids," etc. This gave us an opportunity to tell these Indians that human nature was altogether corrupt, and Br. Kluge told them what the Saviour had suffered in order to deliver us from sin and the power of Satan, and to bring us salvation; that by faith alone we could be saved; that as long as a man did not believe with all his heart and seek the forgiveness of sin with Him, he remained the slave of sin and was unable to help himself; he might do what he would, nothing would do any good. He listened to all this most attentively and in silence (Gipson 1938: 354–55).

Diary Entry, September 15, 1805

25th. We heard that the Wyandottes' message to the chiefs here had no other object than to acquaint them with the wonderful vision an Indian woman had in Woapicamikunk this spring and to beg the Indians in this vicinity to permit the woman to come to them for a while so that they too might learn who among their people was bad and a master of poison. They complained that all men and children in their nation were dying one after the other, and that those who did not amount to much remained alive. Because they had heard that the said woman knew everything, they were anxious to take her with them. When they should bring the woman into their towns, then all Wyandottes should come together, so that the woman might look them over and if she should designate anyone as a bad person and a master of poison, that one should be put to death instantly, etc. The Delaware chiefs excused themselves and said that for the time being they could not spare the woman, because they intended to have sacrifices soon, at which time they would need the woman badly, for they themselves were not in order yet and ever forgetful what the woman had said as to how they should offer their sacrifices. With this the consultation came to an end, and the Wyandottes handed over a large number of wampum strings (Gipson 1938: 382–83).

Diary Entry, January 25, 1806

The teachers of the Delawares said that God had white hands, but otherwise he had the form of an Indian. Their teaching consists mainly of this: they are to sacrifice diligently, then God may hear them. On the contrary, however, if they would not they would all be destroyed within a month by a whirlwind. An old Indian woman, baptized in olden times, named Beate, who is the greatest lying prophet, pretends to have seen God Himself and also an angel. The first asked her if she was clean and when she answered in the affirmative, he said: "We shall see if you are clean. If you are clean the good spirit will enter into you." He then showed her a small white thing, which came to her. Thereupon God said: "Hold up your hands! This is the good spirit. Take it and swallow it." But when she wanted to do it, the little white thing went away again. God then told her to call it, which she did, whereupon it returned and went as far down as the throat, immediately coming out again. She called it again, and when it had again come into her hands, she gently put it into her mouth and swallowed it. The good spirit was therefore inside her and consequently she spoke only the Word of God. Such and similar blasphemous things meet with favor among the poor blind heathen.

The Indians flocked through our village on their way to the appointed house of sacrifice, and spoke with the greatest wonder and respect about these lies. They also promised to drink no more whiskey. This last thing would be well, but they promised the same thing at last year's sacrifices, but unfortunately failed to keep their word, and drank more than ever. They see with their own eyes that, with all their sacrifices, they accomplish nothing, and that all their liars tell them does not go into fulfillment, still they believe and permit themselves to be frightened and deceived, and that under the guise of teaching virtue (Gipson 1938: 402–403).

Letter, February 1, 1806

The heathen teachers appeared with power, and warned the Indians against our teaching. They pretended to have had visions from the Great Spirit, who told them that they should hold to their old customs and mode of life, and that they should have meat offerings, or else they would all be destroyed. Among these teachers, there is also a woman, who went so far as to make the Indians believe that she had actually seen the angels, and even God himself, who had given the Good Spirit into her hands, whereupon she had taken him into her mouth and swallowed him, and that now he was inside of her, telling her everything that God wanted the Indians to do. By means of such and all sorts of trumped-up lies, these instruments of the Devil seek to keep these poor people in the power of darkness, and unfortunately they are only too successful (Gipson 1938: 553).

Diary Entry, September 29–30, 1806

29th and 30th. Many Indians passed through our place on their way to a great heathen festival to be held in the Indian town 20 miles down the river from us. The lying prophetess who had all sorts of foolish appearances was also led there, so that the Indians might sacrifice and do all other things exactly as she had indicated. On an occasion of this sort, at the direction of the prophetess, an Indian dresses himself in a bearskin; over his face he wears an ugly mask, so that a disguised Indian like this makes an altogether horrible appearance. During the festival this fellow has oversight of the Indians because they are of the opinion that he knows everything and is able to bring to light all the bad things done in secret. For this reason he frequently goes from one Indian to the other and looks into their faces while he performs all sorts of ceremonies (Gipson 1938: 451).

CHAPTER THREE

Mid-Nineteenth-Century Accounts

This chapter contains some of the few known mid-nineteenth-century descriptions of the Big House Religion. The first was penned on May 10, 1822, by John Johnston, federal Indian agent at Piqua, Ohio, as a response to a questionnaire listing over four hundred queries into the customs and languages of Indians living in the United States circulated by Michigan Territory governor Lewis Cass (Kinietz 1946: 17; Weslager 1978: 86–87). The account was based upon information provided by an unnamed source. It is part of a manuscript entitled "Answers to the questions proposed in the Pamphlet, By the Delawares and Monsies," on file in the Trowbridge Papers in the Burton Historical Collection in the Detroit Public Library. The following extract reproduces text materials published in Kinietz (1946: 93–94) and Weslager (1978: 114–16).

It is followed by an account written the next year by a Delaware man named Captain Pipe. Captain Pipe was the leader of a Delaware village known as Pipe's Town or Captain Pipe's Town, a community of some sixty inhabitants located about eight miles from Sandusky, Ohio. His identity is unclear. He is the namesake and may be the descendant of the famous Wolf phratry warrior-diplomat Captain Pipe, Hopocan. First mentioned in another journal kept by Christian Frederick Post in 1758, the first Captain Pipe later became a leader of Delawares resisting American expansion into the Ohio Valley during the Revolutionary War. Refusing to end his resistance following the end of the war, he subsequently led his followers to the still British-held territories around the west end of Lake Erie. Whatever the identity or lineage of his namesake, the author of this account of the Big House presented it to Lewis Cass's personal secretary, Charles C. Trowbridge. It is preserved in the Trowbridge Papers in Detroit and published in Kinietz (1946: 94–97).

Rochester, New York, lawyer and pioneer ethnologist Lewis Henry Morgan (1818–81) gathered the next account from the prominent Delaware elder William Adams during a visit to the Delaware reservation in Kansas during the first of four summer field trips to Indian communities in the Kansas and Nebraska territories between 1859 and 1861 (White 1959: 56–57). Morgan conducted these trips to secure comparative information on kinship systems amplifying findings first made in his pathbreaking 1851 study, "The League of the Ho-de-no-sau-nee, or Iroquois" (Morgan 1962). Primarily interested in kinship, he gathered little information on religion or belief. Morgan's field journals, as well as most of his other papers and notes, are currently housed in the library of the University of Rochester in Rochester, New York.

The final account in this chapter is a brief description of Canadian Delaware religious feasts. It was penned by Munsee Christian convert John Wampum under the name Chief Waubuno and first appeared in print in 1875 in the volume, "The Traditions of the Delaware." Mark Raymond Harrington published the extract reproduced below as the only extended account besides his own of the Munsee ritual up to that time (Harrington 1921: 143–45). John Wampum may have been the man of the same name also known as Meni'.towak "Gathered or Bunch of [Deer] Ears." This John Wampum, along with Mohawk Anglican church leader G. H. M. Johnson, is alleged to have defaced or removed some of the Mesingw face-images in the Six Nations Delaware Big House in 1852 (Speck and Moses 1945: 2). Recently, John Bierhorst has found that most of Wampum's information was gathered by Peter Jones, an Ojibwa Wesleyan missionary who worked among the Ontario Delawares during the mid-1800s.

JOHN JOHNSTON'S ACCOUNT, 1822

They have a national worship which they think keeps the world from coming to an end. It is attended with very great expense in procuring wampum and provisions, etc. This meeting is continued for twelve days and twelve nights successively. They have a large building prepared for that purpose about twenty-five feet in width and fifty or sixty feet in length according to the number that it is expected will attend, with a door in each end. Notice is given at what time their worship will commence.

When they are collected and seated in a row round the outside of the building the men by themselves and the women by themselves a man and a woman at each door the man for a doorkeeper and the women to sweep between every exercise, the fires are made in the middle of the building which they make by rubbing two sticks together that it may be pure. The fire they put out every day and make new lest it should become adulterated, they make by rubbing two dry sticks together as at the first. Thus prepared the one that made preparation for the meeting gets up with a turtle shell in his hand (containing pebbles) and he gives it a shake and the whole assembly arises with him he then begins telling a dream which he says he dreamt in his childhood and the whole congregation repeats it after him in one voice word by word till he says he heard a voice singing to him and begins to sing immediately. Upon which two men commence beating with flat sticks upon skins folded together then he stops singing and he with the whole assembly jump ten or twelve jumps in the form of a dance. Then he makes a sudden halt and goes on with his dream as before repeated by the whole in one voice until he commences singing again as before and the players commence beating and the whole jump or dance in the form above mentioned. Thus they continue for the space of half an hour or more according to the length of his dream.

Then they seat themselves and the room is swept by the woman at the doors. The one that first spoke then shoves the shell under his legs to the next one, if he does not feel a disposition to tell his dream he shoves it to the next without shaking it, and it is shoved from one to another till it comes to one who wishes to tell his dream. Then he gives the shell a shake and after some minutes commences telling his dream while sitting but soon arises and the whole assembly with him he proceeds in the same manner as above mentioned. At intervals of telling dreams they appoint one or call one by name and give him a piece of wampum then they call eleven more they go out of the meeting and make doleful noise which is similar to howling but they term it making twelve prayers or praying twelve times. Then they return in to the meeting and the foreman that is the one that was first called divides the wampum among the twelves that went out. They commence telling dreams as before and going out to pray in the same manner thus they continue for twelve days and twelve nights abstaining themselves from women and every thing whereby they think they could be defiled. In these meetings they always have one appointed and dressed in bear skins appearing very frightful to go round and examine and see if there is any improper conduct. If so he points the stick at him or her which he has in his hand, the door-keepers immediately put the person out of the door and those who are put out are not admitted into the meeting any more.

Previous to these meetings they appoint a number of young men to go and kill a certain number of deer which they think will be sufficient to last them during the meeting. These are dressed, their provisions cooked and served to them while in their worship by those that they call their butchers.

CAPTAIN PIPE'S ACCOUNT, 1823

The Grand national worship of the Delawares has already been alluded to, and I come now to a description of it. It is called Engōmeen. There are three or four families in the nation whose duty it is by inheritance to prepare for and invite the nation to this assembly, and to whose care is committed every arrangement respecting it. Each family takes upon itself the performance of these duties once in three years; and as they do so in pretty regular succession, the worship is annual, or performed more frequently. The time and place of meeting is designated by this family, the principal male of which sends a messenger to the chief or head man of each village, who in his turn disseminates the information through the families of those under him. At the time appointed the nation, as well males as females assemble at a large lodge prepared for the purpose, where the females are placed in rear of the men. Here with grave and downcast looks they sit and receive from one of the old men an address upon the importance of a due observance of the ceremonies of the worship, and of abstinence from all unlawful pleasures during the continuance of them, among which any connection with women is counted a polluting sin. After describing at length the customs of their ancestors, among which this worship is placed in the foreground, the principal man of those who prepared the place of worship, having in his hand a small turtle shell containing a few gravel stones, gives it a sudden shake, and at the signal the worshipers all rise. He then commences a history of his early dream, repeating it in short sentences, in a natural tone of voice and being followed in the repetition of each sentence by all who are in the house. At length he commences to sing his dream, being followed by the company as before, and relieved between the sentences by a chorus of singers who are seated apart from the other worshipers, and have a kind of tambourine composed of a deer skin stretched across four sticks, upon which they beat the time. The music is said to be agreeable and very soft.

After this person has finished the tale of his dream, in which is described minutely every circumstance connected with the appearance of his tutelar deity, as well as those events of his life, which being told, have *of course* come to pass, each person in the lodge takes him by the hand in a mystical manner and they all seat themselves. The men then smoke for a short time, preserving the utmost silence and gravity of deportment, during which occupation the speaker takes occasion to push the shell under his legs in a secret manner, to the next person on his right, who declares his intention to speak by giving it a slight shake, or pushes it in the same secret way to the next. When one has accepted the turtle by the shake of accession, he remains in a state of apparent meditation for a few minutes, and then rising gives it another rattle, when, as in the preceding instance, he is joined by all the worshipers and the same ceremonies of repeating the dream, are performed.

The worship is commenced at evening and continued until daybreak, when it ceases for the day during which time the worshipers remain in the lodge in perfect silence. Thus it is repeated from night to night six times, and at the closing of the last night they adjourn for an hour or two, and then finish the worship with a relation of the dream of some extraordinary personage, whose history has been preserved in tradition. They cease at noon of the last day.

LEWIS HENRY MORGAN'S ACCOUNT, 1859

Gum-mween

This festival or annual worship of the Delaware as explained by William Adams and of which he is to write to me more fully, is quite interesting.[1] They

---

1. William Adams was a prominent leader of the Kansas and, later, Eastern Oklahoma Delaware Reservation communities. The later correspondence that is mentioned has not yet been found among Morgan's papers.

believe unless they observe it once a year their crops will fail, and they will lose the favor of the Great Spirit. It lasts six days. It may be repeated by another person or family for a second 6 days, and so on until the feelings are satisfied. It has been known to last a month. The meeting is called by one of a certain class, who I presume correspond with the Keepers of the Faith of the Iroquois. They are called A-la-pa-cte, meaning "Dreamers." The people meet in a large house erected for this purpose and used for nothing else. They build two council fires in the house, and the people assemble by tribes, the Turtles by themselves, the Wolves by themselves and the Turks [Turkeys] by themselves. They use belts of wampum and have many ceremonies. It would seem that this council or religious meeting was called by one person. The door of the house of worship must open to the east.

When they are assembled two singers sit down to two dried and rolled up deer skins, with sticks in their hands to beat time. The leader, who is stationed on the right hand side of the door, gets up and shaking a turtle shell rattle, comes in extemporizing verses which are adapted to the set tune of his choosing, to relate his dream. As he relates his dream in music, he dances, they sing the same time and beat time, and all who enter the dance, dance the religious dance which altogether is called the Gum-mween. This is repeated day by day for six days. But the leaders change. When one has told his dream, he hands his rattle to the next one, who in like singing relates his dream in words of his own making, but sung in an old well known tune of his own choosing.

Before the festival twelve hunters are sent out for deer's meat, as no other meat is allowed. About nine each morning this meat is served to all. At sundown each day they have an exhortation from the oldest wise man of the nation. Once during the six days, about an hour before night fall, they burn incense by throwing on the fire in the center of the house cedar branches, which fills the house with smoke and then ascends to the Great Spirit. If no one repeats the worship, or when all are done, the people all go out in Indian file, and facing the east, in a united voice they thank the Great Spirit for sparing their lives through the year, and invoke him to spare them until the next Gum-mween.

JOHN WAMPUM'S ACCOUNT, 1875

They kept annual feasts—A feast of first fruits which they do not permit themselves to taste until they have made an offering of them to the Manitu-oo-ak, or gods; . . . There is one of the greatest sacrifice offerings of our fore-fathers every six months for cleansing themselves from sin; they will have twelve deers to be consumed in one day and night. At the great feast of the offerings of the first fruits of the earth, which feast the Delawares or Munceys hold annually, they brought a little of all that they raised, such as Indian corn, or Hweisk-queem, potatoes, beans, pumpkins, squashes, together with the deer. The Indian women were busily engaged in cooking their provisions, previous to the commencement of their exercises. They invited all strangers into a long pagan temple prepared for such purposes, there is a door at each end—one opening to the east, and one opening to the west. On entering, they with all the Indians were seated on the ground around two fires; in the center of the temple was a large post, around which was suspended a number of deer skins, and wampum is kept buried at the foot of this post. Near the post sat two Indian singers, each with a large bundle of undressed deer skins which served as drums. There were two young men appointed to watch the doors and keep the fires burning, the doors being closed. Each of the young men brought an armful of hemlock boughs, which being thrown on the fires smothered them and caused a great smoke. In order that the smoke might fill every corner of the temple, each man waved his blanket over the fire; this was done with the idea of purifying the temple and driving out the evil spirits. After the smoke had subsided, the master of ceremonies, an old chief, rose and began to rattle a turtle shell he had in his hand. He delivered a speech to the people telling them the object of the meeting was to thank the Great Spirit for the growth and ripening of the corn. When he finished his speech he began to dance, sing, and rattle the shell, the two singers joining in, beating on their skins. When he took his seat he handed the shell to the next person, who performed in the same way, thus it went from one to the other all night. The purport of their speeches was to recount the mercies of the Great Spirit to them during the past year, and telling any remarkable dreams that they had. In the course of the night a number of them went out the west door, making a wailing noise to the moon, and came in again the east door. In the morning the meat and soup were divided amongst the people.

These feasts often lasted twelve days and twelve nights, and the Indians call it Nee-shaw-neechk-togho-quanoo-maun, or Ween-da-much-teen. No drinking or improper conduct is allowed. The utmost solemnity prevails.

CHAPTER FOUR

Richard C. Adams's Accounts, 1890 and 1904

Richard C. Adams was a highly educated Eastern Oklahoma Delaware writer and activist. Adams was born in Kansas, the son of the same William Adams who provided the information on the Gamwing to Lewis Henry Morgan that appears in the preceding chapter. He was also a maternal grandson of Mekinges, the daughter of the influential Chief Anderson who married trader William Conner before the main band of the Delawares moved from Indiana to Missouri, and then to Kansas in 1829.

Adams was among the Delawares who moved among the Cherokees in Oklahoma in 1867. Educated in American schools and admiring many aspects of American culture, Adams nevertheless remained a tireless defender of his people's rights to the end of his life. A skillful writer and aware of the power of print to mold opinion, Adams published several tracts intended to raise awareness and support of Delaware culture and belief. The accounts that follow reproduce two of Adams's descriptions of the Delaware Big House (Adams 1890; Adams 1904: 8–29). The first contains a schematic outline of the ceremony; the second is a more literary rendition, incorporating story elements evidently drawn from published sources. Regarded as idiosyncratic and flawed by present-day traditionalists and scholars, Adams's accounts nevertheless provide an otherwise unavailable glimpse into an American-educated late nineteenth-century Delaware's views of his own culture's traditions. See Nichols (1997) for a more detailed review of Adams's life and work.

THE 1890 ACCOUNT

The peculiar steps which they use in this dance have caused the name "stomp" or "stamp" to be applied to it. In regard to the stomp dances of our people, we have several kinds of dances; the most important one is the "worship dance" which is carried on in a large building called a temple, which is rectangular and ranges from sixty to eighty feet long, from thirty to forty feet wide, and is about ten feet high. It is built of wood with two doors. The main entrance is at the eastern door, and it has only a dirt floor.

On each post is carved a human face. On the center post or one in the center of the building four faces are carved; each face is painted one-half red and one-half black. All the people enter at the east and go out the same way. When they come in they pass to the right of the fire, and each of the three clans of the Delawares take seats next to the wall, the Turtle clan on the south, the Turkey on the west, and the Wolf on the north. In no case can any one pass between the center post and east door, but must go around the center post, even to go to the north side of the temple.

This dance is held once each year, in the fall, and generally in October, in the full moon, and lasts not less than twelve days for each part. The tribe is divided into three clans, and each clan has to go through the same part, so the dance is sometimes thirty-six days long, but sometimes the second and third clans do not dance more than six days each.

The Turtle clan usually lead or begin the dance. A tortoise shell, dried and beautifully polished and containing several small pebbles, is placed in the southeast corner near the door in front of the first person. If he has anything to say he takes the shell and rattles it, and an answer comes from the south side of the temple from the singers, who strike on a dried deer's hide; then the party who has the tortoise shell makes an address or talk to the people, and thanks the Great Spirit for blessings, and then proceeds to dance, going to the right and around the fire, followed by all who wish to take part, and finally coming to the center post he stops there; then all the dancers shake hands and return to their seats. Then the shell is passed to the next person, who dances or passes it on, as he chooses.

On the third day of the dance all men, both married and single, are required to keep out of the company of women for three days at least. They have a doorkeeper, a leader, and two or three parties who sweep the ground floor with turkey wings, and who also serve as deacons. The ashes from the fire are always taken out at the west door, and the dirt is always swept in the fire. In front of the east door outside is a high pole on which venison hangs. It is a feast dance and the deacons distribute food among the people. The officers and waiters are paid in wampum for their services.

In no case is a dog allowed to enter the temple, and no one is allowed to laugh inside it or in any way be rude. Each person is allowed to speak and tell his dream or dreams or to give advice. It is believed by the Delawares that every one has a guardian spirit which comes in the form of some bird, animal, or other thing, at times in dreams, and tells them what to do and what will happen. The guardian spirit is sent from the Great Spirit.

Traditions say that ten years before white men came to this country (America) a young man told his dream in the temple. This was on the Atlantic coast. He saw coming across the great waters a large canoe with pinions (wings) and containing strange people, and that in ten years they would in fact come. He told this dream and predicted the arrival of the white men each year until they came and were seen by his people. Many of our people still keep up this dance, but the temple is not so large as it used to be, and the attendance now is not more than one hundred persons. Any Indian of any tribe can also take part in the dance, but no white man can.

When the dance is over all the people go out and stand in a single line from east to west with their faces to the south. Then they kneel down and pray, and then go home. We do not know the origin of the worship dance, but the old Indians claim that the Great Spirit came many years ago and instructed it and also gave them the wampum.

In spite of several inaccuracies, such as the statement that the people face south (instead of east) while praying after the ceremony, this account is valuable on account of the additional data it furnishes on several points of interest, especially the tradition concerning the prophecy of the coming of the whites.

Messingq or Solid Face Dance or Devil Dance—The principal leader in this dance is the Messingq, an Indian, who is dressed in a bearskin robe with a wooden face, one-half red and one- half black. He has a large bearskin pouch and carries a stick in one hand and a tortoise shell rattle in the other. He is a very active person. The dance is only for amusement, and men and women join in it. A large place is cleared in the woods, and the ground is swept clean and a fire built in the center. Across the fire and inside of the ring is a long hickory pole supported at each end by wooden forks set in the ground. On the east of this pole the singers stand; on the west end is a venison or deer, which is roasted. About daylight, when the dance is nearly over, all the dancers eat of the venison. They have a dried deer hide stretched over some hickory poles, and standing around it beat on the hide and sing. The dancers proceed around the fire to the right, the women on the inside next to the fire. After the dance is under headway the Messingq comes from the darkness, jumps over the dancers, and dances between the other dancers and the fire. He makes some funny and queer gestures, kicks the fire, and then departs. The Messingq is never allowed to talk, but frequently he visits the people at their homes. He is a terror to little children, and when he comes to a house or tent the man of the house usually gives him a piece of tobacco, which the Messingq smells and puts in his big pouch, after which he turns around and kicks back toward the giver which means "thank you," and departs. He never thinks of climbing a fence, but jumps over it every time that one is in his way. The Devil dance is what the white men call it, but the Delawares call it the Messingq, or "Solid Face" dance. The Messingq does not represent an evil spirit, but is always considered a peacemaker. I suppose that it is from his hideous appearance that white men call him the devil.

THANKSGIVING DANCE, 1904

Traditions of our people as far back as the memories of our tribe are that we always had a Thanksgiving Dance. That many, many generations ago we came from a far-off country in the northwest; came across a land of ice and snow, until we reached the Great Fish River, or Mississippi River, where we found many people living in that valley who fiercely opposed our progress, but, after a long war, we completely overcame them, and proceeded on our journey until we finally settled in that country watered by the Susquehanna and the Delaware Rivers, our country extending from the mountains to the tide water.[1] Here all the Algonquin Tribes lived near them, and they became powerful and rich, so much so that they forgot to give thanks to the Great Spirit.

About that time there was a great famine or drouth. Following this great earthquakes came, rivers went dry, streams and springs started up in places where water had scarcely been seen before. Mountains came and disappeared and great fear prevailed among the people.

About this time there came to the head chief, or sachem, of the Delawares a little boy, who told the chief that his people had treated him very badly; that they would make him do more work than he was able to do and would give him but little to eat; that he had felt very badly about the way he was treated, but had put up with it. Finally, one day his people told him to go out and gather some wild sweet potatoes, which were considered a great delicacy. He went, and, to show that he was industrious, and thinking to get a little praise, or if not that, at least, to escape blame by bringing home a bountiful supply, he worked hard and got all he could carry.

He reached home as early as possible, and his people put the potatoes on to cook in a large kettle at noon. They cooked them until the evening star went down, but before this time they made the little boy go to bed without any supper. After he had been in bed for some time they began to eat the potatoes and other food. They called the boy, and he answered, and jumped quickly from the bed, thinking he was invited to take part in the feast. He was only abused, however, called a glutton and told to go away. So, heart-broken and in despair, he left the house and wandered until he was utterly exhausted. He then went to sleep. Before this he was moaning to himself about his unfortunate lot. He cried out to the Great Spirit to give him relief. He began his supplication with O-oo and heard twelve voices with the same sound.

When he went to sleep there came to him a man with his face painted red, and as he emerged from the darkness only half of his face showed. This man talked to him and told of the great things there were in the world beyond; that his people were wicked, not only his own family but all his tribe; that they had forgotten the Great Spirit, which was the reason why the earthquakes and other trouble had been visited upon them, and that more would follow, if they did not repent. The boy asked why he heard twelve voices answer his prayer, and the spirit to whom

---

1. This passage indicates that Adams was familiar with the Walam Olum legend, which had been published (Brinton 1885) and was widely available. Whatever its symbolic import, most scholars accept the extensive proofs presented by David M. Oestreicher (1994) showing that it was a fabrication.

he was talking replied that he would have to pass through twelve worlds or spheres before he could get to the home of the Great Spirit; that in each sphere there was a Manitou ruling, and that no prayer could reach the Great Spirit that did not come through the twelve spheres; that his cry had reached the first, who transmitted it to the second, and he in turn to the third, and so on until the twelfth delivered it to the Great Spirit himself.

He was told to go to the head chief or sachem and tell him that the people should return thanks each autumn to the Great Spirit, and when the people all met he should say that the Great Spirit sent him to talk to them; that he was a medicine-man, made so this night; that he had received the gift of the Great Medicine from the Great Spirit himself. He was to tell they should never be discouraged when trials and tribulations came to them, for it was under those circumstances, and when in that condition, that the Great Spirit took compassion over mortals, and made them superior and possessed of great influence over their fellow men; that none of the tribe had gone through as great trials as he had.

The chief or sachem called the people together, and renewed the Thanksgiving Dance of the Delawares. The little boy told what he had seen. He told them that they were to prepare a long, large house, and inside this house there were to be twelve posts, each with a face carved on it, half the face to be painted red and the other half black. There should also be a center post with four faces carved on it. These posts were to represent the twelve Manitous who guarded the twelve spheres through which the people should pass to reach the Happy Hunting Ground. The center post represented the Great Spirit, who saw and knew all things.

Every year after that they were to return thanks to the Great Spirit in the time of the autumn full moon, when nature had painted the forest in brilliant hues and the harvest was over. The dance was to last twelve days, which was the time it would take the twelve Manitous to convey their thanks and prayers to the Great Spirit.

All the people are to enter at the east and retire the same way. When they come in they are to pass to the right of the fire and each clan takes its place, sitting on the ground (skins or robes are thrown down for them to sit on) next to the wall.

The Turtle clan on the south, the Turkey on the west, and the Wolf on the north, and, in no case, shall anyone pass between the center post and the east door, but must go around the center post to the north side of the dance house. The medicine man shall lead the dance. A tortoise shell, dried and polished, containing several pebbles, is to be placed in the southeast corner, near the door, in front of the first person, known as the orator. If he has anything to say, he will take the shell and rattle it, and an answer shall come from the south of the dance house from the singers who hit on a dry deer hide. Then the parties who had the tortoise shell shall make a talk to the people, and thank the Great Spirit for their blessings, and then proceed to dance, going to the right and around the fire, followed by all who wished to dance, and, finally, coming to the center post, stop there. All the people shall shakes hands with him, and return to their seats. Then the shell should be passed to the next person, who shall either pass it on or rattle it, as he chooses. They shall have a doorkeeper and a leader, and twelve Oshkosh to sweep the ground with turkey wings, make fires, and serve as messengers. The ashes should always be taken out of the west door. In front of the east door, outside, should be a high pole, on which venison should hang. The Oshkosh shall distribute food among the people. The officers and Oshkosh are to be paid in wampum for their services. In no case should they allow a dog to enter the dance house, and no one should laugh inside or in any way be rude. The orators repeat the traditions, but each party is allowed to speak and tell his dream or give advice. Every one has a guardian spirit. Sometimes representations of it come in the form of some bird, animal, or anything; at times we see it in dreams, and at other times by impression; and it tells us what to do or what will happen, etc. The guardian spirit is sent from the Great Spirit. It is the inward voice.

The last thing, when the dance is over, all the people are to go out and stand in a line east and west, with their faces south, and bow down and thank the Great Spirit, and then go home.

Some of the Delaware Indians still keep up this dance, but the dance house is not so large as it used to be, and the attendance now is not more than one hundred. Any Indian of any tribe can participate in the dance.

At the dance all who take part repeat what the leader says, both the song and the exhortation. The leader often repeats the story of the little boy, comparing our trials to that of the little boy who had met with disappointments, but telling that after a while the Great Spirit sent him gifts, by which he was able to overcome these disappointments, or be strong enough to bear them.

Sometimes in their dreams or visions they see men, sometimes birds or animals, and in telling of them they do not say they had a dream, but say: "There came to me this," etc.

These dreams and impressions are sometimes used as illustrations by the orator before repeating the orations that have been handed down from memory. There are quite a number of these orations. On the following pages are some expressed as nearly as can well be translated.

The historical or opening oration gives one a fair idea of what their faith is. Each night the orations are different, and each night several dances take place; and preceding the dance will be an oration of instructions, an oration of thanks, and oration of praise and encouragement, or an address in which the speaker gives his impressions, and speaks generally for the good of the assembly.

Before the dance closes each night hominy is passed around, and all partake of it and say: "For this we are thankful." Fire is made with the use of fire sticks by friction, which they call pure fire. Smoking is permissible in the dance house, but the smoker must use the fire that is burning in the center, and made by the Oshkosh, which is called pure fire. No matches are allowed to be used.

CHAPTER FIVE

Eastern Oklahoma Delaware Big House Ceremonies, 1907–1910

This chapter and the following one present the first published modern anthropological accounts of the Big House Religion. Anthropologist Mark Raymond Harrington assembled the information between 1907 and 1910 while gathering artifacts for George Gustav Heye, whose collections, first organized within New York's Museum of the American Indian, Heye Foundation, are now curated by the National Museum of the American Indian. Harrington's collections represent the most extensive physical record of the regalia and equipage of the Big House in existence.

Chapter five contains descriptions of Eastern Oklahoma ceremonies based on first-person observation and information provided by Charlie Elkhair (Kokulupo'w'e); Julius Fouts (Peeta'nihink); his wife, Minnie Fouts (Wemeele'xkew); and William Brown. Together, the materials constitute the largest corpus of first-person data from major participants of the Oklahoma Big House. Harrington published their texts and accompanying illustrations of collected artifacts and images in a general monograph on Delaware religion. Library copies of this monograph, first published in 1921 and long out of print, remain one of the most consulted sources of information on the subject. The following extracts from Harrington's monograph directly discuss the Oklahoma Big House (Harrington 1921: 81–116, 122–25).

The Leader

The great Annual Ceremony of the Lenape now in Oklahoma was and is held when the leaves turn yellow in the fall of the year, usually, according to the "pale face" reckoning, some time between the tenth and twentieth of October. It is not exactly a tribal affair, although the whole tribe participates, but must be undertaken by some certain individual of the proper qualifications who takes the responsibility of "bringing in" the meeting and acting as a leader.

The phratry to which this leader belongs determines the exact form of the ceremonies to be held; for each totemic group has a ritual of its own, that of the

Wolf, which is here related, differing in some particulars from the ceremonies as practiced by the Turtle or Turkey people. In former times, it is said, when one phratry had finished its twelve days of ceremonies, another would enact theirs, followed by the third; but at present qualified leaders are so few that it seldom if ever happens that more than one of them feels able to accept such exacting duties in any one year.

This leader it is who sends a messenger forth to notify the people what day the ceremonies are to commence and to invite them all to attend. Several days before the date the wagons begin to roll in and a white village of tents springs up about the gray walls of the old Big House temple, or Xi'ngwikan, standing on the banks of Little Caney River, north of Dewey in northern Oklahoma, far from any human habitation.

Built of rough logs, the Big House is now provided with a roof of hand-split shingles pierced by two great smoke-holes, but in former days the roof was of bark. The length is about forty feet from east to west, with a height at the eaves of about six feet, at the ridge fourteen feet, and a width of twenty-four and one-half feet. Aside from certain ingenuities of construction which can not be discussed here, its chief interest lies in the two large carvings of the human face, one facing east and one west, which adorn the great central post supporting the ridge-pole. Similar carvings, but smaller, may be seen upon each of the six posts which support the logs forming the sides, and still smaller ones, one upon each of the four door-posts. All twelve faces are painted, the right side of each red, the left black. The building is used only for the Annual Ceremony.

Officers

The messenger sent to assemble the people is one of three male attendants chosen by the leader, and these three men appoint three women to serve also. To these six attendants, known as A'ckas, falls all the laborious work of the meeting. Although the duties are menial, it is considered quite an honor to be selected as A'ckas. The attendants camp on the north and south sides of the little open square just east of the Big House, an area where no one is allowed to pitch a tent.

Other officers selected for the meeting are a speaker (usually at the time of the writer's visit, Chief Charley Elkhair), two singers, called Tale'gunük, "Cranes," whose duty it is to beat the dry deerskin drum and sing the necessary songs, and a chief hunter who is supposed to provide venison for the feast.

Preparations

Arrived at the Big House, the attendants begin at once to prepare the building for use after its year of idleness. The first act of the men is to make mortar of mud, in the old style, and stop the cracks between the logs of the house. Then they cut two forked saplings, and set them in the ground about ten feet apart, some

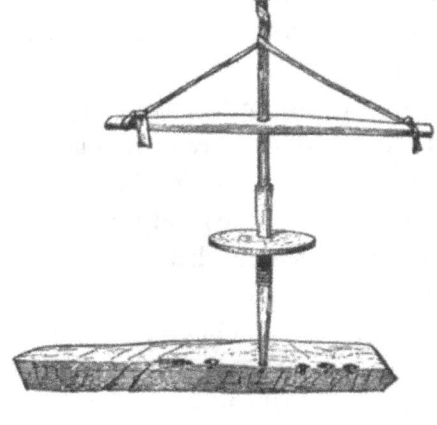

Fig. 4. Ceremonial fire-drill used at the Annual Ceremony, length of shaft 29.5 inches (fig. 8, Harrington 1921: 86). Courtesy National Museum of the American Indian.

distance in front of the Big House; upon these is laid a pole, running east and west, to support the twenty-gallon kettle used in preparing hominy for the feast. After this they gather about a cord of wood for the fires inside the Big House and the cooking fire outside. Then the first night, a fire pure and undefiled by the white man and his matches, is made with a fire-drill [fig. 4]. This is operated on the principle of a pump-drill, like the ceremonial fire-drills of the Iroquois. This fire, and this only may be used in the temple, and no one is permitted to take it outside for any purpose.

Ceremony Commenced

Two of the attendants, a man and a woman, then build the two fires in the temple, so that there may be plenty of light, and sweep the floor with turkey-wings for brushes. The men attendants take turns so that one of them, at least, is always on guard outside the building. When the temple is clean, the fires are burning bright, and the A'ckas have called the people in and all are assembled, the chief arises and delivers a speech.

Chief's Speech

First he states the rules of the meeting, then he speaks along some such line as the following, which was dictated by Chief Elkhair, who frequently made these speeches:

"We are thankful that so many of us are alive to meet together here once more, and that we are ready to hold our ceremonies in good faith. Now we shall meet here twelve nights in succession to pray to Gicelëmû"kaong in the highest heaven. The reason why we dance at this time is to raise our prayers to him. Our attendants here, three women and three men, have the task of keeping everything about our Temple in good order, and of trying to keep peace, if there is trouble. They must haul wood and build fires, cook and sweep out the Big House.

"When they sweep, they must sweep both sides of the fire twelve times, which sweeps a road to Heaven, just as they say that it takes twelve years to reach it. Women in their menses must not enter this house.

"When we come into this house of ours we are glad, and thankful that we are well, and for everything that makes us feel good which the Creator has placed here for our use. We come here to pray Him to have mercy on us for the year to come and to give us everything to make us happy; may we have good crops, and no dangerous storms, floods nor earthquakes. We all realize what He has put before us all through life, and that He had given us a way to pray to Him and thank Him. We are thankful to the East because everyone feels good in the morning when they awake, and see the bright light coming from the East, and when the Sun goes down in the West we feel good and glad we are well; then we are thankful to the West. And we are thankful to the North, because when the cold winds come we are glad to have lived to see the leaves fall again; and to the South, for when the south wind blows and everything is coming up in the spring, we are glad to live to see the grass growing and everything green again. We thank the Thunders, for they are the Mani'towük that bring the rain, which the Creator has given them power to rule over. And we thank our mother, the Earth, whom we claim as mother because the Earth carries us and everything we need. When we eat and drink and look around, we know it is Gicelëmû"kaong that makes us feel good that way. He gives us the purest thoughts that can be had. We should pray to Him every morning.

"Man has a spirit, and the body seems to be a coat for that spirit. That is why people should take care of their spirits, so as to reach Heaven and be admitted to the Creator's dwelling. We are given some length of time to live on earth, and then our spirits must go. When anyone's time comes to leave this earth, he should go to Gicelëmû"kaong, feeling good on the way. We all ought to pray to Him, to prepare ourselves for days to come so that we can be with Him after leaving the earth.

"We must all put our thoughts to this meeting, so that Gicelëmû"kaong will look upon us and grant what we ask. You all come here to pray; you have a way to reach Him all through life. Do not think of evil; strive always to think of the good which He has given us.

"When we reach that place, we shall not have to do anything or worry about anything, only live a happy life. We know there are many of our fathers who have left this earth and are now in this happy place in the Land of Spirits. When we arrive we shall see our fathers, mothers, children, and sisters there. And when we have prepared ourselves so that we can go to where our parents and children are, we feel happy.

"Everything looks more beautiful there than here, everything looks new, and the waters and fruits and everything are lovely. No sun shines there, but a light much brighter than the sun, the Creator makes it brighter by his power. All people who die here, young or old, will be of the same age there; and those who are injured, crippled, or made blind will look as good as the rest of them. It is nothing but the flesh that is injured; the spirit is as good as ever. That is the reason that people are told to help always the cripples or the blind. Whatever you do for them will surely bring its reward. Whatever you do for anybody will bring you credit hereafter. Whenever we think the thoughts that Gicelëmû"kaong has given us, it will do us good. This is all I can think of to say along this line. Now we will pass the Turtle around, and all that feel like worshiping may take it and perform their ceremonies."

Some nights the speaker says more, sometimes less, just as he feels, but he always tries to tell it as he heard it from the old people who came before him.

Recital of Visions

Now, as was stated, these meetings are "brought in" by individuals; that is a certain person, usually a man, undertakes to arrange for the meeting and to lead the ceremonies. This person must be one of those gifted by a vision or dream of power in their youth, and hence, according to Lenape belief, one in communication with the supernatural world.

When the people file into the Big House, the few that still have them dressed in their best Indian costumes carefully preserved for such occasions, the members of this leader's clan always take their seats on the north side, the other two clans in the west end and the south side. Men and women, however, do not mingle, but sit separately in the space allotted to their common clan. The diagram [see fig. 1] shows the seating of the clans when the ceremony is "brought in" by a member of the Wolf division.

After the chief's speech, the leader arises from his place just north of the central post, and, rapidly shaking a rattle (Taxo'xi xowüni'gün) made of a box-tortoise shell [fig. 5], recites his vision in a high monotone, word by word. After he utters each word, he pauses an instant to give the singers sitting at the rolled dry deerskin called Powüni'gün which serves as a drum [fig. 6], ample time to repeat the same word in the same tone, which produces an extraordinary effect. When he finishes, the drummers beat rapidly on the dry hide, repeating "Ho-o-o!" a number of times.

Then the celebrant repeats a verse of his song in the same way, and the drummers, having learned the words, sing them to a dance tune, beating the drum in slower time. After dancing awhile, the celebrator whoops, and they stop; then another similar verse, if not the same, is recited and then sung.

When the leader dances, he circles about the two fires contra-clockwise, and those who wish may join in the dance and follow him.

His dance finished, the leader passes the turtle shell to the next man who has been blessed with a vision. This one has the privilege of singing his vision if he wishes; if not, it is handed to the next "dreamer." After a celebrant has taken his seat, it is customary for those who desire it to smoke until the next man is ready to commence. At this time also it is considered proper for the people to enter or leave the Big House, which is not permitted while the actual ceremony is in progress. When the turtle rattle has thus made the round of the building and

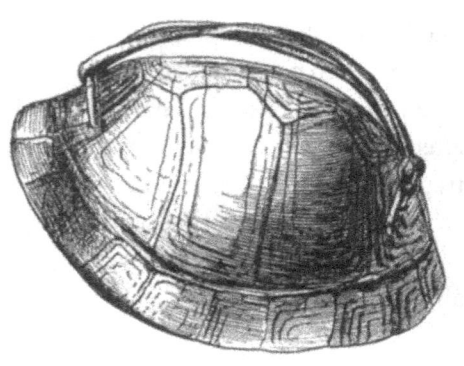

Fig. 5. Box-turtle-shell rattle, length 4.2 inches (fig. 9, Harrington 1921: 93). Courtesy National Museum of the American Indian.

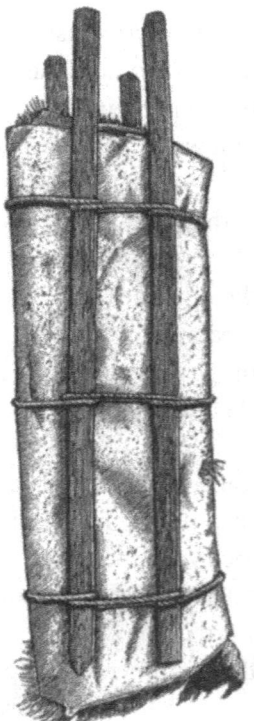

Fig. 6. Eastern Oklahoma–style dried deerskin drum, length 38.2 inches (fig. 10, Harrington 1921: 94). Courtesy National Museum of the American Indian.

gets back to its starting point, the meeting is brought to a close. This is usually along toward morning, the exact time of course being dependent on the number who have sung their visions, and on the length of the intermissions.

Conclusion of Rites

Now, when the man who started the ceremonies begins to dance, that is a signal for two of the women A'ckas, or attendants, to go out and pound corn for hominy or meal, and two of their male colleagues cook it in the kettle hanging on the pole, so that it is ready when the turtle has made its rounds and the meeting is about to close. Then the repast of hominy or corn mush called Sä'pan is distributed, and the speaker says, "We will now pray twelve times," so twelve times they cry "Ho-o-o!" as a prayer. Then they feast, using mussel shells from the river as spoons, and finally the speaker dismisses them with the words, "This is all for tonight; tomorrow night we will meet again."

Departure of the Hunters

When the next night arrives, approximately the same performance is repeated; and the same the next, with little of interest occurring during the day; but on the fourth morning, the leader who has selected a man for chief hunter, gives him a yard of wampum as pay. This master of the hunt then selects as many assistants as he wants, and he and his crew all gather in the Big House, where they are served about noon with a feast prepared for the occasion by the women of the camp, and the attendants tie sacks of the food to the hunters' saddles. When they have finished eating, they arrange themselves in a row, each hunter standing on his left foot and barely touching the ground with the toes of his right, an action whose meaning I have not yet been able to determine.

Then the speaker rises and talks to them, and the Mïsi'ng^{we} who has been seen about the camp from time to time, is in the Big House listening to his words. "When you hunt," says the speaker, "think of nothing but luck to kill deer." As he speaks he goes to the west fire and throws into it, six times, an offering of native tobacco; then to the east fire, where he sacrifices six more pinches of the sacred herb—twelve in all. While sacrificing tobacco, he prays to the Mïsi'ng^{we} to drive the deer up, so that the hunters can kill them. As he drops the last tobacco into the flames, he says, "If you kill a deer right away, bring it in tonight; if not, bring in all you kill day after tomorrow."

What tobacco is left is given to the chief hunter with the words, "When you camp tonight, burn this and ask Mïsinghâli'kün to let you kill deer." The reader will remember that Mïsinghâli'kün, in whose image the Mïsi'ng^{we} is carved, is supposed to have control over the deer, and in fact over all wild animals.

All the hunters that are in the habit of chewing tobacco are now given some for this purpose. When they file out and mount their horses, the Mïsi'ng^{we} follows them and sees them off. After the hunters have disappeared, the people call the Mïsi'ng^{we} back into the Big House and coax him to dance, while two men volunteer to sing for him.

Prayer for the Hunters

The following evening six men are appointed and given a yard of wampum to divide among them, to go out close to the forked game-pole east of the Big House, intended for the carcasses of the deer, and pray there twelve times. The meaning of this, of course, is that they sound the prayer word "Ho-o-o!" which is evidently to help the hunters. This night also a yard of wampum is unstrung and scattered on the ground just west of the east fire, and this the attendants must pick up, crying "Ho-o-o!" as they do so. For doing this, which is called "picking berries," they are supposed to keep what wampum they pick up.

Return of the Hunters

If the hunters are lucky and kill a deer the first day, they send one man back with it. As he approaches he fires a gun as a signal of his coming, at which the singers run into the Big House and begin to sing and beat the drum. Then everyone is happy.

In any case the hunters all return on the third day. If they have killed deer, they shoot their guns; if not, they come in very quietly. When the shots are heard, the singers hasten to their places, and, beating the drum, sing a song that is used only on such occasions. Then when the hunters arrive, they feast, and their leader announces the names of those lucky enough to kill a deer. The carcasses are skinned and hung on the deer pole, east of the Big House, and are used in the feasts at the close of every night's meeting until the gathering disbands.

New Fire

Every night the usual program is repeated until the ninth. On this night a new fire is kindled with the sacred pump-drill called Tuⁿda'i wäheⁿ'ji manïtowük or "Fire maker of the Manï'tos," and the ashes of the old are carried out through the west door of the Big House, which is used only for this purpose (among the Unami), and is usually kept closed. The new fire seems to symbolize a fresh start in all the affairs of life.

Use of Carved Drumsticks

Also on the ninth night, before the singing begins, they bring out the two ancient drumsticks (Puküⁿdi'gün), carved with tiny human heads, one male and one female, to use in place of the cruder sticks used before, which are marked only with a rude cross [fig. 7]. At this time, also, twelve prayer sticks (Ma'tehi'gun) are distributed—six plain and six striped ones—by two of the male attendants, each with six, one man starting from each end of the Big House and proceeding in a trot to distribute the sticks while the drum is beaten, and the people, holding up their hands, cry the prayer word "Ho-o-o!" Both drumsticks and prayer sticks are used every night from this time on. If it so happens that the plain sticks do not fall opposite each other (or on opposite sides of the house), they must all be picked up again and redistributed. After this, those who have received a stick raise that instead of their hand, when they repeat the prayer word "Ho-o-o!" and carry it when they dance.

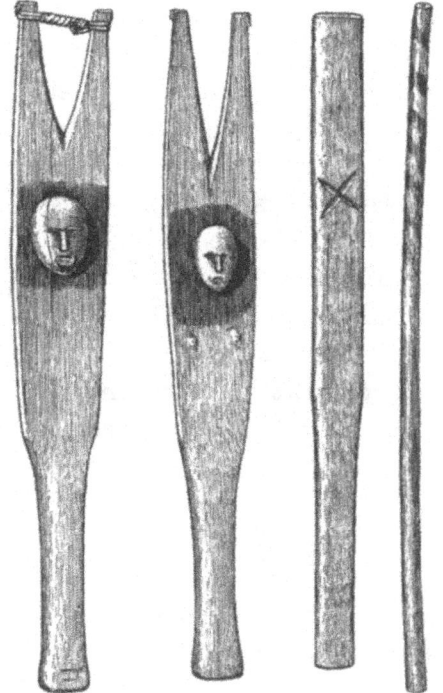

Fig. 7. (*Left*) Sacred drumsticks, length 18.6 inches; (*center*) plain drumstick, length 18.6 inches; (*right*) prayer stick, length 18.9 inches (figs. 11 and 12, Harrington 1921: 102). Courtesy National Museum of the American Indian.

Turtle Rattles

At this time, too, all who own turtle rattles such as are used in singing the visions, are requested to bring them in to the meeting, when they are placed in a row on the north side, in front of the man who, as the Indians phrase it, "Brought in the meeting." The backs of the turtle shells are all measured with strings of wampum, which are cut off in lengths corresponding with the lengths of the backs.

Then the owners are called to get their turtles and wampum, which is supposed to be their pay for bringing them to the meeting. As each takes up his turtle, he shakes it, and if it does not sound well, then the people laugh, and the owner, abashed, takes his property out of sight as soon as possible.

Phratry Prayers

Then they call up six men, two from each of the three phratries—Turtle, Turkey, and Wolf. Each goes outside and cries the prayer word "Ho-o-o!" twelve times, holding up his left hand. When the first one returns, he is given one yard of wampum, and divides it with the other five. This is done each night until the end.

Women's Night

The twelfth night is reserved for the women to relate their visions; but before they begin, the speaker orders the attendants to burn cedar leaves in the two fires and the people are supposed to inhale the smoke and purify themselves. Then two women are ordered to take, one a little bark dish (Aⁿsipla'gün) of red paint, the other a similar vessel of grease, and the two start from the door on the north side of the Temple and go to each person present. One dips her fingers in the paint and touches the color to the person's left cheek, while her companion similarly anoints the person's head with a little of the grease. This done, two men attendants take the bark vessels and paint and grease in the same way the twelve Mïsi'ng^{we} faces carved upon the posts of the building, also the drumsticks, the prayer sticks, the deerskin drum, and the turtles. A variant has it that both bark vessels contain paint, the customs differing according to phratry.

Each woman who takes part on this night receives a share of the venison, if there is any,—the biggest and fattest buck the hunters kill,—and the attendants cook it for them at the fire outside.

Conclusion of the Ceremony

Next morning the men resume the ceremony and continue until the sun is high. Two men are then appointed to close the meeting, for which each receives one yard of wampum. Their duty is to sing twelve times while the people dance about the central post, the women in a circle next to the post, the men in another circle outside that of the women. These two singers stop dancing in front of where the chief is sitting, and announce, "We will now pray twelve times." They go back to their seats and cry "Ho-o-o!" twelve times. Then the attendants serve the last feast. Two women then go around with wampum in a wooden bowl, giving everyone two or three beads.

Payment of Attendants

Then the attendants, three men and three women, stand in a row and receive six yards of wampum on one string, which they hold in their hands the first in the row holding the end of the string, which stretches along from one to the other. Then the chief says: "We thank you attendants of this meeting for your kindness in sweeping our Temple for these twelve nights, and the attention and care you have given. We have heard our old parents say that, if you sweep this Meeting House twelve different times, you will sweep up to where our great Father is, as he is up in the twelfth Heaven above the earth."

The attendants then circle about the fires and go out to the cooking fireplace, where they divide the wampum, taking a yard apiece. At last, when the shadow of a person is nearly under him, that is, about noon, the speaker or chief arises, and says, "All of us kinfolk must now go out and end our meeting, which has been going on for twelve days and nights." Thereupon they all file out—men, women, and children—and form a row extending north and south, facing east, just east of the Big House, the hunters taking with them the skins of the deer they killed.

Finale

Here they all pray, or rather cry the prayer word "Ho-o-o!" six times standing, holding up one hand, and six times kneeling, holding up the other hand. The meeting is then ended. The deerskins are given to poor old people, who need them to make moccasins.

One informant stated that instead of crying "Ho-o-o" twelve times in closing the meeting, it was customary to use this word only ten times, and then cry "Ha-a-a" twice, completing the sacred number twelve; but such discrepancies are probably due to the variation of ritual among the three phratries before mentioned, the Turkey, the Turtle, and the Wolf. This kind of prayer was noticed by Zeisberger as early as 1779. The suspicion that Zeisberger mistook the conclusion of the Annual Ceremony for a separate rite is strengthened by the fact that he gives its name as "'ngammuin," which seems to be a form of Ga'mwing, the modern Lenape name for their Annual Ceremony.

Payment of Officers

All of the officers of the meeting receive pay in wampum for their services, except, of course, the leader—the man who has caused the meeting to be held. The speaker receives a yard for every night of the meeting; the drummers get a yard between them each night; there are also the payments to the attendants, hunters, and others, already mentioned. The attendants have other sources of profit, too, for they serve meals three times a day in the Big House to the leader of the meeting and all his near relatives, also to the speaker and the drummers.

When they have finished feasting, the leader calls the attendants to come and get their dishes and pans. Each has a cup in which he brings coffee, and the leader puts twenty-five wampum beads in each cup for every meal. Moreover, when any one in the outside camps is hungry, he may go to an A'ckas and obtain a meal for twenty-five wampum beads. The attendants have a table near the tent of one of the woman A'ckas, and here they eat.

Valuation of Wampum

For ceremonial purposes the wampum (white) is held at one cent a bead, one hundred to the dollar. Before the meeting the people give a yard or so apiece, if they are able, to show their appreciation and to be prayed for, or subscribe money for its purchase and for the other things needed at the meeting. The wampum is afterward redeemed at the same rate and is kept to use again.

Indian Comments on the Ceremony

Some explanations and remarks concerning the annual ceremony, as furnished by the Indians themselves, may prove of interest here:

Julius Fouts (or Fox), the interpreter, remarks "When the Delawares complete this meeting, then they claim they have worshiped everything on this earth. God gave the Powers Above authority to go around and give all the tribes some way to worship. They say these things were as if carried in a bundle, and when they come to the Delawares, last of all, there was a lot left in the bundle and they got it all—that is why the Delawares have so many different things to do in their meetings."

In explanation of the prayer word Ho-o-o, he said, "Did you ever hear that noise out in the woods, in the fall of the year? 'Ho-o-o,' it says. What is it? It is the noise of the wind blowing in the trees. When the Delawares pray in the Big House, they raise their voices and cry 'Ho-o-o,' to God, and the Mïsi'ng^{we} hears it and understands, for he is of the same nature as a tree, and there are twelve Mïsi'ng^{we} carved in the Big House who will carry the prayers to the twelfth Heaven. The Indians call the Mïsi'ng^{we} 'Grandfather,' because the trees were here before the Indians. The Big House is going out of use now, because only the old people have had gifts or visions of power to sing about. The children of today are not Pi'lsu^n, or pure; they are reared like the whites, and the Powers Above do not speak to them any more."

Chief Charlie Elkhair, or Elkire, who frequently served as speaker in the Big House, said, "The Delaware meeting helps everybody in the world, for they pray for good crops and everything good, even wild fruits. About ten years ago the people thought they would give up holding these meetings,[1] and the following year they had high winds and big rains, and everyone was frightened. Then grasshoppers came in swarms, but they came in the fall a little too late to get all the crops. So the people held a council and talked about the Big House again. They finally decided to resume it, before any more bad luck came; so they began the ceremonies again in the fall.

"Then it seemed as if all the trouble stopped. Of late there has been talk of again giving up the meeting, but if we do give it up we are likely to have a tornado or maybe dry weather to ruin the crops.

"Once the Delawares owned a great deal of land, but that is nearly all gone now, and the people seem to have no power to do anything. When God looks down from Heaven, he sees but very few Delaware people, and the reason for this is that they cannot follow the Meeting House ceremonies now. When I was a little boy, I heard my people say that this thing would happen just as it is happening now. You see, the young people raised during the last thirty years do not believe in the old ways. We are having good times yet, but we don't know when we shall catch it. If anything happens to us, and once [it] really begins, we can not stop it—it will be too late. Even if they take up the meeting again—they can not do right, even when the ceremonies are going on.

---

1. Sometime between 1900 and 1910.

"They can not accomplish anything in the Big House; they can not raise it up, because there are a lot of young folks who do not even try to do what the speaker tells them, for they do not believe in it.

"The people could get along fine, if they followed the rules of the meeting—not only the Delawares, but the other people round about. For when the Delaware prays, he prays for things that will benefit everybody; he prays for the children as well as for himself; he prays for the future time. But if anything comes to destroy the world, it will be too late to think of starting the Big House then."

Another Form of the Ceremony

It appears that in former years there was, in addition to the rite just described, another form of the Annual Ceremony practiced by the Lenape, before their removal to what is now Oklahoma from Kansas, where the last man to "bring in" such a meeting was John Sarcoxie, now dead.[2] The ceremony, which was called Muxhatol'zing, seems, from the accounts given the writer by his informants, to have taken place in a similar building, and to have been similar in ritual to that just described, except that it was held for only eight days instead of twelve, and that, after the return of the hunters the skin of one of the deer they had brought in was stuffed with grass and stood up by the central post of the Big House, antlers and all, while about its neck hung a string of wampum—perhaps as a propitiatory offering.

Moreover on the morning of the last day of the ceremony a large sweathouse was built and stones heated; then about noon the men who had been reciting their visions went into it, each taking one of the hot stones with him. This privilege was not confined to the actual celebrants however, for every one blessed by a guardian spirit even if they had not sung their visions in the meeting, was entitled to carry in a stone and join them.

The entrance was then closed and water poured upon the stones; and while the steam rose and the sweathouse grew hotter and hotter the perspiring occupants prayed to their guardian spirits and recited their visions. These finished, with a shout of "There go our prayers to Those Above," the cover was suddenly snatched from the sweathouse so that the steam it had contained rose in a puff. If the steam cloud went straight up into the air it was thought that the prayers would be heard and answered, and that all was well, but if it broke and spread out the people felt that something had gone wrong, and that their prayers were of no avail.

In endeavoring to explain the presence of such variations of the Annual Ceremony, it should be remembered that the Lenape now in Oklahoma whom the writer has called for convenience "Unami," are not really pure descendants of this

---

2. John Sarcoxie was chief of the Delaware Turkey phratry living in Kansas and, after 1866, in eastern Oklahoma (Weslager 1972: 408–409, 422).

tribe, but probably have a large proportion of the blood of the Unala'tko or Unalachtigo, whose dialect, according to Heckewelder, was very similar, and a smaller proportion of Minsi and even Nanticoke blood. Perhaps then the first form of Annual Ceremony described may have originally been purely Unami, and the second Unalachtigo, or Minsi, or vice versa; but later, when the remnants of these tribes became amalgamated their mixed descendants inherited both forms.

The second form seems to be a variant of the rite mentioned by Zeisberger. That this is really the same ceremony is shown not only by the details as related but by the native name of the rite, the Machtuzin of Zeisberger corresponding with the Muxhatol'zing of the present writer.

The M̈isi'ng^{we} or Mask

The Unami version of the myth explaining the origin of their great ceremonies is intimately interwoven with the story of the M̈isi'ng^{we}, or mask [fig. 8]. The myth is therefore presented herewith, as related by Chief Charlie Elkhair, the Lenape master of ceremonies, with only such additions as later questioning brought forth.

Fig. 8. Carved wooden M̈isi'ng^{we} mask, height 14.5 inches (fig. 1, Harrington 1921: 32). Courtesy National Museum of the American Indian.

Origin of the Mask, and of the Big House

This is the way the Lenape found out that there is a living Mïsinghâli'kün above us. Many years ago, when the Delawares lived in the east, there were three boys who were not treated very well. Their relatives did not take care of them, and it seemed as if it made no difference whether the children died or not. These boys were out in the woods thinking about their troubles, when they saw the Mïsinghâli'kün or Living Solid Face. He came and spoke to them, and gave them strength so that nothing could hurt them again. To one of these boys he said, "You come along with me and I will show you the country I come from." So he took the boy up in the air to the place whence he came, which is rocky mountains above us, reaching out from the north and extending toward the south. It is not the place where people go when they die, for it is not very far from this earth. A long time ago people could see this country of Mïsinghâli'kün, but none can see it now.

While he was showing the boy his country, the Mïsinghâli'kün promised him that he would become stout and strong, and would have the power to get anything he wished. Then he brought the boy back.

Afterward, when the boy grew up and went hunting, he used to see the Mïsinghâli'kün riding a buck around among the other deer, herding them together. Thus it happened that there were three men in the tribe, who knew that there is a Mïsinghâli'kün, because they had seen him with their own eyes.

The Delawares had always kept a Big House (Xi'ngwikan) to worship in, but in those days it was built entirely of bark and had no faces of the Mïsi'ng^{wt} carved upon the posts as it has now. Here they used to sing about their dreams (visions of power); but some time after the three boys talked with the Mïsinghâli'kün, the people gave up this worship, and for ten years had none. Then there came a great earthquake, which lasted twelve months and gave great trouble to the Lenape. It came because they had abandoned the worship their fathers had taught them. In those times the tribe lived in towns, not scattered about the country as they are now; and in one of these towns a chief had a big bark house, and here the people met to worship, hoping to stop the earthquake, while they were building a new Big House. When it was finished, they began to worship there, and sang and prayed all winter for relief. After spring came, they were holding a meeting one night when they heard the Mïsinghâli'kün making noise, "Ho^n-ho^n-ho^n," right east of the Big House. The chief, who did not know what was making the noise, called for somebody to go and see what it was. Then these three men offered to go, because, as they said, they knew what was making the noise and would find out what he wanted. So they went out and found Mïsinghâli'kün, and asked him what he wanted. He answered:

"Go back and tell the others to stop holding meetings and to attend to their crops. Do not meet again until fall, when I will come and live with you, and help in the Big House. You must take wood and carve a face (Mïsi'ng^{wt}) just like mine, painted half black and half red, as mine is, and I will put my power in it, so that it will do what you ask. When the man who takes my part puts the face on, I will be there, and this is how I will live among you. This man must carry a turtle rattle and a stick, just as I do now." Then he told them how to fix the twelve carved faces on the posts of the Big House, and the faces on the drumsticks, and taught them how to hold the ceremony.

Then he said:

"You must also give me hominy every year in the spring. I take care of the deer and other game, that is what I am for. Wherever you build the Big House, I will keep the deer close by, so that you can get them when you need them.

"Never give up the Big House. If you do, there will be another earthquake, or something else just as bad.

"The earthquake stopped that time; that is why the Delawares have kept the Mïsi'ng^{wt} and the Big House ever since. The Mask is left in charge of some family who will take good care of it, and burn Indian tobacco for it from time to time."

It will be seen that, according to the above tradition, the Mïsi'ng^{wt} was, first of all, a personal helper, or guardian Spirit, that afterward became more or less of a tribal deity, and that his cult became engrafted on the Annual Ceremony among the Unami, the rites of which were already ancient among them. That this engrafting really took place seems possible from the fact that among the Minsi there were no masked performers at the Big House ceremonies, and that, while the central post of the temple was provided with carved faces, the masks had an entirely different function among this people. The innovation, if it took place at all, must have been before Brainerd's time, however, for he found the Mïsi'ng^{wt} and Big House in use, as among the Unami today, as early as May, 1745, while traveling among the Delawares living at that time on Susquehanna river.[3]

Mïsi'ng^{wt} Dance

Besides the part taken by the Mïsi'ng^{wt} in the Annual Ceremony, he has certain rites peculiar to himself which were held every spring. As the Indians put it: "When spring comes, the Delawares are glad, and they are thankful that their helper, the Mïsi'ng^{wt}, is still among them. For this reason they give a feast and dance to make him happy too."

Notification—So at the time of the full moon (about May), the keeper of the mask gives another Indian a yard of wampum to ride around to all the Delaware houses, wearing the mask and bearskin costume to let the people know that the time for the Mïsi'ng^{wt} dance (Mïsinghâli'kün) is at hand. The Mïsi'ng^{wt} rides horseback, and another man, also mounted, follows him to see that he comes to no harm. At each house the impersonator dismounts and enters, making known his errand by signs, but saying only "Ho^n-ho^n-ho^n," and everywhere they

---

[3]. As mentioned earlier, Brainerd almost certainly was visiting a Conoy Indian community.

give him tobacco, which he puts in his sack. At this time the people frighten disobedient children with the threat that, unless they behave, the Mïsi'ng^{wt} will carry them away in a sack full of snakes.

Preparations—The dance-ground customarily used for this purpose has meanwhile been put in order, a cleared place in the woods selected for good shade and pleasant surroundings, and the logs which serve as seats arranged to form the reserve as seats arranged to form the rectangle within which the dance takes place. A great pot of hominy is also prepared; this constitutes the main dish of the feast.

The Ceremony—When the people have gathered on the night appointed, and the impersonator has returned from the bushes where he retired to dress, wearing the mask and bearskin suit, the speaker addresses the people and relates the origin of the dance, then addressing the Mïsi'ng^{wt}, says, "Take care of us while we are dancing, so that everything goes smoothly." Then they have a dance in which the Mïsi'ng^{wt} joins, but he dances around the outside of the circle of people, not with them. When they have finished, he dances twelve changes alone, which occupies the time until morning. When daylight appears, the hominy is brought out and everyone eats, including the Mïsing^{wt}, after which the speaker says, "Now we have eaten with our Mïsi'ng^{wt}. We will have this dance again next spring." The people then disperse to their homes, the Mïsi'ng^{wt} is put away and the impersonator paid a yard of wampum for his dancing. At this dance the singers keep time by striking with sticks on a dry deer-hide rolled over and stuffed with dried grass, very similar to the "drum" used in the Big House.

Other Functions of Mïsi'ng^{wt}

The *Mïsi'ng^{wt}* the Indians claim, "takes care of the children," as well as of the deer, for as before related if any Delaware has a child who is weak, sickly, or disobedient, he sends for the Mïsi'ng^{wt} and asks him to "attend to" his child. On his arrival it does not take the impersonator long to frighten the weakness, sickness, or laziness out of such children, so that "afterward they are well and strong, and whenever they are told to do a thing, they lose no time in obeying." This is the only trace of the doctoring function of the mask found among the Unami.

When the keeper of the Mïsi'ng^{wt} burns tobacco for him and asks for good luck in hunting, "it turns out that way every time;" and the Lenape say moreover that if anyone loses horses or cattle, either strayed away or stolen, he can go to the keeper of the Mïsi'ng^{wt} with some tobacco as a gift and get them back. He explains his errand to the keeper, who in turn informs the Mïsi'ng^{wt} that they want him to look for the horses or cattle. The loser then goes back home, and after a few days the missing animals return, driven back by the Mïsi'ng^{wt}, who if they had been tied or hobbled by the thieves, frightened them until they broke away and came home. When the Big House meeting is held in the fall, the Mïsi'ng^{wt}, as before related, is seen going around among the tents of the Delawares assembled, and in and out of the Big House, always coming from the woods, where the impersonator has a place to change his clothes. The Indians say: "He helps the people with their hunting, and also helps in the Big House while the ceremonies are in progress. If he finds anyone there who has not done right, he informs the three guards of the meeting, who take that person and put him out. In all these ways the Mïsi'ng^{wt} helps the Delawares."

CHAPTER SIX

Canadian Munsee Big House Ceremonies, 1907–1910

Mark Raymond Harrington compiled the information presented in this chapter while visiting Ontario Delaware-Munsee communities at Munceytown and the Six Nations Reserve at various times between 1907 and 1910. Traditionalists James Wolf ('Tayeno'xwan) and his nephew, Nellis F. Timothy (Tomapemihi'lat), were Harrington's main informants at the Munceytown community; his primary informants at the Six Nations Reserve were Michael Anthony (Na'nküma'oxa), Isaac Montour (Kapyü'hüin), and Monroe Pheasant.

Some of the artifacts gathered by Harrington at Munceytown and Six Nations are currently stored and maintained at the American Museum of Natural History in New York. The remaining part of the material collected by Harrington is preserved with his field notes in the collections of the National Museum of the American Indian in Washington, D.C.

The accounts of Canadian Munsee ceremonialism in this chapter also first appeared in Harrington's 1921 monograph on Delaware Religion. The 1921 monograph included both original material (Harrington 1921: 127–42, 158–61) and an extract from an article published earlier in the American Anthropologist (Harrington 1908).

Myth of Origin

At first, it appears, the Indians did not know how to worship, so Kë'tanï-to'wët, the Great *Manï'to* or God, now called *Pa"tümawas*, came down and told them what to do. After following his instructions, they watched him when he ascended. He carried twelve sumac sticks in his hand, and they could see them shine far up in the air. Every now and then he dropped one, and when he dropped the twelfth he disappeared, while they heard the heavens crack like thunder behind him as he went in. After this the Lenape began to hold these meetings according to the instructions he had given them.

Number of Ceremonies

There were two of these ceremonies every year, both held in the Minsi Big House (W'a'tekan), which was quite similar to that of the Unami. One of these, performed about June when the wild strawberries were ripe, lasted only a single night; the other, early in winter, covered twelve days and nights. This latter corresponds to the Annual Ceremony of the Unami.

At the June ceremony fresh strawberries were made into a drink for the people, which reminds one of the Iroquois Strawberry Dance, or Dance of First Fruits, as it is sometimes called. Strawberries were dried at this time to make a drink for the Winter Ceremony.

Arrangement of the Big House

Like the Unami Big House, that of the Minsi had a large central post bearing carved faces; but, unlike that of the Unami, there was a second short post, near the central one, upon which was hung, for each ceremony, a raw fresh deerskin with the head and horns at the top. This feature, however, corresponds with the second form of the Annual Ceremony noted among the Lenape in Oklahoma and also recorded by Zeisberger in Pennsylvania. Near this central post the singers sat, and beat with four carved sticks upon a dry deerhide folded into a square, in lieu of a drum, differing from the Unami form, which is a rolled dry deerskin upon which are tied several slats of wood [fig. 9]. The drumsticks are flat, resembling those of the Unami, as each bears a face carved upon one side, but differ from them in the form of the forked end, and in width. Some, it is said, represented women, the breasts being indicated as among the Unami, but this feature does not appear in the set collected by the writer at Grand River reserve, which the Indians said were representative of the Minsi type.

There were two poles laid along on each side from end to end of the Big House to divide the dancing place in the center from the sitting places on the side, which were covered with a special kind of leaves. Along these poles twelve little sumac sticks, peeled and painted, were laid for twelve people to hold in their hands, and tap on the poles in time to the music. There were also provided a turtle rattle, which was placed at the foot of the central pole; a fire-drill which Nellis Timothy thinks was worked on the "pump-drill" principle, like that of the Unami, and a lot of entirely new and unused bowls and spoons of bark. Unlike the Unami custom, both doors of the Big House were used, the people always going in at the east door and coming out at the west, and here also (like the Unami) the ashes were carried out. "The Sun and everything else goes toward the west," say the Minsi, in explanation, "even the dead when they die."

Fig. 9. Munsee-style square dried deerskin drum in the E. T. Tefft Collection, American Museum of Natural History, length 16.7 inches (fig. 14, Harrington 1921: 129). Courtesy National Museum of the American Indian.

Canadian Munsee Big House Ceremonies, 1907–1910

Preliminaries

The first act remembered by the informants preparatory to holding a meeting was to send to each man in the tribe who had been blessed by a "vision of power," a little stick which represented an invitation to the ceremony, the time of which the messenger gave out, before which date the people leaving their scattered homes gathered and camped about the Big House. Meanwhile hunters were sent out, appointed before, not during the meeting as among the Unami, to bring in for the Winter Ceremony, if possible, exactly twelve deer, which were cooked by four young men who served as attendants in a small separate house, built for the purpose.

Fire—The fire was made with a fire-drill by a group of old men for use in the Big House, but, as among the Unami, none of it could be taken outside during the ceremony.

Purification—When the two fires had been built, but before the crowd had gathered, the house was purified by the smoke of hemlock boughs thrown on the flames, and by sweeping the floor with turkey-wing fans, which cleared away both dirt and evil influences.

Opening of the Ceremony

Chief's Speech—The next step was for the attendants to call in all the people from their camps, except the women in their menses, who were not allowed to enter. When all were seated, the speaker rose and addressed those assembled in terms like the following: "We are now gathered here, our house is purified and clean, and Pa"tümawas is with us, ready to hear our worship. We must thank Him for all the things that we enjoy, for He made them every one." Then he proceeded to tell the people not to drink liquor, nor to do anything wrong in the Big House or in the camp about it, and advised them to be always honest and kind and hospitable. He held virtue as something to be followed, at the same time condemning evil, every vice that he could think of being mentioned.

The chief then gave thanks for everything he could remember, from the heavenly bodies to the animals, trees, and herbs of the earth, not forgetting corn, beans, and squashes; and prayer for successful hunting and good health for all the people. At the summer meeting he prayed for good crops also. When he had finished, bear's fat was thrown on the two fires, and the smoke rose and filled the place with its odor.

Ceremonial Drink

At this point it was customary to pass around a vessel of drink made of crushed wild strawberries, from which each person present swallowed about a spoonful, a drink made at the Summer Ceremony of fresh fruit, but in winter necessarily of berries dried for the purpose.

Recital of Visions

The first man to relate his vision (my informant did not remember whether he was the one who "brought in" the meeting or not) took up the turtle rattle from its place at the foot of the post and began to shake it rapidly, while the singers struck the drum of dry hide. He then recited the story of his vision of power, still keeping the rattle shaking, following this with his dance song, at the same time dancing and rattling the turtle-shell.

Any one who wished to dance was supposed to give wampum to the vision-teller for the privilege. Some who were well off would give him an entire string, others merely a few beads. These the vision-teller would take, when he had quite a handful, to two officers who sat in a corner of the building, whose duty it was to count the wampum, after which it was kept by the chief or leader. Sometimes if a poor person who had no wampum wished to dance, they would give him some to pay the vision-teller.

When the dream-teller finished the first verse of his dance song, he exclaimed, "E-ye-he-ye-ë!" whereupon the singers took up the strain and sang the verse several times, for the benefit of those who wished to dance, omitting, however, the final exclamation, but those who had bought the privilege rose and danced where they stood, instead of circling around, as among the Unami. Each "set" ended with a whoop, "Kwi!"

When the vision-teller finished dancing, he went around the house and shook hands with everyone; then the turtle rattle was passed to another man who had been blessed with a vision, and so on, until all those qualified, who wished to recite their visions, had done so.

Features

The Prayer Cry—From time to time during the night the prayer cry "Ho-o-o!" was repeated twelve times, and the twelfth cry, they say, was heard by the Great Manï'to.

Feast—The people were accustomed to eat a light supper before going into the meeting; then about midnight the four attendants carried around baskets with boiled meat and corn bread, and in the morning, before leaving the Big House, a regular feast of venison was served in new bark bowls and eaten with new bark spoons especially made for the purpose.

Final Address—Before the meeting closed, the speaker again addressed the people, telling them to do right, and prayed that the hunters about to leave for the winter hunt might be successful, and that all might live to meet again.

Conclusion of Rites

In the morning after the ceremonies in the Big House were finished, the people filed out through the west door, circled about the building, and lined up, facing eastward, to the east of it. Then they raised their hands and cried "Ho-o-o!" twelve times, and the twelfth time, it is said, their cry reached Heaven.

In comparing this form of the Annual Ceremony with that of the Oklahoma Lenape, the most noticeable difference is that here no masked impersonator of Mïsinghâli'kün was seen in or about the Big House, the Masks among the Minsi, as with the Iroquois, constituting a society with its own separate rites.

Grand River Version

Such was the version of the great ceremonies given the writer by the Minsi of Munceytown, Ontario, which is similar to, but more detailed in parts than, the account previously obtained from the Delawares of Grand River Reserve, published by the writer in the *American Anthropologist* which we will reproduce here.[1] It will be noticed that this description gives fuller information in some places where the first is deficient; so that between this and the preceding account, a good general idea of the Minsi form of the ceremony can be reconstructed:

In the old religious ceremonies of the Delawares at Grand River a very peculiar drum was used, a dry skin folded in rectangular form and beaten with four sticks, each bearing a tiny human head carved in relief. I secured the set of four original sticks from Michael Anthony (Na'nküma'oxa), and employed him to make me a reproduction of the drum as the original had been destroyed. This he did, and in addition made six painted sticks also used in the ceremony. The

---

1. The present-day Muncytown and Six Nations reserves in Ontario. See Harrington (1908: 414–16) for the full text of the *American Anthropologist* article.

description of how these articles were used, pieced together from several Indian accounts, may prove of interest here.

It appears that the Delawares of the Six Nations Reserve formerly held what was known as a "General Thanksgiving" ceremony called in Lenape Gitctla'kan, twice a year, once in the spring and again in the fall. At these times it was customary to meet in the Cayuga long house, borrowed for the occasion. At a certain point in the proceedings (I shall not attempt a consecutive description from hearsay testimony) a man stood up and recited, in a rythmical sing-song tone, his dream—the vision of power seen by him in his youth. Na'nkuma'oxa remembered how one old man was accustomed to tell about a duck, half black and half white, which had appeared to him. Between the verses of the dream four musicians kneeling at the drum (Pw'awahe'gün) began a plaintive song, beating time with the carved sticks (Pw'awahe'günük). As they sang, the reciter swayed his body to and fro, while a group of dancers gathered on the floor behind him danced with a sidewise step. Before the ceremony, poles were laid lengthwise along both sides of the council house, and against these, at intervals, three on a side, the painted sticks, called Mkäähi'gün, were laid. If anyone in the crowd felt "especially happy" he was privileged to strike with one of these sticks upon one of the poles in time to the music. The carved heads on the drumsticks meant that human beings were giving thanks; the lengthwise painting of the sticks, half black and half red, implied that men and women were together in the thanksgiving, the black representing the warriors, the red the women. The fork at the striking end of the sticks was to give a sharper sound. The dyes for producing the colors were made by boiling bark, the black being soft maple (Sexi'kiminsi), and the red, red alder bark (Wito"pi).

In another part of the same ceremony wampum was used in the form of strings and bunches, both of which were represented in my collection from the Delawares. At least thirteen of the strings were used, each one made different by different combinations of the white and purple beads. These thirteen, it is said, represented respectively (1) Earth; (2) Plants; (3) Streams and Waters; (4) Corn, Beans and Vegetables; (5) Wild Birds and Beasts; (6) Winds; (7) Sun; (8) Moon; (9) Sky; (10) Stars; (11) Thunder and Rain; (12) Spirits; and (13) Great Spirit. At the ceremony these strings were laid upon a bench before a speaker, who picked them up one by one as he made his address, each string reminding him of one part of his speech. He began, my informant told me, by explaining that the Great Spirit had made all things—the earth, plants, streams, and waters—everything. Having thus enumerated all the things represented by the wampum, he proceeded to speak to each of the remaining twelve directly, holding the appropriate string in his hand. Thus he gave thanks to the Earth for the benefits it gives to man, and prayed that its blessings might continue; then thanked in the same way the Plants, the Streams and Waters, the Winds; the Corn, Beans, and Vegetables—each one in turn. As he finished each string he handed it to an attendant, who laid it aside. When his long speech or prayer was finished, he announced, "We will now enjoy ourselves," and selected a man to distribute little bunches of wampum, three beads in each, which served as invitations to join in the dancing that followed. These bunches were delivered only to a certain number of those known to be "sober and honest" among the crowd in the long house. If any person wishing to dance failed to get invitation wampum, it was his privilege to ask for one of the bunches, which was given him if he was considered qualified. The first man receiving wampum arose first; then the others, until the dancers were all on the floor. It is said that this dance, which sometimes lasted all night, did not circle around like most of the Iroquois dances, but each performer remained in about the same spot.

I was told that in this dance a small rattle without a handle and made of turtleshell was used, probably like the box-turtle rattle still used in the annual Planting Dance by the Seneca and Cayuga.

Masks of the Minsi

The Minsi Mizi'nk (cognate with the Unami Mïsi'ng^{we}) was a mask made of wood with copper or brass eyes and a crooked nose, according to my informants at Munceytown; and judging by Peter Jones' drawings they were provided also with hair, tufts of feathers, and jingling copper cones or deer-hoofs.[2] The Mizink at Grand river was of Minsi type, judging by the specimen obtained by the writer.

Such masks were made to represent Mizinkhâli'kün, who was "something like a person, but different from the Indians, and was powerful. They saw him first among the rocks on a hill, and he spoke to them and told them what to do to get his power. When a man put on a Mizink he received the power of this person or spirit; he could even see behind him, and would cure diseases."

The Mask Society—The men who owned these masks formed a kind of society which Nellis Timothy says originally had twelve members, but which, before it disbanded, dwindled to about five. Sometimes only two appeared in costume.

The society had a meeting-house of its own where its dances, Mizinkï'nlïka, were held, for, unlike the Unami custom, no Mizink ever appeared in the Big House. The members appeared wearing their masks and clad in rough bearskin and deerskin costumes, while some, at least, where provided with a turtleshell rattle which they would rub on a long pole, crying "O^n-o^n-o^n!" the while.

Ceremonies—While no consecutive account of their ceremonies is now remembered, it was said that they sometimes put down their rattles, heaped up the ashes from the two fires, then threw the ashes all over the house to prevent the people assembled from having disease.

Should any sick person appear, he or she would be especially treated with ashes. Sometimes the performers would pick up live coals and throw them about,

---

2. As mentioned earlier, Peter Jones was an Ojibwa missionary who worked among the Delawares and other Indian nations in Ontario during the mid-1800s. See Jones (1860) for details of his experiences among the Munsees.

frightening the people. At other times the whole company of them would go around to the different houses begging for tobacco, and would dance in any house where someone was willing to sing for them.

Nothing was said among the Minsi about the Mizink bringing back stray stock or driving deer, characteristic attributes of the Mask Being of the Unami. The writer obtained but one mask among the Canadian Lenape, and this was from the Grand River band; it has been described by him in the following words:

But one mask (Mizink) was obtained. It differed from those of the Iroquois chiefly in being cruder, and also in decoration, the lines being burnt into the wood instead of being painted or carved. The original use of the mask had to do, in part at least, with healing the sick, but Isaac Montour (Kapyü'hüin), from whom I bought it, failed to make himself clear as to the details.

It will be seen that the Minsi beliefs and practices noted above resemble those of the False Face Ceremony of the Iroquois tribes much more than they do the customs connected with Mïsi'ng^{we} among the Unami.

In fact, a vague tradition exists to the effect that the False Face Company of the Cayuga once put a stop to an epidemic of cholera among the Minsi. While this was not given to account for the origin of the society among the Minsi, it at least shows that they were familiar with the Iroquois practices in this line.

CHAPTER SEVEN

Charlie Elkhair's Text, 1912

Eastern Oklahoma Big House adherent Charlie Elkhair dictated the following text, printed below in its entirety for the first time, to Smithsonian Institution Bureau of American Ethnology ethnographer Truman Michelson in 1912 (fig. 10). Elkhair, whom Michelson noted was sixty-two at the time of their interview, was born on the Delaware Reservation in Kansas in 1848. He served as ceremonial chief of the Delaware tribe after the death of Colonel Jackson from 1904 until his own death in 1935. His duties as ceremonial chief included service as speaker in the annual Big House Ceremony. As subsequent accounts show, Elkhair loomed large as an authority on Oklahoma Delaware tradition.

Michelson's original notes of Charlie Elkhair's text, cataloged as MS 2776 (folder 10:1–18), are on file in the Smithsonian Institution's National Anthropological Archives in Washington, D.C. The origin story that appears at the beginning of this text has been published in Bierhorst (1995: 107–109). James Rementer transcribed and edited the unpublished remainder of the text in 1994 and annotated the material for this book. A brief account of the function and significance of the Big House center post and notes on band rights to dances, seating locations, and membership in the Big House, collected by Michelson in 1912, appear at the end of Elkhair's account.

Delaware Meeting House

The Delaware church was given the tribe when all nations were given churches in case they wanted to live a good life and be with God. This Delaware meeting is in the beginning of Spring. Then the people plant the crops. Everybody is glad because the crops are good so in the fall they give thanks to God at this meeting house. For what good they have seen they attend the meeting house to extend it for another year. The back generation always said it has been known that this meeting is to be held twelve nights. They have the twelve days because the sky is divided into twelve tiers, and the supreme being is in the twelfth tier. So they have twelve wooden faces, [each is] one half black, the other half red. Made of

Fig. 10. Charlie Elkhair. Courtesy James Rementer.

sugar-maple. White marks represents the eyebrows. Each represent a being not seen on earth except at certain intervals. Each can take our service to the next tier till it reaches the Supreme Being. The suit is made of bearskin. There was one time during a war they had a war so long that the Delaware could not hold their meeting on that account. Then there was no meeting house. So in the meantime, the earth shook for one year. So the Delaware not having a meeting house, knew of no way to check this. So the Chief had two bark houses combined. So they held their meeting there. After they started this meeting up, all day long they shook hands with each other. The earth continually shook. Trees sank down. Directly big pools of water could be seen. After they held the meeting for six months, the earth began to stop shaking a bit. After that in the meanwhile they built a meeting house like the one across the river.[1] They held meetings in the barkhouse until

---

1. This is a reference to the Big House near the Little Caney River in Copan, Oklahoma.

they completed this meeting house. During the time they held this meeting about March or April at this time they held the meeting in the new meeting house. So one night they heard those deities represented by the wooden faces coming for several nights. Every night they came closer. They could hear them hollering. So in the meeting house one night, the older people got up and said "If there's anyone here in the meeting house that knows those parties" (i.e., had a gift from those people). So one fellow said "Yes. I can go and talk with them. I've been gifted by them." So two other old men went along with the fellow and when they got over there where the wooden faces were this fellow who said he had a gift from them, asked them what they came for (those deities represented by the false faces left, but the old men and fellow followed them and entered into conversation).[2] So they said that God sent them down to tell the people to stop the meeting at this time; it is time to plant your corn, your garden, anything to live on. The earth had stopped shaking; and not to hold another meeting till the coming fall. Then those false faces told those three men that hereafter they must never quit this Delaware meeting we have. They came to assist the tribe in carrying on the meeting; also they had control of all the deer and these deers are to be used in carrying on the meeting.[3] And at the time of the meeting in the fall they would drive the deer close to the meeting house so they could be easily found by the hunters; and for the Delawares to also make faces out of wood representing the authorities' looks identically in the faces. "So when you get the faces down representing our looks, we will put the power in them same as the power in us."

The rulings of this Delaware meeting, after four nights of meeting that day right at noon the boys get ready who want to go on the hunt just as many as want to go. And they elect a leader and all the boys hunting are to listen to what he says, he is to give the instructions. So they will all march in the meeting house who go hunting. They eat their dinner in there; all who camp nearby. After dinner they form in a line and the chief instructs them. When they are in the line they face the north, the right foot of each will be placed on the left foot of the next. The gun is held in the hands, the butt on the ground between the feet. So the chief gets up and instructs the head leader. The head leader carries a (bucket), brass kettle on his back to cook meat in. He carries the supply of grub to be taken. It is in sacks, etc. Then the chief has tobacco. He instructs the boys, encourages them, and tells them to have nothing on their mind but killing deer. Then he walks to the fire in the meeting house, he stirs up the coals; then he has in his hand tobacco which had been plug tobacco but it has been cut up fine. About this time the false face with the bear skin on comes in. He goes to the far end of the building and stands about in the center, and he hears the instruction that's given by the chief. The chief then burns this tobacco asking those twelve false faces that as these

---

2. Elkhair's reference to false faces identifies Mesingw.
3. This is probably a reference to the Mesinghalikun's role as "Keeper of the Game."

young men going off on a deer hunt, they must drive all the deer right in the way of those hunters. He repeats those words as he drops the tobacco on the coals of the fire. And the false-face wearing the bearskin listens to all that has been done. And this is the way the Delaware were instructed by the false faces in case they wanted anything for sure and in earnest, that they must burn this tobacco, and they will get their wish by doing this. After that the hunters march out after the attendants raise the sheet up.[4] There are two men who sing and beat on a deer skin. Those singers sing a song about the false faces and drive deers in the way of the hunters. Those fellows who hunt them get right on their horses. They are to hunt for three days. The third day at noon they are supposed to return at noon. That's the day they will have a lot of good grub in the meeting house for the hunters. Those hunters are instructed any time they kill a deer in those three days, one man could bring it home, or if more, then enough [men] to carry the meat. But the head man is not to return till third day at noon. When they come back, after eating their dinner then each begins to tell how many deer he saw, why he didn't kill one, etc. general talk about the hunt. So then that same day, those singers sing songs till the fourth day the hunters have been out hunting. After the sixth night meeting, they make everything new. The meeting is then generally ended; straight business now takes place: wants and wishes. They build a fire by a revolving stick. (There is a wheel with buck skin strings; by pulling up and down revolves shaft of mulberry. This shaft rests on a block of mulberry). After the fire is built before the starting of the meeting, new hay is spread where the people sit down along the edges inside. Then they repaint those false faces. Everybody then comes in—twelve sticks of sassafras about one and one half feet long are distributed. There are a few turtle shells striped (prairie turtles). Those are distributed. They are lined in a row right in front of the leader of the meeting (he will be on the north side of these shells). The leader takes a string of beads fully a yard long called wampum, he measures the length of the back of the turtles, he cuts the beads so as to correspond [with the length of each shell]. Then the nearest relative walks up. Then they take beads off each turtle shell, and then after he (she) takes those beads, he (she) hands the turtle shell to the leader of the meeting, keeping the beads. Those attendants (sweeping, getting wood, etc.) are three men and three women. They are called up by the leader [as] a yard of beads is to be poured out in the center of the church building. Those six attendants all kneel down and kind of hum, pick up the beads with the left hand and place those beads in their mouths. After the beads are so gathered, they go to the door where they are supposed to stand (on the east end of the building). There they count how many beads each got. After that the meeting starts in for that night. The headman he shakes one of the turtle shells (they have shot or rocks in to make a rattle). It is answered by the singers across the building by three strikes on the deer skin (on

---

4. James Rementer (1997: personal communication) points out that this is a reference to the canvas wagon sheet used as a door to the Big House.

the south side: the building runs east and west). The leader tells the people what he saw when a child. This will be about some animal who turned into the appearance of a person. He will tell what this animal told him. What help will be rendered him. Meanwhile he shakes the turtle-shell slowly with the rate of his talk. He will tell what caused him to see the animal, maybe his parents abused him or ran him off home. At this point, then he starts to singing. Then he will say "That's the way I heard them sing." So then he will go on telling this dream again. The next time he sings again he gets up. Then he will tell further what he saw in his dream. And he will sing again. Meanwhile the singers across the room keep time beating on the deer skin. When he [the leader] stops singing, the singers will sing the same song in the same time but as a second (like musical instruments T. M.).[5] When the singers sing the leader will dance. All will look at him. Others can volunteer, young men and women, and dance behind him. When he's through telling his dream and singing, all go and sit down. He will remain at the main guide-post at the center of the building. He will be standing. Then he will extend his kind thoughts to the people in the meeting house. And then he will tell them he thanks them all, thanks God he is able to perform his duty in the meeting house. And then he will sit down on the north side of the building. Those two attendants (men) will go out and cook one or two deers whole. Another man will follow suit with a turtle shell and tell his dream. They will go on till the turtle shell goes around the house to where it started from. Then the chief (not the leader) gets up and tells them the turtle that's been long here has returned [to the starting point]. Then those attendants are told to bring in the meat that they have cooked. That meat is put in brass kettles, sometimes baskets, before the leader (not the chief) to divide it to the old people first, not young men and women. Those attendants are then notified to distribute the balance to all the people in the meeting house as far as it will go. Those two singers across the hall get the deer heads. (The new fire will be used till the ninth night, when a new fire will be used till the end, till twelfth night. Next morning they take it out and clean up the meeting house). That will go on two more nights. Then the last night the women have their innings, tell what they have seen and sing. Before the women start, cedar is burnt, and every one is painted on the left cheek. The paint is out of weed in a little wooden bowl. First the men paint the false faces, deer skins, and sticks and turtle shells. They paint with paint and grease from the marrow of deer with one finger. One man paints—another greases. Then two women paint all persons in the meeting house, grease on left side of head, paint on the left cheek (paint dark red pe. kon; crimson; grows in timber).[6]

---

5. The initials in this parenthetical note are a marker reminding Michelson that the passage is a note to himself.
6. Puccoon is *lithosperum canescens*, a plant rendering a reddish dye color. Speck suggested that bloodroot, *Sanguinaria canadensi*, may also have been used for this purpose. Citing the fact that elders did not permit young people to accompany them while gathering the plants, Nora Thompson Dean and other Delawares have been unsure of the exact identity of plants used to make paint for Big House rituals (Rementer 1997: personal communication).

Then the chief tells the women to go out and get ready for their part, to form a line outdoors and elect two men. They will be each side of the woman who is going to lead. Then the women they tell when they're ready. Then the two men will cry out Kwia first, and women answer hu! twelve times. They raise the flap up, those singers beat as [they] cross the floor; as the women enter the men inside will cry ho! And everybody will hold up their right hands. The flap will be let down. The two men and women fall back. One man will [be] on the southside of the first woman, the other man similarly for [the] next woman. The woman-leader has six songs which must be sung which were gifted to her [in a vision by a spirit helper]. Then the turtle will be passed and all those that can sing will have to sing. The second woman sings four songs, the third sings two songs. The others can sing one or let it go if they can't sing (more than one if they want to).

When that's over it will be twelve p.m. All those attendants three second men, three first women will take a hand in this singing. If [a person] can't sing the songs, they must hire a substitute. The substitute will get one yard of beads. After this, this part is ended. After they get back to the head man, the head man of the women will be told to end the services. He will sing twelve [times]. Those two deer skin singers across the building they follow after him with a second. He dances, twelve stops in his dances. At the twelfth stop he will be at the entrance door. The women will dance following him. At the twelfth stop, the chief will call the attendants to raise the (wagon) flap sheet. They all will march out in a line as they came in. Then as going they will cry hi! with the right hand upraised. The deer skin beaters will beat time. After [they] exit, the flap is dropped. The two men that followed accompany the women. The deer meat will be in baskets outdoors. All those that sang, men and women, will get a share in the deer meat. The two men distribute the meat to those that sang. That part of the services is over. Then the attendants are called in. They sweep the building with turkey wings, one man and one woman. They use the left hand. The woman sweeps on one side, the man the other (next time the man will sweep the woman's side and she his). After the hall is swept the attendants have the privilege of going out if they want to. Still the chief tells them "You mustn't all go out, if you can help it, come right back in again." So then he tells them, "our meeting is getting short. It will be over tomorrow at noon." Then this head man, after all are in, takes this turtle shell, and tells about his dream, sings again in the usual way, the turtle goes from hand to hand. Anyone who has had a dream can sing. And the deer skin drummers sing a second to his song. Then he is ended and begins dancing. They beat the deer skin while he sings before. When the turtle shell reach[es] the two deer skin drummers, the turtle will stop right there and remain all night (it will be the twelfth night). Next morning, the fire will be taken out and the trash will be cleared up. Then they will proceed with the meeting again. When the turtle gets to the headman, the chief then says "this turtle is back here again where he started from last night." So there'll be a man seated supposed to sing twelve songs. He'll be the last man to sing. While he sings the twelve songs, at the tenth song every one will rise to their feet and he will dance about the main post, every one crowding up towards him. After the twelfth song all hold up their left hands crying hi! ho! Then all will be told to sit down where they came from. Then one of the attendants, a woman, will distribute beads (wampum) in a wooden plate. Each gets two or three beads. They are given because it is extending thanks to God. So then those attendants are notified to bring in the deer hides of the slain deer. Then those deers hides will be piled up in the middle of the meeting house. The chief asks the head-hunter (supposed to be one of the attendants) who were they who killed the deer. The oldest woman or man of the band (Wolf, Turkey, or Turtle) of the slayer will get the hide. The rest of deer (which are left) will be out of doors cooked in baskets. The attendants will be instructed to bring it in the meeting house. Then the close relatives of the head man will get and distribute the meat to their nearest relatives, then to the older people that are in the house, then the attendants will take the meat and distribute the meat as far as it goes to all in the meeting house. Then those attendants two men, one at the east end one at the west, will begin he! The two singers will beat the deer skin. Then the two attendants will go, one on the north side, one on the south picking up the sassafras sticks, and deerskins. They are piled up in the middle of the meeting house. Those six attendants are called to the head-man. They are in line. There will [be] two men with six yards of wampum. Each attendant will get one yard. Each near relatives, usually four-five, will hold the beads up with their hands. So then the chief tells them what good they have done since they were there, and during the time they were in earnest about their work, and their good-will will be a benefit to them from heaven. So those attendants hold those beads instead of cutting them up. The head-man will have hold of the end [of the strings]. They start out doors. When they be out doors, quite a way from the meeting house they hold the beads up and pray by crying out he! ho! twelve times. Then they go back to the fire in front of the meeting house, where they cooked the deers, there they distribute the beads, each getting as much as the other (that is one yard for [each] attendant). In the meantime the chief rises, makes a speech that they have all fulfilled their work in regard to the meeting's regulations and rulings. Then all will proceed to march out of the meeting house and they will go out and pray on the east side. All will form a line north and south. They will kneel down, cry with right hand upraised, cry six times ho! Then they will stand up and cry ho! four times. At [the] South end of the line the man will cry he! and the man at right also he! Then it is carried north and south, each taking it up. When they meet, the meeting is over.

The Center Post of the Delaware Meeting House

The Meetinghouse was used to keep anything down that was injurious to the people, such as floods, earthquakes, or anything injurious to the people, such as droughts, famines, etc. So as long as they kept it up we would raise good crops and everything else that was beneficial to the people. So that guide post in the center is what protects the people on the earth. So long as that stands up the earth will stand. It is that pole that holds the earth down. So when that Delaware meetinghouse whenever that is quit and the house destroyed, the world will come to an end. And that's the belief of the Delaware tribe. All the instructions given about the meeting house are true.

Miscellaneous Notes

The Doll Dance belongs to the Wolf Band. The Feast or Otter Skin Dance belongs to the Turtle Band. The False Face with Bearskin—essentially that is the F. face mask with bearskin called Mesingw—Belongs to the Turkey Band. The head-man would have to be a member of the Turkey Band. The men attendants will have to have father or mother in the Turkey Band. And the women attendants the same (that is on both sides, Father and Mother). In the Delaware meeting house: The Turkey bands sit at that southeast corner. The Turtle Band owns the entire north side of the meeting house. They are ones who can start the performance. On southwest corner belongs to the Wolf band. They sit over there. No exogamy or endogamy. Female descent: Child by right belongs to mother's band: sits regularly with mother's band at meeting house; can however visit father's band at meeting house and sit with them. (The divisions of Unami and Unalachtigo apparently completely obliterated today).

Each band has a chief, a [illegible] (messenger), a counselor (weighty in council, supposed to be smart), a brave (hard to kill; shot at, will be missed; takes lead).

CHAPTER EIGHT

The Charlie Webber [Wi.tapano'xwe] Text of the Oklahoma Delaware Big House Ceremony, 1928

The following account presents what is probably the best-known and most widely read description of the Gamwing. It was first published in University of Pennsylvania anthropologist Frank G. Speck's 1931 monograph, "A Study of the Delaware Indian Big House Ceremony." The heart of Speck's book, a lengthy text in Delaware with interlinear English translation, was dictated by a Delaware man named Charles C. Webber (also known as War Eagle) over a four-month period in 1928 while Webber was working in Philadelphia as an herbalist (fig. 11). Webber, whose Delaware name was Wi.tapano'xwe, "Walking in Daylight," was a member of the Turkey phratry. He told Speck that he was born about 1880 in the Cooweescoowee District of the Cherokee Nation to a Cherokee father and Munsee mother. He went on to claim that "he was elected to the Council of the Fowl or Turkey division of [his mother's] tribe in 1902, and re-elected secretary of the Delaware executive council by the combined Delaware and Munsee tribes in 1921" (Speck 1931: 9).

Portions of Webber's text were retranslated by Smithsonian Institution linguist R. H. Ives Goddard, III, for Elisabeth Tooker's source book on Eastern Woodland Indian religions (Goddard 1979: 104–24). Goddard did more than cast the text in a more modern idiom. Employing the most recent developments in linguistic theory and method and drawing upon more than two centuries of linguistic research and the results of his own fieldwork in Delaware communities, Goddard's retranslation of Webber's text revealed numerous differences in meaning and interpretation. Many could be classed as relatively minor semantic differences. More significant were major syntactic reassessments showing that original translations such as "My defunct parent was exceedingly grieved over the thing" were more properly translated as "He caused me great sorrow."

Fig. 11. Charlie Webber. Courtesy James Rementer.

Webber's expertise in matters concerning the Big House has been questioned in recent years. Jay Miller attributes discrepancies between Webber's accounts and those of other Oklahoma Unami traditionalists to two main causes. First, as a Munsee, he may not have fully understood the Unami rite. Second, although present-day Eastern Oklahoma Delaware traditionalists remember him with fondness, and many remember the prominent role he played in attempts to revive the Gamwing during the 1940s; none recall his active participation in the traditional Big House or regard him as an authority on Delaware religion (Miller 1976: 83; 1980: 111).

Despite these criticisms, Webber's Delaware text, Goddard's retranslation, and Speck's analysis of documentary and ethnographic evidence remain indispensable sources for anyone interested in the Big House.

Origin of the Ceremony and Formal Preparations

The[1] first beginning of this Big House was the beginning long ago of that worship that the Delawares now call Ngamwin, when there was a quaking of the earth throughout where the Delawares lived. And even all the animals were frightened; people could do nothing because the earth was shaking greatly. And for great distances came crevices in the earth. Everyone was greatly disturbed of mind when they saw how huge the gaps were, of unknown depth, extending here from the world below; there was utmost disturbance of mind. Even the animals were terrified; they say, even the animals prayed. And accordingly, everyone came into council to consider a possible way to proceed so that we might please that Pure Manitou, our Creator.

Now at the time the earth quaked, a great cracking, rumbling noise arose here from down below the ground, and there came issuing out dust and smoke, while here and there came issuing out something looking like tar. It was a black fluid, that substance which flowed from under the earth, where great gaps opened in the ground, in our mother's body here where we dwell.

To this day it is not known what was the purpose of the black fluid substance that issued forth from below, where the earth split open and dust and smoke were seen. They say that was the breath of the Evil Manitou.

And then when the men were called together, it was said: "The Delawares ought to pray, for it would seem that we have very seriously angered the Great Manitou. That is why he frightened us." One after another, people arose and said, "This is my dream and I can explain and sing everything for sure the way I saw it.

"Now," it was said, "first of all we are to build a house." And also it was specified how that house should look, and how big inside and how high, and also, it was said, "This is the size of that door. It will have doors in the direction of the setting sun and in the direction of our sunrise. And at the sides of the logs will join end to end three times and three posts will be used. Two posts will be at each door, opposite each other, reaching to the height of the top of the roof. In the middle shall be the big post, and it shall be as high as the height of the house. All the posts shall be notched on top, and those at the sides where the logs join shall stand as stud-posts opposite each other, and held together at the top with short cross-ties. And up at the top of the posts [rafter] poles run across, and that ridge pole is in two pieces that join in the center. At a little more than a person's height, the roof shall be begun. Everything shall be of wood, including the rafters and flat boards. Also, bark shall be used for roofing.

"And on opposite sides of the center post is where the fires shall be made. Directly above each the roof shall have an uncovered hole, where the smoke will go out. And on every post at about a person's height there shall be carved a Mesingw, and half the face shall be painted red and the other half black.

---

1. Beginning of Goddard retranslation (Goddard 1979: 104).

"And around the sides where the people sit, hay shall be used. And three men and three women shall be selected—one each from the Turkey group, the Turtle, and the Wolf to be appointed to labor as long as the Ngamwin. For ten and two days people pray. All this time they furnish sufficient well-dried wood. But it is those women who are appointed to grind up corn and cook meat."

And[2] the Attendants all together feed in the house. And they pay them one shoulder-length of wampum every time they furnish food. And it is the rule that the people shall use wampum when purchasing food from the Attendants. There everyone who recites visions in the House will eat there with his family three times each day.

No iron or nail is used when building the House, and no wooden floor. It has a dirt floor inside the House. Deerhide is used when the drum is tied together and two drum-sticks are cut forked. And small faces are carved on one side, alike in appearance. Another different pair of sticks are made plain and these are used when the cranes are singing. And a wooden bowl is made ready when they mix up the tobacco and Kinnickinnick. Another different wooden bowl is provided when they carry the red paint and Puccoon and also there they put cedar.

And ten and two sticks are made, called "means of earnest prayer." And some are marked with spots. Whoever wishes to sing in company shall also use this when helping to lift up the prayer, it is said, with concentration of spiritual force far above to the ten and two sky-levels where dwells the Creator.

And now this Big House when first built, they say of it, was the one great prayer-creed, that this carved post in the middle of the House, standing there reaches to the above through as many as ten and two strata. And the strata of sky light are as high as that post, it is said, this being the fastener. That is the Creator's staff. From that very staff, branch off all prayer-creeds of the red-people given to them, whence come all other prayer-creeds of the world.

And there was given to the Delawares something which is used when they make fire. It is called "ringing noise-instrument." Whomever they chose as fire-maker, any of the Attendants, was of moral habits or spiritually clean, for that one shall drill for fire in the House. Sometimes flint is used when they make fire in the House and pith is used when they make fire with flint.

Now therefore in the beginning the Delawares came to be blessed with religion together with the Munsee; so the prayer worship proceeds for ten and two days. Now that very log-house itself is called Big House. Right here toward the dawn-direction and sun-set direction it lies extended. And the doors are opposite each other. Right here in the direction of the sun-set, it is the rule that the Bringer-in come, bringing the ceremony into the House.

---

2. Beginning of Speck translation (Speck 1931: 85).

Everything was provided for the Delawares in the Gamwing. There was also wampum supplied by rule, it is said. Each person gives one shoulder-length for helping to prepare this food and also for when they pay the Attendants. And, so it is said, the Attendant is pleasing to him our father the Great Spirit, even the Creator.

When the workers purify everything, these women with the Attendants, it can not be conceived how sacredly valuable those labors are. It has been destined for the Delaware that very wampum he uses becomes his heart. And moreover when purchasing food, or when anything of value is bought, he employs wampum. And then a quantity is gathered. Here at the left side of the House where the Bringer-in sits, at a certain height above the ground, there a white cloth is hung along the wall. There is suspended all the wampum, as much as has been gathered together each day over again.

And it was said, long ago in the beginning at the Gamwing, inside the Big House, they built a great sweat-house. They heated rock and put it inside that sweat-house. There the shamans crawled in. And water was used here for pouring upon the rocks. That was called testing with heat. Everyone going in there and staying for any length of time was said to be a great man. Some person would be exhausted in a little while for which reason they took him out. Those enduring it for a considerable length of time, those are the great men.

A turkey's wing is used when they sweep out in the Big House. And besides, the Attendant carries a long stick as a poker and that is used when they stir up the fire, and it is the rule that they shall light a good bright fire every night as long as they perform the ceremony. And the Attendant-leader every evening walks around all over where they are camped about this Big House holding a whip. And any person that they find that is causing unnecessary noise they correct. And the children are instructed. And he notifies them, telling them thrice "Come in! Come in! Come in!" And just recently they selected an officer from the Delaware Agency who is on guard all the time here while they are assembled, so that no one brings in liquor.

When any one of us considers the rule with all the obligations and instructions as these are properly carried out, it should be forbidden for one thing that those of our women who when they cannot cook are not pure, be allowed to trouble about the cooking. And should not come in the Big House as long as they are affected with the sickness, because some pure children might be much contaminated, especially when they perform the Gamwing. And it is the rule that persons should abstain from bringing into the Big House any animals of whatever kind they may be which are domesticated.

And right here opposite from the door on the outside over there at a certain distance they make the fire. Two forked poles are set upright and a pole laid across, upon which they hang the big buckets in which they cook. Near here standing upright is a many-forked tree where meat is hung. And a big shelf is there at one side of the fireplace with two floors where they put the corn that is used. When hominy is made the female Attendants have for their duty every morning and

THE CHARLIE WEBBER [WI.TAPANO'XWE] TEXT, 1928

evening to grind and make corn flour and hominy. Sometimes two or four mortars are used together with those long pounders.

Here on each side three tents are provided. In the first there camps the leading Attendant, from here outwards the rest of the Attendants. When any one of these Attendants does not serve, he can hire a substitute to provide fire-wood or to sweep in the Big House, and occasionally to cook.

The Delawares were given the Mask-image so it became the rule that whoever owns that mask should take it into the Big House each year, that mask, because it is he who has complete control over all the wild animals. And it is said that our grandfather is believed to walk around early each morning. Now here he goes about frightening unruly children. When the "one who is our grandfather" begs, the child is taught that he shall pay a plug of tobacco so that he will not scare them.

If the person who assumes to wear the mask is able to see clearly for a long distance it is said that he is a man of power. He carries a turtle-rattle and a staff of twisted wood. When the mask makes his utterance it resembles a horse whinnying, and when he makes signals using his turtle-rattle, then they give him tobacco. Every child customarily is taught that he gathers snakes and throws them into that pouch in order that no one may steal our grandfather's tobacco. And it is also said that our grandfather keeps guard over all so that no one may be overcome by disease. That also is the teaching in reference to the spiritual doctrine of the Mask-image.

When the worship ceremony begins everyone is instructed to wear things conforming strictly to Delaware style, such for instance as the deer-tail or horse-hair when made into a roach. And everything is beaded including moccasins. And if any one wishes it he goes there to the Attendant where he may choose paint of whatever color he prefers. And those desiring it wear eagle feathers. All the old men customarily have the head-band when going into the Big House.

And anyone may choose his style, but red paint and yellow, by custom, are more frequently used. A person does not rub it on his face all over. A person usually paints his cheek or at the sides of his eyes lightly. But the relief-drummers can, if desired, paint black or paint fancy. All the women if they desire may paint red when entering the Big House. And also when the ceremonial leader first enters the Big House that is the time when all those Face-Images are painted.

Two shell-rattles they make of a wild creature. One they call the leading rattle and the other, greater in size, is called, traditionally, timber-terrapin. And those are used when they pray every night. Here just at the right hand side of the door they place these shell-rattles. When the Master of Ceremonies arrives he says, "Now then, my brothers and my sisters, now as we begin we are approached and touched by those Man.i't.u who are carrying this ceremony of worship." That is how they employ them there. And both the dance-leader and his follower each hold in their hands these shell-rattles when they are dance-leading. The leading shell-rattle does not have a great sound, but that of the follower has a great sound, it is said traditionally, for he does answer when they are rattling.

Every year the old men hold a council. The day is named, it is talked over, and they decide who shall bring in the ceremony. And they name the person who shall carry the six yards of wampum. And generally they name three men and three women Attendants going to see them. They select the one who is willing to act as leading Attendant for the two Turkey group representatives, and the two Turtle clan representatives and the two Wolf group representatives are chosen.

These leading Attendants, one and the same, belonging in the group of the Master-of-Ceremonies, he who opens the ceremony. Now when the Attendants have accepted the call, forthwith a shoulder-length of wampum they are given as a symbol of being blessed. And announcement is made of what day in the future they shall go into camp at the Big House. When they finish cleaning this House they also plaster it with clay and all then about outside rake it clean. Then and there preparation is made for beginning the Gamwing. And besides, everyone who is to relate a vision and lead a dance, if he had prepared his rattle of turtle shell, shall see to it to bring it with him for the ceremony.

There, in the ancient times the beginning of their worship the Delawares went into camp every month. They worshiped in the Big House for a ten and two day period. But then in a few years a different rule made it every three months. And again it was changed. It was said, "We are hindered in our labor," because of our ceremony. Whereupon for the last time they changed it. It was said, "From now on every six months, the Gamwing will be." But indeed it was discovered that they had become by now too much like the white man in their life. The young Delawares were ashamed, seeing what their elders did. And so by this time it is very difficult for the Delawares to assemble when ready to perform the ceremony.

Such was the ruling long ago how several different kinds of spiritual forces were existent, how, it was said, all the wild animals and birds as well as the creeping wild creatures are the ones to be mentioned in the Big House.

The pure animals and birds only are used when they prepare meat. This is the reason why every one of them, even that Mask-Spirit, and all their kind including the Tortoise, are called Man.i'.t.u. It is because he it is who carries our mother's body. And the bird is used there to be eaten. And these feathers of him are ceremonially used when they sweep clean the beautiful-pure White Path, our father's, the Great Spirit's road.

Wherefore a person will appear fine when dressing-up for the ceremony, because anyone who earnestly prays in worship to even the deer and the antelope as well as the bison or any other wild creature whatsoever, that is said to be pure spirit. And also those twelve face-images in the Big House, and those prayer-sticks, and the maize and fruit, all things indeed used in the Gamwing, it is said, are helpers when it comes to lifting up to the twelve levels of heaven above us where he dwells, our father the Great Spirit.

And also there is a ruling of custom. The religious obligations sometimes require that the speaker, when talking, it is said, names over all these spirit-forces wherever they reside around the earth, calling upon them, as it is said: "Truly we are thankful that we have lived long enough to see the time come when these our grandfathers the trees bloom forth, and also the coming up of vegetation.

"Now as well for this water and for him our grandfather fire, and again this air, again this sunlight. When everyone has been blessed with such gifts it is enough to make one realize what kind of benevolence comes from our father, because he it is who has created everything."

And now furthermore one more spiritual-force is said to be a part of creation up above. The first being mentioned is called day-moon, and the night traveler is called night-moon. And of several kinds of stars, the first one seen is that one from the sunrise direction, called Great Star. Again seven stars, it is said, are sometimes at the noon-point seen after dark. Those stars called the Bear; also the head of this one is separate. Now it is said that whenever that Bear shall catch up with his head, then will be the end of the world. And again another group is called Bunched-up, seven is their number. And again here in the direction of sun-down, that evening-star is called Kwe^{e}tci'pene^{e}s.[3] Thenceforth are other stars and moons. And there are also these Thunders, our grandfathers, even coming to those clouds, all called spirit-forces. And the sun, our elder brother, is considered a leading spirit-force up above, because he is a great person. By his breath he warms all the universe, and it is he also who lights up the day-time, and the night-sun. It is he who lights up the night-time. And those stars, in accordance with the strength given them, in proportion that serve and aid our father's, the Great Spirit's labors.

And so this is what the Delawares understand; namely that some spirit-forces are able to control everything whatsoever, and some are created with less strength. Therefore when a person acquires the strength of a vision of some object or living being, he will obtain it in accordance with the strength imbued in the spiritual power which gives it to him.

And now of the several kinds of spirits when they are spoken of, the tortoise is said to be a powerful being because he is able to bear up this our mother's body. That is why it is said he slowly moves, walking deliberately, because he carries the whole earth. And he starts out, beginning walking from the direction of sunrise. It is said that when he arrives at the edge of the earth, it will seem like but a short time, namely, for instance we may say like one eye-wink. But because of his slowness of movement afoot; that is why it seems so long before he shall have traversed this world. For, whenever they see him in the wilderness he is going toward the direction of sun-set. And now it shall be, when he has completed his road, then shall come to end this earth.

Some persons when endowed with shaman power, it is said, can use it against anyone when they are angry. And that is the cause of some persons' disability or the cause of persons going blind. And he may even decide that he can kill with it. And that is called evil conjuring.

---

3. Speck wrote, "Unfortunately the informant was unable to give a translation for this term."

Now the non-beneficent spirit-force has shaman power wherefore a person can employ that Spiritual force for evil purpose. For it is said by tradition, evil things belong to the Evil Spirit, the cat, panther, or long-tail and the snake, and also the lizard and insects, for example, the spider, and also the scorpion, and these birds; the screech owl and the horned-owl and also the chicken-killer, the red-tailed hawk.

Now what is called the state of being a clean, pure child is the source of a person acquiring something as his spiritual vision. Anciently there the children, little boys, it is said, were given a bow and taught how to make arrows. Before daylight they obliged him to go in swimming. Now after, when he appears to be older, far off into the wilds he is driven. "Now must you hunt birds!" Food is not eaten until he kills something. And in the evening as well, the person sleeps without being fed, because, it is said, a child lying exposed in a pitiful state would cause some occasional spirit-force to have pity on him when passing by visiting all the children in the world. Because here from the sunrise direction, or from up above and sometimes from the northern direction or the south, are the directions whence they are visited by spirit-forces. On account of this it is called pitiful abuse.

Long ago it was called correction. Some persons when sick in any way, persons in perplexity and distress, would accordingly experience a dream-vision of something, or some would acquire a revelation vision. It is that [by] which one is blessed, whence one becomes useful or becomes a healer or the reciter of a vision in the Big House.

First Night of the Ceremony

The Master of Ceremony says when he goes into the Big House, when rising to his feet, he speaks saying, "Truly I am thankful, my kindred. It is exceedingly good that we have lived on through to see each other, that we are in good health. I am truly thankful to bring forth the blessing, my brothers and sisters and those there, our children. I bless you all with every kind of blessing. Truly it is unbecoming to me because I feel incompetent when instructing you what to do. Pitiful am I, indeed, as it is said. It rests very heavily upon my mind when I see each year how at present this our way of living has become pitiful. But nevertheless we must all try, my brothers and sisters and also even those children. Let everyone use his mind earnestly when we lift up our prayer of appeal to that one, our father, the Great Spirit and Our Creator. Indeed it is with great sadness of mind that we look back and see the past of our cultural-life as it is said to have been. Formerly, but a few years ago, it is said, here the seating space in the Big House was overcrowded with our now deceased relations. Indeed it brings sadness of mind when we see here now how few of our relatives are seated around that space. It is enough to make anyone ponder over the cause of it. I myself never did think that I would live long enough, as a survivor, living as I am right here, instructing in sacred things where other sacred-teachers, our deceased ancestors, so thoroughly inspired in worship, taught. So I pray that everyone help. If accordingly everyone does all in his power, earnestly praying with all his heart, it might occasion those spirit-forces to hear our pitiful appeal, those who carry the power of blessing. And right here this evening in a little while we shall begin to feel ourselves being touched by our grandfathers who move this our prayer-worship.

And now when worshiping, these Turkey-group people, because they enter the Big House with the ceremony, that group is our old man and our chief. "He-Walks-Turning-Around-Slowly" is the one who brings in the ceremony.[4]

When the enterer begins the ceremony everything is prepared. Here at the middle of the right hand side, directly opposite where the studpost stands, right here he conducts the worship—the Enterer. From this place is where they perform the vision recitations. These turtle-rattles are called our grandfathers. When they reach the place where the Master of Ceremonies sits, he shakes the rattle, the leading rattle, and the follower answers him.

Then these "cranes," or drummers, beat three times the drum. First the dance leader strikes the drum once, and then the follower-singer, and the leader again. And then also he will say, he who is about to recite his vision dance, "I now must worship!" And all the old men answer. They say, "Hau! Indeed it is truly fine, my brother!"

Recitation of Vision by Ko"kwel.epo'xwe (Charlie Elkhair)

I[5] must now come to the point of relating my narrative about Kansas River when I was a child, when my now deceased father told me, "Now, indeed, for your younger brother's life is ended." He caused me great sorrow, since I really grieved for my younger brother. For I used to think that later on I would play with him. Truly indeed it bothered me very much. I did not know what to do. That is why I began to wander away, and walked along there toward the edge of the timber. I was unaware that night was beginning to overtake me, and more and more my thoughts bothered me. I really did not know what to do. Then, suddenly, I made up my mind to let whatever might become of me happen. Then under a tree I doubled up to the ground. In a short time I began to feel that my grief had begun to flow out. I seemed as though I were not asleep, for I thought: "I don't care if I die right here; I don't have a younger brother now anyway." It was not long before I heard something land on the ground nearby. I did not realize that I had apparently gotten up halfway while looking over toward the north.

---

4. Speck wrote, "The performance is to be recited as though it were being conducted by the present chief of the tribe, Charles Elkhair who has held the office since 1898, whose Delaware name is Ko^{u}kwəl.əpo'xwe denoting someone who is walking along slowly then turns around in the opposite direction. The same chief was the host to the ceremony described by Harrington in 1912 (Harrington 1921: 85–87). The informant planned the text to follow Elkhair's manner of conducting it because he had participated in it frequently under him and had a clearer recollection of his addresses and details of management."

5. Goddard's retranslated text begins here (Goddard 1979: 109).

Pitiful me, I saw nothing although I could hear the being well. From right over the ridge I heard him say: "Do not think that you are not cared for, my friend!" Then he was walking about! Indeed, the being really startled me when I looked over. Then I saw him stretched out; he seemed to me to extend from the north. He was kind of red looking. And he said, "My friend, pay close attention! Look at me! This is what I do when I walk about in this place!" Every little while he would start running. When he started running the sound he made was tammmmm, tammmmm![6] That being looked as odd as could be.

When I thought about him when I looked at him, it was over the edge of the southern land where he apparently came to ground. And every time that being started running, he sounded like ooooo ooooo.[7] And he said when he landed there, "This is what I do when I pass by here bestowing my blessings." There in the direction of the north I heard him. That being every so often started running. More and more I was concerned by what the being said.

Truly thank you, my kindred. I am glad that we have so far had good health and that I can bestow on you all kinds of spiritual blessings, even including all of those grandfathers of ours. And before long we shall shake hands with these drummers,[8] who are lifting up the worship of the Delawares with song. More and more clearly could I see that being. I took him to be over there in the north where he originated, and he seemed, as I saw him going by, to be of red appearance.

Truly I am utterly inadequate to do it, my kindred, but I shall nevertheless do as well as I can and with all my heart, pitiful me! For that is what I thought when I heard that being saying, "My friend look at me carefully. I too bring blessings when I come here!" My kindred, I am glad that I have reached this Fine White Path, our Father's Road.[9] And now we have come here to where our grandfathers stands.[10] And also we used to hear our now-deceased ancestors worship in the proper manner. They said: "This is how many times we dance around the place where our grandfather stands." So let us, too, state it: It will be four times. And then for a while we shall cease talking about that being. But if only I have good health a little longer, we shall never cease for good talking about that being.

Truly indeed my kindred we are enjoying very good fortune when we are given an abundance of pure game animals as our spiritual meal, as a result of which all of us shall become glad when he our Father, the Great Manitou, comes to our aid. But still, we pitiful people, that is why our pitiful utterances are heard here in our Father's House.

---

6. Speck wrote, "Here the drummers beat the drum in response."
7. Speck wrote, "At this point, the drummers strike the drum rapidly."
8. Speck wrote, "The reciter in his circuit of the Big House is approaching the drummers. When he is almost in front of them, he stops and shakes hands with them. All those dancing behind him do likewise."
9. Speck wrote, "The oval dance path in the Big House. It symbolizes the path of life."
10. Speck wrote, "A reference to the center post on which two faces are carved."

Now, my kindred, we have gone once around our Grand-father, the Mesingw. Truly thank you for taking care of us until now and for our being in good health, including these our children. Now greet our grandfather. Twice we shall lift up our appeal, hooooo, hooooo! And again, my brothers and sisters and also my children, we have danced up to where stands this grandfather of ours. All together there are twelve of our grandfathers, by whom every Manitou alike is represented: Here is our grandfather Fire, and here is our mother Water, and all the food that supports our life. It is enough, my kindred, to make us happy when we are given all the things that are growing. All of that which our Father, the Great Manitou, has provided, which is why it is possible for us to see it.

And that being appeared to me right there in the south; he appeared to me and he seemed to possess power in all things. Truly, my kindred, one more time we dance around where our grandfather stands. And this will be the last time when we shall go around. And then also will everyone lift the prayer twelve times up to where his worship of the Delaware belongs, to the twelfth level of the sky, where dwells our Father, the Great Manitou.

Truly thank you, my kindred. Now here we have come here to where our grandfather stands. Now the time has come for us to offer up our adoration, to lift up our prayer ten and two times to where dwells he who owns us, the Great Manitou, our Creator.

Truly thank you that I shake hands with you, my brothers, my sisters, and these our children. I give thanks that I bless you with all and every kind of spiritual blessings. Truly it greatly oppresses my heart when I see how we are orphans now. Many times we have heard how pitiful our deceased ancestors sounded when they recounted how pitiful were the conditions then. I make myself grieve very much, my kindred, when I see what happened in the past. But, nevertheless, still try your utmost, let us every one be helpful. Maybe if our pitiful plea is heard by the Great Manitou, we would sometime earn something good that he might do for us.

Truly my kindred, I feel utterly unable to give blessings from here where our grandfather stands. And I am truly thankful to greet all those Manitous, all of them sitting round about and above. And when we remember how our now-deceased ancestors so thoroughly took care of the obligations of this worship, it is very good that we can still perform the ceremony as we used to see our now-deceased ancestors do it. This is sufficient for this occasion. Thank you.

Now[11] the leader goes and sits down. When he has properly seated himself and swept it clean then "These who are painted red" say "Let us all smoke, Let us all smoke." So the tobacco has been placed in a wooden bowl and should be mixed with sumac leaves (Kinnickinnick), because it is the rule that sumac shall be used

---

11. The Speck translation begins again here (Speck 1931: 127).

by the Delawares when smoking. And besides the cedar and paint are all kept there at one place close to the drum. And when anyone lights the pipe in the Big House, he will then use our Grandfather because that one also is called pure, clean fire.

Two Attendants sweep clean the House. The man goes to the far end from whence he begins to sweep, while the woman begins to sweep from the door. Turkey wings are used when sweeping. Both Attendants finish sweeping at the same time when they arrive at the door and then for a while put away the wings.

Now it is permissible for anyone to go out, and quickly to come back inside because in a little while then again will begin to stir those tortoise shell rattles, our Grandfathers. When they have come to where sits the next following Reciter-leader, or to anyone else feeling able to recite a vision and lead, it is permitted by the rule that he shake the rattle and, if desired, recite and lead.

Recitation of Vision by Wi.ta'panoxwe

All[12] of you, my kindred, are acquainted with where I spent my childhood, at Raccoon Creek, where lived my now-deceased parents. Once my now-deceased mother really scolded me. She drove me away because I was continually looking at books. That is why she scolded me. She told me, "Go away somewhere into the wilderness, since all you seem to do is look at books." And she said, "For all the days to come you will be pitiful because the book blocks your path. Never will anything be revealed to you in a vision, for you live like a white man."

Truly, my kindred, great sorrow did my late parents cause me. Then and there I began to walk aimlessly toward the direction of our sunset here, toward the timber. My grief was heavy when I thought about myself: "Truly that is really so; my parents spoke the truth in saying that never would anything be revealed to me in a vision." And I thought it very likely that I would never be blessed the way that the Delaware is blessed. Indeed, my kindred, I was humble in spirit for many years.

Now, when I became a grown man, far away in the country of the Creeks when I was camping with a group, one time after dark, in the course of the night, I heard some beings coming towards me in the midst of the clear sky. It was here from the direction of our sunrise that they were coming.

And when they came and stopped right here above where I had collapsed in sleep.

I well remembered what my now-deceased mother had said to me, and I thought, "There it is. It must be that those are the Manitous my parent had talked about." I do not know just how my mind acted, when I looked toward them. I saw nothing, pitiful me, although I well heard those beings. I thought there must be four of them, and I thought they must look terrible, for they greatly upset me

---

12. Goddard's retranslation begins again here (Goddard 1979: 114).

when they said to me: "Do not think that you will never be blessed the way the Delaware is blessed!"

I am truly thankful, my kindred, and happy that I have attained this our Father's Road, the Fine White Path of the Great Manitou. I am utterly inadequate, pitiful as I am, because never did I think that I would be able all of a sudden to perform in this our ceremonial House, where I heard our now-deceased old people, who worshiped properly. But still I will do my utmost. Take heed, my brethren. Help me, because now we know that we are growing weaker and weaker. So perhaps if we help each other earnestly, we might quite unexpectedly earn blessings, if the Creator hears us with pity.

Truly thank you that I address you, you men, you young men, you women, and also you our children. I address you with every form of this blessing. I am glad that so far we have enjoyed good health while we are gathered here in this House of ours. Truly, I make myself grieve when I recount how my parent used to instruct me, and I well remember how pitiful the old men sounded long ago, when they described their life in the past and what happened then. When I listened to them it was really that way, but now it is worse. At this time it looks hopeless, considering how few we are. Even a few years ago, my kindred, there were quite a few people sitting all around. But nevertheless I shall try my utmost.

Truly I am quite inadequate. I never even thought that I would survive long enough to suddenly be instructing from this spot, where long ago our now-deceased ancestors who performed the worship so well have instructed. And thank you, my kindred, when you help me in my recitation, for that has been the strict rule since the beginning of the world, that people should help each other. For even a little child may suddenly remind people of something. That is why it is a great help when anyone is assisted in his recitation. There might very well be something more I should say, but thank you that you and I are addressing prayers to all our grandfathers, around here, and all over the earth, and up above where they dwell. All of that our Father, the Great Manitou, has arranged, and it is why we are happy when he does something good for us.

This is all I have to say for a while.

Second Night of the Ceremony

THE[13] PROCEDURE OF THE SECOND NIGHT'S PERFORMANCE FOLLOWS THAT OF THE FIRST NIGHT AS RESPECTS THE RECITATIONS BY THOSE WHO DESIRE TO CHANT THEIR VISIONS AND TO DISCOURSE.

Here now, when the last Reciter-Leader has finished, and when they have swept the House well, then the other male Attendants bring inside the Big House the hominy. Everyone eats the hominy in company. Each and all of the women

---

13. The Speck translation begins again here (Speck 1931: 137).

comes bringing a dish to dip it out with. The Attendant has authority to give out the amount allotted to each, so it is said. The boys carry mussel-shells[14] which are used the same as when spoons are used. Now when everyone has eaten his share of the hominy, he feels happy for it, because the Bringer-in always says that this grain-food brings a spiritual blessing of strength when we set out to appeal to our common Father in the sky above. These Attendants first set apart a portion for each individual in his dish, because that is strictly understood to be the rule since long ago in the beginning of the world.

Third Night of the Ceremony

Thanks be given, my kindred that still we are blessed with good fortune. Now it is the third evening since here we have performed the ceremony in our temple-house. Now we beg, everyone of us, at his utmost that we may be favored by the pure spirit-force, by him the mask-spirit because he is the one who owns and controls all the wild animals. Now tomorrow morning all must be ready to accompany the hunt because to do so we concentrate our minds in order that we may be favored with success. The Hunt-Leader and his assistant and also the cook must all be selected, and also the tobacco together with the rations for the journey. You Attendants must see to it with care that plenty of rations for the journey are furnished for all the hunters;—the bread.

Address on the Fourth Morning to the Hunters About to Leave: The Mask Performance

Here now, my kindred, we have come to the fourth day since we began, in this place, to perform the ceremony. And each and every one of us know the ruling of this our form of Prayer-Worship. Now we are using the tobacco our grandfather, while we are pleading earnestly with the Great Spirit. And the Mask-Spirit also, when we are giving thanks to him our grandfather Fire. This is how it is done by the Bringer-in: "I thank all the Spirit-Forces on top of the earth and all the Spirit-Forces up above. Wherefore we earnestly plead with grandfather when we give you to eat this red man's tobacco. Have pity on us here your grandchildren. They are begging you, Oh Mask-Spirit, that we may have success. Give us the wild animals since you control them, all the wild animals because we need that we may be blessed with this meat. And that one, our mother the corn, because of all the food given us I thank you Spirit Forces that we are given the blessing of your spirit-power. Now give us all we ask of you Great Spirit that you are and, our creator, think of your children."

---

14. Speck wrote, "The single shell of the fresh-water mussel (*Unio companatus* in the east, *U. gibbosus*, in the west) employed as a spoon is *ees.e'm'h@n*."

Brothers! Now the Hunt Leader, and he who is assistant, and also the cook, you must all remember the instructions and traditional rules that all persons who hunt observe as they journey. Here now being under our power, you are taking as you go the spirit-power of the Mask-Spirit, and tobacco is given the Hunt Leader and his assistant which they carry. Now when you have been gone two days it is permissible that any one who had killed something, they may use the meat.

Now when they return from the hunt, the Hunt-Leader when now he has come near even if it is midnight, shall shoot a signal once for as many deer as were killed, shooting so many times. And now when the Cranes hear the signal-shot of the Hunter they shall immediately run into the Big House and begin to sing for these hunters. All the Attendants must be ready to feed the hunters and all the horses unsaddled and fed, for that is the rule and act governing the Attendants.

First the Bringer-in prays, using tobacco. He bestows a blessing when offering praise to him our Father. This is sufficient for this time.

There is also, my kindred, an ancient custom that we beg the Mask-Spirit to dance for us. You Cranes, you know how and you understand those songs which are used for this occasion when singing for the Mask. Every person who wants to go in the Big House is permitted to look on while the Mask dances in the Big House.

Fourth Night of the Ceremony

The Attendants call the men, "Red Horns must be hereabouts!" The Attendant calling out, "Red-Horns! Red-Horns! Good-Horns must be hereabouts!" If he answers, the Attendant says, "Now he has answered; 'Looks-like-a-Man' must be hereabouts! Now he has answered; 'Rises-at-Daybreak' must be hereabouts! 'Leaf-Man' must be hereabouts; Now he has answered; 'How-the-Weather-is' must be hereabouts; Now he has answered."

The Bringer-in says, "Brothers, here is the one shoulder length of wampum. You, the first ones called, take it with you and pray outside, ten and two times. Lift the prayers on high and where he dwells our father, the Great Spirit. And while these praying ones are outside you Attendants must be ready to 'pick berries.'" Attendant come here, take one shoulder length of wampum right over there on this side where stands our Grandfather. There do you unstring these wampum beads. All Attendants come in, because here, soon they are going to pick berries.

Here they begin "picking berries," the Attendants, saying this, "m+!"

The speaker says, "My kindred, now it is the fourth evening since we have been worshiping here. And should any one of the hunters whatsoever have good fortune all of a sudden, some one of the drummers be careful and watch for them at once. Because you know the rule. If you hear the signal-shot run inside the Big House at once. You must sing for them."

The Fifth and Sixth Nights of the Ceremony

The performance of the usual recitations and dances of the previous nights is repeated.

Seventh Night of the Ceremony: Return of the Hunters

Now, my kindred, it is the seventh evening come since we have brought in this pure prayer-worship. Now it is very pleasing that we have had good fortune, that these our young men and that he my son "Walking-Four-Abreast" and "With-Wings"[15] have killed game. I am indeed thankful. On account of it at least we feel pleased, and we use the animal that we offer up as a sacrifice when we are pleading with the Great Spirit.

And it is truly grand that we are having good weather each and every day, on account of which we enjoy good health. When we wake up to another day, when we see him our elder brother the sun how he lights up all this earth, which causes an emotion within us, when we feel the coming warmth of his breath of life. And we are truly thankful when we acknowledge the blessing of the Night-Traveler, our elder brother the Night-Moon. For we have heard the deceased, our ancient people of the past while they were explaining these many things say, according to tradition, "Night-Moon and also those stars, all of them were put in place by him who owns us. That one, our father the Wind, and that one, our mother Water, flowing stream and that one, our grandfather Fire, all are sitting around us; the Spirit-forces. Truly, my kindred, I feel very discouraged, pitiful me. It is unbecoming for me, I feel unable, as it is said, to instruct my own kindred in blessings, so difficult is it now and so heavily are we oppressed. For instance now, when we are about to be touched by these Spirit-forces, the shell-rattles, be careful, my kindred, we must remember that we are praying for a blessing to the Great Spirit. And it is wonderful that he feels sympathy for us, he our father, also our Creator, in those wild animals which he has given us.

Eighth Night of the Ceremony

The usual performance is repeated.

Ninth Night of the Ceremony

Now[16] Attendants, you know the rules of this teaching, that you keep in mind, all of you, that a person must act in purity. All of us have heard the instructions of

THE CHARLIE WEBBER [WI.TAPANO'XWE] TEXT, 1928

---

15. Speck wrote, "The narrator of the text is assuming that the ceremonial hunt has had a happy conclusion; that the two young men named have been blessed with game."
16. The Goddard retranslation begins again here (Goddard 1979: 117).

our now-deceased ancestors. They said that a pure person shall make fire. Because when those fire-making Manitous are used, if someone cannot make fire, it would clearly be seen to be a fact that the one trying to make fire is not pure. Nevertheless, my brothers, everything is easy when done right. Now you know to purify these two places where fire always is. All the ashes shall be carried out there through the west door. That is what it is used for. Such is the rule of our prayer-worship.

I thank you, my kindred, that I greet you. I am really happy when I address you with every form of blessing. Now, my kindred, we have lived on to the point where we are purifying this fire here in our ceremonial House. Indeed thank you that we have come in good health to this evening. For tonight we know how we used to see our now-deceased aged people properly carry out the instructions and the regulations.

And, my kindred, everyone who owns a turtle rattle should bring it with him when coming into the Big House. And right here in front of where the Bringer-in sits all those turtle rattles should be put in a straight line. And, attendants, you know that you are to prepare and make ready everything, for those drum sticks,[17] and the cedar, and also the red ochre, blood root, and the prayer sticks, everything that is used now on this night, has to be all ready. Now, the first thing, the leading attendant takes one yard[18] of wampum. Carefully measure those turtle rattles. Everyone will be given a string of wampum beads as long as the back of his turtle rattle. And, my kindred, now we have lived to the Calling of Names. Attendants, summon those people whom I send for. (Here the names of the men selected are called by the attendants, and those summoned gather before the sponsor).

My brothers, here is one yard of wampum. My kindred, go give the prayer-call outdoors. When twelve times you shall have lifted up the supplication then you shall divide the wampum equally among you. (The men whose names have been called now file outside by the east door and facing east raise their right hands giving the prayer call Hooooo six times and Haaaaa six times).

Attendants, build up a bright fire. Now is the time when everyone who owns a turtle rattle goes and takes it and the turtle rattle is shaken. It is just a little while before everything is ready, including those forked drumsticks, and all those prayer sticks are scattered in an even number on each side of the Big House. Now, my kindred, again these Manitous are beginning to touch us, those who carry our prayer-ceremony.

Now the Attendants sweep the Big House clean. Now the leading Attendants make fire and burn cedar.

---

17. Speck wrote, "Referring to both the plain drumsticks and those with carved faces on them. The latter are used on the ninth and following nights."
18. Speck wrote, "Literally 'one back length,' measured from the point of the shoulder to the fingertips of the extended arm."

Speech Before the Fires

Thank you, Oh Great Manitou, that we have lived until now to purify with (cedar) smoke this our House. For that has been the firm rule from ancient times since the beginning, when anyone recalls how fortunate his children are, and when he sees them enjoying good health. And this is the cause of a feeling of happiness when we consider how greatly we are benefitted by the benevolence of our Father, the Great Manitou. And also we can feel the strength of our grandfather Fire, which is why we please him when we purify him and take good care of him, and when we feed him this cedar. All of this we offer in prayer to our grandfather, because he has compassion with us when he sees how pitifully we behave while we are pleading with every Manitou above, where they were created, and with all those all over the earth. Do everything for us, our Father, that we ask of you, Great Manitou, our Creator."

Now the leading Attendant shall carry around a wooden bowl of wampum beads. Every person shall be given equally three wampum beads. But the woman attendant who follows shall carry around a bark bowl in which she has ochre and bloodroot; everyone shall be painted.

When all is ready then shall either one of these Attendants paint every Mesingw in the House. That, my kindred, since long ago has been the rule and conduct of the Delaware when they intended to please our Father, the Great Manitou.

Attendants, bring into the House your cooking and your dishes. Each one who brings a dish is to be given some hominy and meat. When the eating is finished, then shall everybody who desires to sleep in the House bring something, whatever he uses, it is up to him what kind of blankets. Now it is nine evenings since we camped.

Tenth and Eleventh Nights of the Ceremony

The[19] performance of the usual recitations and dances is repeated.

Twelfth Night of the Ceremony: The Aᵃteho'mwi.n

I[20] am thankful, my kindred, that we have come to the point where we bring to a close our worship, which is so greatly esteemed. I am indeed thankful that so far we have enjoyed good health from way back when we started camping, for, my kindred, there are many more things that we have to do tonight. I am glad, my brothers and my sisters and also my children, for the extent of our good fortune, including how much good weather we have had day after day. For in addition, our grandfather Fire and our grandfathers sitting around here[21] make us feel joyful this evening.

---

19. The Speck text begins again here (Speck 1931: 155).
20. The Goddard retranslation begins again here (Goddard 1979: 120).
21. Speck wrote, "Referring again to the carved images on the posts of the Big House."

And, my kindred, this night it is permitted for someone to "Sing-the-Fires-out." For that has been the firm rule since ancient times when the Delawares first began the Ngamwin. It is and is known to be that the twelfth evening is the time that our women and any other person who feels competent among our young people take part and help. If his mind is made up, anyone truly is permitted to "Sing-the-Fires-out." For there are those older men who have been assigned the duty to help this our prayer-worship. For truly indeed this performance is a heavy burden because it is a very great thing. That is why our elder brother, the white man, considers it a wonderful thing. Because they see us earnestly perform pitifully in this our house of worship,[22] on account of it the government has great wonder. And that is how we obtain help and also are supplied with a police officer to look after us. And, my kindred, it is evident that we have help, this Delaware tribe, and it has been known since ancient times everywhere the Delawares successfully migrated from. Because truly indeed, in the ancient world since the beginning of the earth, the Great Manitou used to arrange it, back in the direction of our sunrise on the coast where our now-deceased ancestors lived. All of this should make us joyful, because tomorrow when it is morning, before we reach noon-time, we must conclude the ceremony.

Thirteenth Morning of the Ceremony: Final Dance Around the Center Post

Here[23] now the time has come for all these our sisters to join and dance, and join in a single file outdoors. And all the men and children besides, everybody may wear Delaware garb and go into the Big House. Yet whatever anyone wears it is the rule to go in. But women, from right here next door, shall begin to form in single file. When they have formed a line then the Assistant Concluder[24] should shake the Leading Tortoise-Rattles. Ten and two times he shall shake them and shall say when shaking them, 'Kwi/ya!' And all of the women from the leading one through to the end of the row shall answer, all of them, and say "Hu+!"

I am thankful,[25] my kindred, that again I greet you all, my brothers, men, young men, and my sisters and also all those our children. It is truly fine that we have good weather this morning, that we are so well treated by our elder brother, the sun, when he sheds illumination down here on all the earth. For now it is ten and two days that we have been doing this here when pleading earnestly with our Father, the Great Manitou. We all know it. It is truly fine and I am glad when we are helping each other. And really great things are said about this prayer-worship of ours. And marvelous is the service of our attendants, which will soon finish.

---

22. Speck wrote, "That is, perform with humility."
23. The Speck translation begins again here (Speck 1931: 159).
24. The master of ceremonies is so designated now.
25. The Goddard translation begins again here (Goddard 1979: 121).

And there is one yard of wampum for each one that we pay them, although their services are worth much more, because exceedingly heavy is this that we are doing.

Hardly, for example, can I tell you how precious it is. But still we have heard what our now-deceased ancestors spoke about. They said, "The labor of the attendant, when he makes fire, when he feeds us, when he provides plenty of fire wood, and when he sweeps—all of these acts of purity with which we bring joy to the One who owns us."[26] For now our work has come to where we conclude the ceremony. Let us consider, my kindred, if only we have good health, that we do this next year right here again.

Oh, and my kindred, there is one more thing I want to say. Bear it well in mind. It is said that when any one meditates on good, the thought is formed in his heart, and when he thinks of good it is easy to behave well. But when he does wrong, it is exceedingly hard. For we want to prepare the soul-spirit, so that we shall be able to take it back home again to where it belongs, to our Father, when it is no longer used here where we live. But here the body shall remain always, because here below is where it belongs.

Indeed, my kindred, that is why I beg you that someone help me or tell me, since sometimes I forget something. That is how I have always seen it since long ago. Yet at times I feel I have not studied it enough. That is why I am pleased when anyone calls my attention to something.

The attendants must prepare wampum in a wooden bowl. Every person shall be given three beads, and anyone, if he wants, when all are now leaving, there is a hominy mortar outside, and he may deposit there those wampum beads that he was given.

And now, my kindred, when for the last time we are touched by those our grandfathers, the turtle rattles, now is the beginning of our concluding the ceremony. Now at last we are ready to end this our Father's service. And, my kindred, from now hence as we are going home, you must keep it firmly in mind. For you are carrying with you the worship of the Delaware, whereby for one year we shall be happy. For all the Manitous given us on top of the earth, and those up above where they were created, come to our aid, as well as our Father, the Great Manitou, Our Creator. This is all for this time.

Now, my kindred, for the last time we go out to pray, everybody with all his heart. And you know that we shall all go out to the east and carry with us the wampum that is left unused (because that is our heart) when we address our prayer to our Father, up to where the soul belongs. And let us study it. Everyone earnestly addresses his prayer up above, and we express our prayer with this wampum, our heart. Through ten and two levels of sky we lift our prayer to where dwells him our Father the Great Manitou, Our Creator.

---

26. Speck wrote, "Another designation for the Great Spirit; as the explanation runs, 'We are his children.'"

CHAPTER NINE

Additional Notes on the Big House Ceremony, 1937

Frank G. Speck published the research notes that follow as a single section in a general book on Oklahoma Delaware religion, feasts, and ceremonies six years after the appearance of his major study of the Big House (Speck 1937: 15–26). The notes both fill in and amplify information from the first study and serve as a status report and prospectus for Speck's projected research among the Delaware people in Oklahoma.

Much of the text reads like a grant proposal. It begins with the tantalizing possibility that traditionalist leader Joe Washington may be able to provide a substantial body of new data. Following a discussion of some of Washington's observations on the Big House, Speck reports that further funding will be needed to fully support the development of an account of the ceremony by Washington. Unfortunately, Speck was never able to secure the necessary support, and Washington evidently passed on before his knowledge could be recorded.

The greater part of the account is a discussion of information provided by Oklahoma Big House adherents Tom Half Moon and Tom Anderson. It ends with a surprisingly prescient structuralist comparison that examines the concept of duality expressed in numerous aspects of the ceremony and the symbolism of that duality. Recently, Jay Miller has built upon Speck's approach to develop what he terms a three-part structural model, dividing Delaware thought into male and female principles mediated by the concept of mind (Miller 1980).

THE HARRINGTON TEXT

The great recurrent and communal ceremony, the Big House or Gamwing, has been covered in a preceding study (Speck 1931). At the time it was recorded, most of the topics prepared and discussed were treated with the understanding that a continuation of inquiry into Delaware religion would contribute supplementary material to our knowledge of the spiritual functionings of this festival. Accordingly the way was left open for an extension of its treatment as occasion arose. It is true in particular, and was so recognized in the version of the ceremony published, that variations in performance and in the obligations enforced upon its participants were understood to exist in accordance with the procedure as conducted under sponsorship of the three ceremonial groups, Turkey, Tortoise, and Wolf. It has been previously shown that the ceremonial if not the social structure of the Delaware Nation is, in certain respects, founded upon these groupings. I may repeat the important comment that the version of the Big House Ceremony recorded in the volume referred to was a type-performance of the Turkey group, of which the narrator, Wi.tapano'xwe, was a council member.

An opportunity has since arisen for me to interview, in Oklahoma, Joe Washington, Ni.ka'ni.paxoxwe, "Walking in Advance, Leader," the hereditary master of ceremonies of this rite when its celebration falls into the hands of the Wolf group. The occasion of questioning him resulted in substantiation of the details previously recorded and printed concerning the general aspects of the ceremony. But it became clear that in the history of Delaware institutions something has been going on, either, *a*, to integrate the religious observances of formerly separate local bands of the tribe, having more or less distinct customs, into a national ceremony which through time has retained some original features of a distinct character, or, *b*, that it was in earlier times a uniform ritual which has broken up into variant forms with changes of time and place in the expansion of its influence. For the present time it seems hardly safe to interpret the circumstances that may have contributed to change the manner of its celebration. My impression is at present, nevertheless, that the three social divisions of the Nation, Turkey, Tortoise, and Wolf, were in an earlier period indistinct areal groups whose fusion created the Nation. The Nanticoke, for instance, have been repeatedly referred to as being of the Wolf identity in the sense of a sub-tribe, and something similar is true of the Mahikan, giving evidence in the direction of the above supposition. As regards the local-group types of the Big House Ceremony, an opportunity to record the version and rulings of the performers as carried on by the Wolf group, would be an important addition to our knowledge of religious history among the eastern tribes. And Joe Washington's dictation of the Wolf group's regulations becomes a necessary task for the future. Through lack of support at the time to undertake this study its completion will have to remain postponed. Washington offered to dictate a full account of the Big House rite as carried on by the Wolf group, and through conference with him the following notes were secured covering some of the particulars in which it differed from the Turkey group rite. His observations bring out a point in question, namely, that the details of the Turkey and the Wolf group ceremony probably differ as much as they do when the Turkey group rite is compared with that of the Munsee recorded in Canada by Harrington.

The Wolf group ceremony lasted only eight days whereas the Turkey group rite as recorded consumed twelve. The last time that the Wolf rite was performed by the father of Joe Washington, he was told not to repeat it unless the spiritual obligation took possession of his mind with such compelling force that he could not decline his mission. He was also enjoined not to give away to the insistency of members of the Wolf group or others of the Nation that the rite be carried out merely to maintain the customs of their respective ancestors. This move would be insufficient, even a sacrilege. The spiritual preparation of its participants was made a matter of prime importance and the purity of those concerned in it was to be insisted on. Joe Washington has since felt that these serious injunctions were of so drastic a character that until the present time they could not be complied with. It seems, therefore, that there is little prospect for anything more than a dictated version to be obtained, which will have to await necessary support for its accomplishment.

Upon the occasion of my expedition to the Delawares in Oklahoma some time was spent in interviews with Tom Half Moon.[1] He had experience as an attendant, or A'ckas, of the Big House Ceremony as performed in recent years by his group, the Turkey group. The notes offered are, therefore, advantageous in respect to the details furnished by one who had the teachings directly from those who were responsible for its proper conduct. These notes should accordingly serve as a supplement to that section of the ceremony published in the Big House Ceremony volume dealing with the duties of the attendants. They are in effect as follows:

The attendants who sweep the White Path, or the path around which the dancers proceed when performing in the Big House after each dance, do so with turkey wings, using only the left hand in holding the fans, since the left hand is the holy hand, the right the unholy. The male attendants start sweeping at opposite ends from the women. When they have swept the dancing path twelve times they have cleared away the obstacles of an unfavorable spiritual nature lying between the worshipers and the Great Spirit. As was noted in the published account, the attendants each receive a yard of wampum at the end of the ceremony. He also noted that those who attended the ceremony received two wampum beads each to be kept by them as tokens of good fortune until the next performance. These beads were, he added, held in the mouth as sacred objects when the members went outside at the termination of the rite to pray, forming a line at the west door of the Big House. Why they prayed with the wampum beads in their mouth, figuratively with their "heart" in their mouths, is not explicitly known to the informant, but we are told that wampum is the "heart" of the Delaware.

Reverting to Wi.tapano'xwe's version of the origin of the Turkey group rite, Half Moon added a most interesting supplement to the tradition which I quote as follows as nearly as possible in his words. The origin tale narrates the occasion of the earthquake and bursting forth of black fluid as in a volcanic eruption, as a sign of the anger of the Great Spirit aroused by the evil doings of men, and that the ceremony of the Big House was revealed in a vision to some good men as a

---

1. Speck wrote, "His Delaware title-name was Axkwe'lpango'xwe, 'Overturns Mountains when Walking.'"

means of appeasing the anger of the Supreme One. Half Moon added to that that at the time of the cataclysm the women in terror trying to shelter themselves from the downpour of destruction, took the little children under seven years old and held them under their arms. They knew that children of this age could not be guilty of wrong and so attempted to shield themselves from the Great Spirit's wrath. Finally, we are told, one of the innocents cried out in terror, "Ho, Ho; Hä, Hä," which became known at once as the revealed prayer-call by which the Great Spirit should be addressed. The distracted people knew that it was the mission of this child to inform them of the means by which the Great Spirit might be invoked in prayer to stay his anger. This most interesting narrative accounts for the origin of the sacred prayer-call so often employed in the procedure of the Big House as recorded in the published work, which for the student of the history of religions we have in it another instance of the ruse of the guilty hiding from wrath behind the shield of innocence.

From Half Moon as a source comes another most significant tradition bearing upon the history of the Mask and the carved images in the Big House Ceremony. According to the Delaware conception of the events in the history of their ceremony the images and the Mask Spirit episode were formally introduced into the rite shortly before or about the time of the arrival of Europeans. A transcript of the informant's version is as follows:

> It was relatively late, just about the time when white people were first seen by the Delawares, that they adopted the carved images as part of the ceremonial equipment of the Big House. The images were not made on the posts of the building before. A man of spiritual power had a vision of a monster residing in the East, its body covered with hair, with a face half red and half black. To prove the reality of his vision he induced a companion to accompany him traveling to the East where they finally reached the dwelling place of the monster, proving his existence. Upon this discovery they returned to their people. Having identified the monster and desiring the power to call upon him for spiritual aid when they desired it, they induced the other Delawares to allow them to carve the likenesses of the monster upon the posts of the Big House. Further more they innovated the rite of the false face or Mask image (Messingk) as personified by an actor who wore the Mask and who was garbed in the bear skin coat and leggings carrying a pouch of the same material and a large snapping turtle shell hand-rattle. Henceforth the Mask Image figured as a potent Spirit Force in the hierarchy of the Manitto assemblage in the Big House celebration. The black- and red-faced hairy monster possessed latent power to effect evil in the lives of men. Hence those to whom he reveals himself in a vision acquire the power to do harm, and since his presence is tolerated among the Big House spirits they may find a place

among the worshipers. That is why it is not all for the exercise of the power of good. In the development of Delaware religion as it appears in the Big House, a fault crept in.

What the meaning of this particular legend may be as regards the actual history of the Big House Ceremony, one is at a loss to say as yet. It would seem that the position of the Mask Spirit as a canonized Spirit Force amid the benevolent congress of Delaware deities corresponds to that of the Devil's advocate. Before, however, we can admit the tradition as one having historical significance, a wiser analysis and wider comparison of the elements of the major ceremonies of the eastern Indians will have to be invoked. Nevertheless there seems to a feeling current among some of the religious men with whom I talked that the Big House Ceremony has absorbed some imperfections like this one. Half Moon himself even went so far as to declare that the decline of the ceremony as well as the Delaware Nation, was due to the transgression of accepting an Evil Force as part-sharer of the worship in the Big House. I might add, as contributing a view-point on the same perplexing question, that early in the eighteenth century the missionary Brainerd, then living with the Delawares on the upper Susquehanna in their village near Sunbury, reported a conversation with a man of the Nation in which was embodied a similar opinion as regards the False Face.[2]

In a section of my study of the Big House Ceremony I indulged in quoting some estimates of the religious spirit among the Delawares adding some of my own impressions in the matter. An opportunity to add to these, since it comes from the writings of a contemporary witness over a century ago when the tribe was resident on the Scioto River, comes from John Brickell (1842). He says, "I know I am influenced to good even at this day more from what I learned among them than what I learned among people of my own color.... They worship the Great Spirit whom they call Manito, which signifies or conveys to them the idea of all strength or rather all sufficiency."[3] This commentary may be adjoined as a supplement to the section of the work referred to (Speck 1931), dealing also with the native concept of the Great Spirit, as something corroborative of the early belief of this tribe in the existence of a supreme deity and is intended for the eyes of authorities such as Dr. Schmidt who have devoted so much attention to the nativity of the concept in American [Indian] culture [see below].

In the study of the Big House Ceremony some space was devoted to the construction of the belief regarding the path taken by the soul on its journey from earth to the spirit realm. The assumption was made that the Milky Way was considered to be the path in question. Yet the inability on the part of several sources

---

2. The Brainerd account appears in chapter one. As noted there, the observation occurred at the Conoy town at the mouth of the Juniata, many miles to the south of the major Susquehanna Delaware town of Shamokin in present-day Sunbury, Pennsylvania.
3. See Brickell (1842). The Scioto River, a major tributary of the Ohio River, runs through central Ohio.

to furnish the native term applied to the Milky Way and their uncertainty as to what symbol in the sky represented the path of the spirit left the matter in a state of doubt. The fact that among other Algonkian peoples the Milky Way is "Spirit or Ghost Path" has some bearing on the point that we are trying to clear up in Delaware belief. It remained for inquiry among the Delaware-Munsee of the Six Nations Reserve, Canada, to furnish a Delaware appellation for the Milky Way, which turned out to be Ane'i, "path." This determination would seem to bridge the gap in the previously obtained data. As a corroboration, likewise, of the Delaware belief that the Milky Way is the path of ghosts, we discover in the confessions of belief of the Delawares while residing in the Ohio region that the Milky Way was the path over which souls traveled; after the teachings of several native prophets who in about 1762 stirred religious revivals in the tribe (Hulbert and Schwarze 1910: 133–34; Heckewelder 1876: 291–93). Whether or not this belief was derived in that time from a still older native concept is not said, yet something of this sort is implied. Thus the Delawares coincide in belief with kindred peoples in the East to establish the antiquity of the concept just dealt with.

George Anderson, Kwu'tepagi.'kamen, "Rustling Leaves (when Walking)," also of the Wolf ceremonial group, offered the following details of information on the procedure of his group when celebrating in the Big House. The Wolf group rite may be conducted within an eight-day period. He had heard that the sweat lodge had formerly been erected in the Big House at a point just to the left of the drummers. As noted in the volume on the Big House Ceremony, the sweating rite was held as a test of endurance for the men who had spiritual guidance. Anderson also added that he had heard of deer skins as offerings being hung inside the Big House during the Ceremony near the east door. Several additions were made by him to the information recorded in the volume referred to among which may be noted that when the fires are removed from the Big House the ashes from both are thrown out through the west door. Furthermore, he emphasized the regulation that no women or children were allowed to be present within the Big House when the new fire was being made. He said that the rite of making new fire performed by the male attendants was one of spiritual intensity, that sometimes they failed trying with all their might to make fire with the fire drill one after another and had to resort to making it with flint and steel. He attributed such failure to the attendants having violated the rules of continence during the Big House period. He himself felt that it was becoming more and more difficult for the Delawares to perform the ceremony on account of increasing moral laxity among the people.

Anderson corroborated the tradition of the earthquake and associated physical disturbances as accounting for the cause of the Delawares instituting the Big House Ceremony. He added that there was a tradition of falling stars occurring during the disturbance and also a tornado. Anderson expressed the feeling of the Delawares that the performance of the Big House Ceremony was intended to avert physical catastrophes, saying that upon several occasions in the past the ceremony had been performed after a tornado in the country to preserve the people from another such visitation of anger on the part of the Creator.

It might be expected that the performance of the Big House Ceremony when sponsored by the Tortoise ceremonial group would differ in some of its particulars from what we have previously recorded. This investigation will undoubtedly have to be considered and it will be possible to do so should the Big House Ceremony ever be repeated by Frank Wilson who is a member of the Tortoise group.

Among the notes of information which Anderson made to extend our knowledge of details of the Big House Ceremony, he called attention to an error in the color plate illustrating the interior of the Big House while one of the dances of vision recitation was in progress, in Harrington's monograph on Delaware ceremonies.[4] The color plate shows the people in the Big House seated while the dance and recitation are going on. Anderson pointed out that the audience should be shown standing during the dance-recitation.

Duality of Symbolism in the Big House Rite

In my former study of the Big House Ceremony I did not become aware of the significance that seemed attached to the fact that upon the center-post of the structure there were two faces carved on opposite sides, one facing the east, the other the west, and that also there were two fires, one on the east, the other on the west side of the center-post. These are evident symbols of duality, and it becomes plausible to suspect, as did Dr. P. W. Schmidt, that the symbolism of duality in these features of the Big House might refer to sun and moon worship. Dr. Schmidt, in correspondence with me, also suggested that the two fires may represent the luminaries, and the double image representations on the center post a dual personality vested in the Supreme Being idea which in turn he proposes may be a fusion of the male and female concepts as tribal progenitors (*Stammeselternpaar*). We lack, however, supporting native testimony for the establishment of Dr. Schmidt's elucidation of a historical background for these mysterious symbols so far as the Delawares are specifically concerned.[5]

I was unable to take up this question with Delaware informants before the publication of my earlier study but since that time I have had the opportunity to discuss the point with Anderson. While he was unable to speak in positive terms of the dual symbolism of the two fires, two center-post images, two doors

---

4. Here Speck is referring to a painting by the Shawnee artist Earnest Spybuck. Readers interested in his work can consult a catalog of his paintings published by the Museum of the American Indian, Heye Foundation (Callendar and Slivka 1984).

5. Wilhelm Schmidt (1868–1954) was a leading member of the *kulturkreislehre*, a school of German sociological thought that tried to identify historical developments and relationships by tracing geographical distributions of culture traits and complexes. See Vogt (1975: 348–55) for an assessment of the kulturkreislehre in general and a brief survey of Schmidt's work in particular.

of the Big House, two paints, red and black, on the carved images, he offered a rationalization in attempting to explain the matter. This I consider well worth reproducing as an example of Delaware explanatory thought on a point concerning which tradition in the tribe is not definite enough to be canonical. Our own speculation on the matter, when such fails to coincide with speculative attempts of the natives who themselves *profess* the principles of the religion in question, can hardly be considered as having equal weight with theirs.[6]

I would accordingly present Anderson's explanation of the dual principle in Delaware ritual as being connected with the division of sex in the realm of life. Anderson pointed out that the balancing of functions between the male and female elements of human society was implied in the Delaware ritual performance. He began by referring to the requirement that there be an equal number of male and female attendants in service during the ceremonies; that the duties of the females should coincide with and supplement those of the males; that one fire, theoretically, was in charge of the female attendants and represented their contribution to the worship, the other the males; that a similar division extended through the Big House, one door and the image on the center-post facing that door "belonging" to the men, the other, the opposite to women. He also pointed out in explaining the principle of dualism that when the attendants swept the dancing path encircling the fires after each dance performance to purify it, with turkey wing fans, a male attendant starts sweeping from the west door toward the east door and a female from the east door to the west door on the opposite side; that when the east door is reached by the male attendant sweeper and the west door by the female attendant sweeper, each places the fan-sweeper in a crevice in the logs above the door where he or she stops. Furthermore, at the conclusion of the next dance when the sweeping is repeated for the same purpose of purification, the male attendant sweeps his half of the dance path with the fan previously used by the female and leaves this in the logs above the door on her side. She does the same with the fan left over her door by the male attendant the time before. Thus the two fans are relayed by men and women attendants successively on opposite sides of the Big House after each dance. One of the fans, moreover, is associated with male attendants, the other with the female. Anderson used this illustration to bring out his idea as implied from the teaching of the old people that while there was no definite doctrine of sexual duality taught in the Big House, that the same might be implied as a hypothesis. He pointed out another fact in demonstrating this likelihood which is clearly evident on the surface, namely that the two forked drum sticks, those of highly ceremonial significance used only from the ninth night of the ceremony to the end, bear carvings of human heads, a male on one, a female on the

---

6. I think what Speck means here is that Native speculation is more valid than ethnographic inference.

other, the latter having also the representation of female breasts below the face. This leaves no doubt of latent trend of thought in the basic symbolism of duality based upon sex in Delaware. The two drum sticks in question are definitely designated male and female.

I might mention also another piece of native reasoning along the same line of explanation of the black and red half-painting which is so characteristic of Delaware sacred coloring. It has been assumed and with good reason that these colors represent the states of life and death, respectively red and black. I would not discard this theory since it is one present in the minds of some Delawares, but would rather find an explanation for the confusion in idea of the black and red symbols as an overlapping of several vaguely fused symbolisms; one designating sex, the other life and death. The whole question, as it now stands, amounts to a problem of symbol interpretation in Delaware religion in which the supposition of sexual duality must be given primary consideration.

Reverting for a moment to Anderson's explanation of the two fire, two door, two center-post image peculiarity in the Big House arrangement, it should not be inferred that he intended to point out that these were exclusively or definitely sexual segregations or that they reflected duality in the conception of the deity. He also wished especially to avoid fixing the idea that the two center-post images represented the Creator. He tried to make clear that the two branches of service represented by the men and women worshipers were made convenient and kept separate in accordance with the division into male and female functions by the dual arrangements just noted.

The whole question of sex differentiation in Delaware religion and natural thought is one which may have to be worked out through evidences beneath the surface, perhaps in almost forgotten but deeply significant principles of thought, since it is only hinted at in deliberate explanation by the people of today, though preserved in the equipment and furnishings of their worship.

An arrangement of symbols and functions associated with sex in Delaware thought could be shown as follows:

MALE	FEMALE
Abstract Associations	
The color red	The color black
life	death (the beyond)
east	west
day	night
right-hand side	left-hand side

Big House Associations

East half	West half[7]
east door	west door
east fire	west fire
image of Great Spirit on east side of center post	image of Great spirit on west side of center post

Functions and privileges

Balanced participation in all rites and dances
Balanced ritual and dance leadership (approximate)
Balanced sponsorship of ceremonies
Balanced performance of offices as "attendants"
Balanced dance path sweeping
Balanced reception of "payment" (sacrifice) of wampum for ceremonial services
Balanced control of ceremonial equipment in east and west sides of Big House

MALE	FEMALE
Conducting ceremonial hunt (Symbol of animal economy as male sphere)	Preparing ceremonial food (Symbol of plant economy as female sphere)
Singing and praying aloud	Silent supplication
Giving ceremonial prayer-call	Occasionally giving prayer-call
Conducting harvest rite (Corn Harvest Ceremony)	
Dancing on outside of dance column in Big House (inside in Doll and Buffalo dances)	Dancing on inside of dance column in Big House (outside in Doll and Buffalo dances)
Formal recitation of visions	Recitation only allowed on last day of Big House Ceremony
Use of musical instruments (hide drum and rattle)	
Moral "purity" during ceremonial periods	Moral and catamenial "purity" during ceremonial periods

---

7. Speck pointed out that the "dichotomy of sex in seating arrangements during ceremonies in the Big House is subordinated to the classified grouping of the ceremonial divisions, Turkey, Wolf, Tortoise, and secondarily to which of the three groups is sponsoring the celebration."

CHAPTER TEN

The Nicodemus Peters [Nekatcit] Account, 1945

This chapter presents the results of what is probably Frank G. Speck's least known and most fascinating Big House research. It is based on a text provided by Nicodemus Peters (Nekatcit, "Tame Little Fellow"). Peters was born into a Delaware-Mahican Star clan (Ala'ngwe) family in the Smoothtown district of the Six Nations Reserve in Ontario, Canada, in 1859. Although the last Munsee Big House rites at the reserve ceased some ten years prior to his birth, Nekatcit preserved in his memory the stories and traditions told to him by elders who had officiated the services of the old religion. From 1932 until his death in 1938, Nekatcit shared his knowledge with Speck. Both men were aided in this work by Delaware-Mahican traditionalists Jesse Moses, Sr. (Teo'kali "Blackbird"); Jesse M. Moses, Jr.; Joseph Montour, chief of the Delaware nation at Six Nations until his own death in 1938; and his grandson Josiah Montour (Xko'kwsis "Little Snake"). The results of this collaboration, published in 1945, represent the most extensive known surviving body of information documenting traditional Delaware religious life in Ontario. The extract that follows contains Speck's translation of Nekatcit's text of the "Last Performance of the Bear Sacrifice Ceremony" and Speck's commentary on the ritual (Speck and Moses 1945: 60–78).

THE NICODEMUS PETERS TEXT

Twenyucis had a dream. Then she told the chief, about the time of the new moon when we celebrate the feast, "I know where the bear is living. So you call these young men to go and bring the bear." The chief went and brought Maxkok. The chief told Maxkok, "Twelve men will go with you. All twelve men of the Big House." Then Twenyucis told Maxkok, "Very near daybreak you will reach there. Then you will see a little creek which runs by. And the tree standing there is an oak. A little hole will be visible. Then the bear's nose will appear as though it comes out of the hole pushed through, his nose icy about the edge. Do not bring him. That is not a good one, it is a smooth bear. You will go on, down past him. Then you will see an elm tree leaning toward the east. Then you will look up. You will see a hole.

That is the bear's home. Thence you cannot come back. There, accordingly, you stay all night. And then standing by that tree there, you are all standing around. Then you hit that tree standing up with your bow on that tree. Three times you will hit that tree. You tell the bear, "I find you." Then nothing will be heard. Then also you hit that tree three times. Tell the bear, "I find you."

Then they heard him moving about. Once more the tree was hit. He told him, "You we have found." All these men look upward. All saw the bear's head sticking out. Then Maxkok told the bear, "Come down! The chief wants your body." Then that bear climbed down. Then that bear came down on the ground. Then that bear let his head hang down on the ground. "Surely like a dog he was ashamed of something." Maxkok told the bear, "The chief wants your body." Then he told the bear to turn around. Then that bear turned around. Maxkok told this bear, "That's enough." He told him, "Now you go and take the lead." The bear went on ahead. Then these men all came behind him. Then they reached the little creek here. Then that bear lay down. Maxkok told him, "What is wrong! Get up!" Truly the bear did not move. Then Maxkok told these men, "The bear will come to the Big House." Then Maxkok appointed one man. He told him, "So, you will tell the chief that the bear refuses to come. You will go there yourself." Then the chief came there. Then Maxkok told him, "The bear will not come to the Big House. So no more will there be a feast dance. Therefore you will have to kill the bear right here." Then the chief told the bear, "Right here we will have to kill you. We want your body for the Big House." Then that bear got up. His head was still hanging down on the ground, his eyes were closed. The chief hit him. Then he died. He never kicked. Then these men skinned him. Then that Maxkok picked up the bear skin. He gave it to the chief. Then the chief told these men, "Now we will go to the Big House. You men carry the bear. We, with the dead bear, will take the lead. You will come behind."

Then they reached the Big House. Then they went into the Big House, to the middle of the building. Then they lowered that bear on the ground.

Then that chief untied the old bear hide and put the old bear hide down on the ground. Then he wrapped the new hide around the center post, a little below where these False Faces were hanging. Then that chief told the woman and one appointed man, "You cut up that bear. Help these women in the cooking."

Then that chief stood in the center of the house. "Therefore indeed we are thankful, all of us, that God should help us. All of us people, we should help one another, that we do not steal, not to steal you brother's wife."

Then all of us people came into the Big House. A new moon elevated as high as the tree tops sets and goes down. Then the chief stands right in the middle of the floor of the Big House and talks to these people. He tells them, "All be good to one another, do not cheat one's living companions." Then the moon goes down. Then the chief tells them, "Go home, don't be trifling, be good to one another."

EXPLANATION AND AMPLIFICATION OF THE TEXT NARRATIVE, AND DESCRIPTION OF THE CEREMONY TO ITS CONCLUSION

The person denoted by the name Twenyucis was an old woman of Delaware and Tutelo tribal descent. The name is untranslatable. She had come with the band from Dunnville[1] early in the nineteenth century. She is remembered as the last woman to have been favored with the dream revealing the resting place of the bear destined for sacrifice. The dream revelation was considered as a blessing, falling upon some woman of the company qualified by her virtue and devotion. Every year someone would dream where the sacrifice was to be found. Her address to the chief of the band is the informant's paraphrase of the pattern speech of announcement that the preliminaries of the ceremony had taken form.

The twelve men referred to are the chief's executives. The individual Maxkok, which means "Red," was the last of the spiritually blessed men, as chief, remembered who conducted the Bear Sacrifice Ceremony in the Delaware Long House on the Six Nations Reserve. Nekatcit figured the event to have occurred about 1850.

The instructions that follow represent the peculiarly definite character of the dream revelation received by the blessed woman. The bear designated is a specific animal ordained by supernatural selection for the sacrifice. Not any animal of the genus would do as a vicarious offering. Note the distinction between the "smooth bear" and the predestined bear. The smooth bear was explained as being an animal characterized by having a skin covered only lightly by a growth of hair, and has reference to the myth of the Boy-Bear or Bear Abductor. The narrative referred to explains how a boy child was lured by a female bear to her den and lived for some time with her cubs, at last to be restored to his people. A peculiar mythical association developed from the incident, which resulted in some bears having less fur on their skins than others, and these derived their peculiarity from the temporary familial relations with the bear-boy of the tale. The taboo against killing them rests upon their possession of humanized psycho-physical attributes.

Nekatcit later stated that the location of the den sought was near Canfield, in the neighborhood of Dunnville, about one and a half days walk from the Big House on Boston Creek in the Reserve (fig. 12).

The short formal address to the bear when called from his winter hibernation quarters is deeply significant of an underlying concept of the spiritual nature of bears. The use of the bow in the formal attack upon the creature, in this case to summon the victim forth from hiding, is, in other narratives given by Nekatcit, varied by reference to the ax being used to deal the fatal blow. Particular stress is to be laid upon the address made to the bear by the chief of the hunting party bidding him come forth to be slain. It is one of the definite evidences of historical unity of a custom in such instances widespread over Asia and northern North America. That such a concept is common property in the

---

1. Dunnville, Ontario, in the Six Nations Reserve.

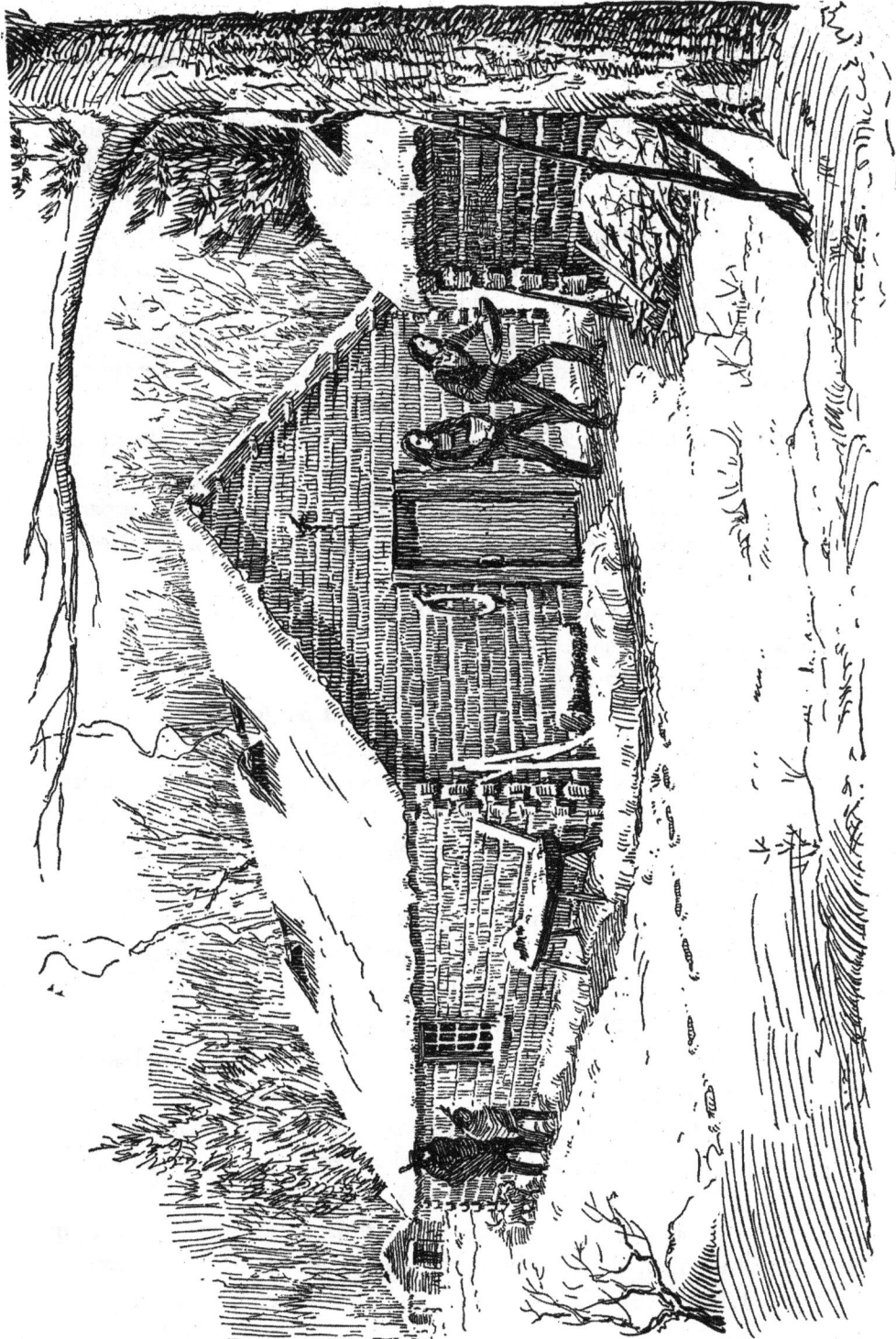

Fig. 12. Artist's conception of the Boston Creek Big House near Hagersville, Ontario, ca. 1850 (frontispiece, Speck and Moses 1945). Courtesy Reading Public Museum.

religious systems of peoples throughout northern Asia and northern North America has been strikingly demonstrated by ethnologists and travelers for more than a century. So far as revealed in published literature, this is the only reference to the conciliatory address to the bear recorded for the Munsee-Mahican (cf. Hallowell 1926).

The section following portrays the emotional disturbance of the bear about to be lured away for sacrifice. The willingness of the bear to submit to being driven from his den to the place of his death at the Big House, and his subjection of spirit is a point difficult to discuss. Leaving out of consideration the convictions of a people in regard to the authenticity of traditional miracles, one could only comment upon the incident by saying that such behavior on the part of the creature is to be taken with a large dose of faith. The actuality of the act seemed to be wholly acceptable not only to the narrator of the event but to others of people. The unquestioned sanctity of traditional testaments would seem to be the only reason for credulity in respect to animal behavior unknown under normal conditions.

The next section of the same paragraph brings us to a specific fact apparent in connection with the bear's submission and death in conformity with its destiny. The text designates a "little creek" where the creature halted and beyond which it refused to advance in its procession to execution under escort of chief and twelve holy attendants. Nekatcit had been shown the precise spot at which the defection of the bear on this last occasion took place. It was at a bend of Boston Creek a few hundred yards from where the Big House then stood. So definite was his information derived from elders who had shown him the spot that he conducted a small party of us to the shallow part of the stream where it ripples over a little sand bar. It was near where the gypsum plant now stands. Here he stopped and pointed out the crossing where the events described occurred. Several photographs of the scene were made. At this point Nekatcit repeated the speech of Maxkok in which he sent an appointed man to summon the chief who was waiting at the Big House for the procession to arrive to culminate the sacrificial rite. He indicated the spot approximately on the sand spit where the bear, with closed eyes, gave up before crossing to complete the crucial portion of the journey to the place of demise at the Big House. Here the bear was killed by the chief and skinned by the ceremonial attendants. In the act of skinning, the cutting began at the throat and proceeded to the tail. This procedure reversed the direction of cutting of animals killed for food or fur; it was a formal mark of respect for the remains of the sacrifice.

In the next paragraphs the account of the ritual performance proceeds in the customary manner. The dried bear skin, which had remained tied about the center-post of the sacred edifice since the last occasion of sacrifice, was untied and the skin of the fresh sacrifice fastened in its place. The note was added that the "fresh bear skin was hung on the east side of the center post so that the tip of the nose of the animal reached to and touched the bottom of the white mask hanging on that side of the post."² Mention has been previously made of the reason for hanging the fresh hide on the east side of the center-post. Here the sacrificed bear's spirit slept in death, just as the earth bear sleeps through winter in its hibernating den on of a tree.

In the text narrative no mention is made of certain acts performed by the chief when, under normal circumstances, the bear submitted to being driven by the twelve magical-men directly to the door of the Big House. Nekatcit gave these particulars on another occasion. It was understood that the bear victim would be driven to the center-post entering through the east door of the Big House. There the chief killed him by a blow on the head with an ax. He then delivered a lecture to the creature telling him that they would later all meet above (in the sky). He admonished him to go in advance of his slayers and to inform the spirits in the sky that everything was right on earth, that men are faithful to their obligations toward each other and to the spirits of the deceased. This being done the bear's body was taken out of the building through the east door and carried to the cookhouse at the east side of the Big House. This smaller structure where the food was prepared for ceremonial feasts was called Lin-I-'kan, "man's built house."

The official appointment by the chief of certain women and a male helper to cut up and prepare the body of the sacrifice for the feast at the termination of the rite has a formal quality which accords with the data given us in other feast preparations of the Delawares. To serve in the capacity of attendants, cooks, and helpers is a privilege in festivals among the Iroquois as well. "The head of the sacrificed bear was stewed with the rest of the carcass and eaten with it by the participants in the ceremony."³ There is no further reference to special treatment bestowed upon the bear's head as is customary among other northern Algonkian peoples.

The ensuing duties of the attendants, or helpers, as they were also called, were elaborated by the informant as follows: The two Sweepers, whose stations of duty were at the east and west doors of the Big House, were expected to appoint two helpers to carry the body of the bear outside. Here the two Sweepers superintended the cutting up of the carcass, the two helpers aiding. The same Sweepers appointed two women to wash and boil the meat. All take place at the termination of each night's ritual. The remaining mass of sacrificial flesh was to be consumed by the participants at the final feasting occasion on the sixth night of the ceremony. Reference to the final acts of disposing of the remains of the sacrifice will be made farther on in this section.

The narrator's attempt to insert a sample of the type of sermon he had heard delivered by the chief at the opening of festivals is characteristic of the Delaware ritual pattern in general. We have similar examples of moral admonition from

---

2. Speck wrote, " This passage by Nekatcit was quoted by Jesse Moses."
3. Speck wrote, "This information was provided by Jesse Moses in 1935."

rituals recorded among bands of the Delaware Nation in Oklahoma and Ontario (Munsee) in which even the wording is curiously alike. Nekatcit, however, made but a feeble try at sermonizing; it was not in his repertoire.

The entrance of the ritualists into the Big House marks the next stage of the ceremony. It is the point at which the formal procedures inside the edifice begin with full stride. The narrator goes only so far as to picture the chief as standing near the center post before his bench on the north side of the post and preaching again to the assembly (fig. 13). From this point the narrative falls off into a blank. A mere glimpse of the termination of the ritual comes out in the words of dismissal spoken by the chief. When Nekatcit had reached this point, I could only conclude, that his muse had forsaken him suddenly. The intention to resume the narrative at a more favorable time was never carried out, for circumstances delayed matters too long, and then he passed away.

Continuation of the Ceremonial Program

From here on, the description of the ceremony must proceed as based upon the questions and answers given by [Nekatcit] in the course of elaboration of details, during the time when information was being taken down concerning the Bear Sacrifice Ceremony and other rites in the religious cycle of the Munsee-Mahican group. The sequence of events comprising the ceremony as a whole and the explanation of their symbolisms will follow independently.

A statement in the final paragraph of the narrative, however, requires immediate attention, since it is actually a part of the account and yet is so vaguely

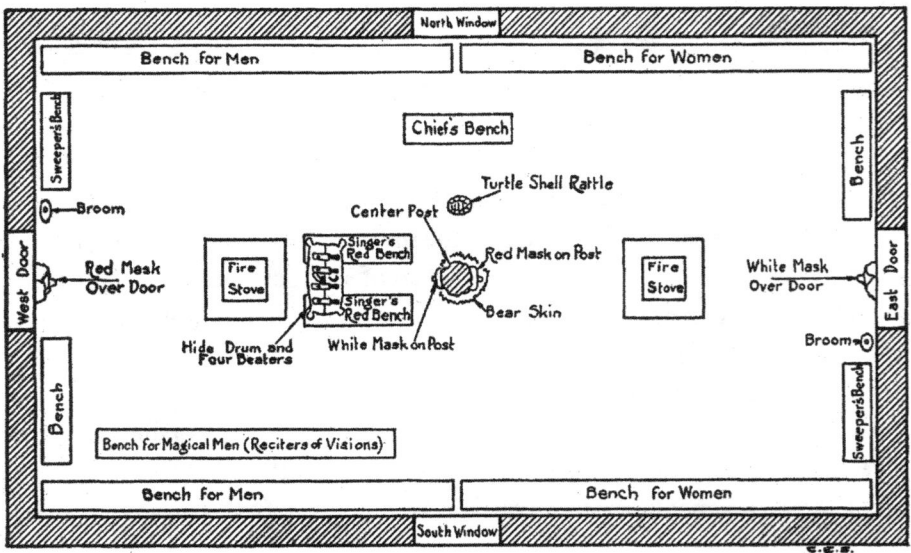

Fig. 13. Floor plan of the Munsee-Mahican Big House (fig. 1, Speck and Moses 1945: 38). Courtesy Reading Public Museum.

expressed that its symbolical portent is totally lost in the text as it now stands. The statement in question refers to the moon and its appearance above the tree-tops. It was separately explained by the narrator that the night prayer-service, occupying the first five nights, ceased when the new moon came into full view above the top line of the forest bordering the clearing in the midst of which stood the Big House. This meant that the prayer session of these nights began and ended in the dark and that it began about an hour later each night of the first five. The length of the preaching periods was automatically shortened, it would seem, by about an hour on each successive night. What a picture of ceremonial regulation by a celestial time-piece in the coordination of human and spirit associations! Why the period of preaching restricted to darkness? Could one venture the explanation that with the illumination shed by the moon the spirits descended to earth to fraternize with the living in the festivals? No explanation came from Nekatcit.

THE ORDER OF SERVICE FROM THE FIRST TO THE TENTH NIGHT OF THE CEREMONY

We now depart from the text narrative and take up the account of the rites as they occurred in the sequence of the ensuing night's programs.

Procedures from the First Night to the Fifth Night

PREACHING BY THE CHIEF

Having entered the Big House, the company of worshipers arranged itself in the prescribed manner of seating for the sexes—the women in the east half of the building, the men in the west half. All, however, entered by the east door on the first night of the performance at the time when the bear's body was carried inside. During subsequent sessions of the ceremony the celebrants used the doors appropriate to their sex.

As a preliminary to the preaching on the first night after the company had entered the Big House, there was enacted a ceremonial game called the Tug-of-War or Pulling Contest. A short account of the contest given by Nekatcit explains that the opposed teams consisted of six picked men on each side. These men represented the two halves of the congregation, the men and the women who occupied opposite sides of the Big House. Wagers were placed upon the outcome of the contest, the women betting against the men. The stakes were objects of use or beauty, such as cakes, silver brooches, handkerchiefs, knives, and the like, not money. The two parties of players faced each other, holding fast to the ends of a long pole. The chief stood at the center of the pole and, when all was ready, gave the signal to start pulling. The side pulling its opponents past the middle point was accorded the victory, and the stakes went to their backers. In this contest we have a counterpart to a similar ceremonial contest taking place in the Cayuga Long

House ritual of the mid-winter ceremony. In both instances the contest lacked a seemingly mercenary quality which another people might attribute to it, possessing rather the elements of a kind of sacrifice in which the losers of the wagered materials gained a vague blessing by "the presentation of gifts through the defeat of their team to the team of the opposite sex." It is unfortunate that Nekatcit was only able to reproduce a few brief passages of these extenuated sermons as he remembered hearing them repeated in outline in after years. They were evidently of a stereotyped character, monotonous and repetitious.

I may revert to the observations in the last paragraph of the text and the short discussion in the last part of the explanation in reference to the timing of the events of the first five nights by the appearance and by the size of the moon. The new phase of the moon of late January and early February, as the case might have been at the time referred to, was the time-piece of the Bear Sacrifice Ceremony. It has been pointed out that the ritual service of the first five nights began with the chief's moralizing discourses during that part of the night before the luminary crescent appeared above the tree-tops. In the words of Nekatcit, "the chief kept on preaching as long as the moon was not in sight for each of the first five nights. When the moon appeared he stopped and the company of worshipers dispersed for that night." We also note as being significant that, while the preaching period opened about an hour later each successive night, the moon was waxing larger each of these nights from the first quarter phase to the second or near half-moon dimension. In short, the preaching formed a first half of the ten nights ceremony, and was correlated with the period of darkness and with the weakest phase of the luminary, seemingly as a prelude to the second half of the ceremony devoted to the dancing and singing rituals which were timed to the third, nearly full and the full, phase of the "night sun."

Nekatcit's observations, it must be noted, were based upon oral testimony on matters which, under closer checking, could be tested as possibilities for lunar movements a century ago. One can hardly expect the tradition of timing to possess astronomical accuracy over this lapse of time.

The provisions made by the Creator for the care and nourishment of his human children is expressed in a saying which Josiah Montour had often heard repeated among the old people in his youth, "God hangs a kettle and there is plenty of food. You go there and serve yourself." His father had further said in the meetings which were held to strengthen the religious sentiment of the people, "Do not take the kettle away. God has left the kettle with you. If you take it away, he will put it somewhere else." Only fragments like these do we have as memories of the long preaching sessions in the ceremonial assemblies, which seem to have occupied so much of the time spent in the Big House.

Among the Delawares who finally settled down in Indian Territory [Oklahoma] among the Cherokee after 1867, there is still a tradition of the intensely religious nature possessed by the Munsee when they all dwelt as neighbors and relatives in the Eutopia [sic] of the Atlantic seaboard. Nothing in the ceremonial gatherings of the Oklahoma bands seems to show the amount of time given over to preaching to the degree that marks the festivals of the Munsee-Mahican. I feel quite sure that the preaching period of the latter covering the first four nights and part of the fifth night of the Bear Sacrifice Ceremony would impress the other groups of the Delaware Nation as being of maximum proportion.

The Sacramental Feasting on the Bear's Flesh

The flesh of the bear was made ready to be eaten at the conclusion of one of the first of the four nights of preaching or at the end of the fifth night. It was passed around the assembly of worshipers as a sacrament, the formalities of its distribution being of particular significance. Nekatcit was not clear in explaining some points in this part of the proceedings. Whether the feasting on the bear's flesh began on the first night of the preaching or was postponed until the fifth night at the conclusion of the period of service was left in doubt by him. Accordingly I enter the description of the feast of the flesh as an episode taking place on one or all of these nights without stating its exact time.

The first serving of the meat was offered by the two Sweepers who entered the edifice with bowls of the boiled viands by the east door, outside of which stood the cook house where the cutting up and cooking was done. One Sweeper went down each side of the Big House with the offering. The women seated on the north side of the east half of the building were served first, then those on the south side. Next the men in the west half of the house were passed their portions. Everyone was expected to partake of the sacred flesh. The Sweepers always used the east door in their movements during the eucharistic ritual.

On the last night of the preaching period the last of the bear's flesh was thought to be consumed by the company. This was the last feasting period of the ceremony, as we understand the facts given.

Ceremonial disposition of the bones of the sacrificed bear was made, Nekatcit explained, when the last night of preaching was over. When the chief had closed his discourse that night, the bones were all gathered up and burned in the east fire, or in the east stove of later times. Only the skin of the sacrificed animal was left hanging on the center-post for the ensuing year.

No salt was used in preparing the meat for ceremonial consumption. Nekatcit further explained some interesting facts of food portioning in the feasting ritual of the Indians there. He said that the liver of any animal they killed was considered as "red," and that deer liver, moose and bear meat and grease were ingredients of the feast food served in the ceremonies.

An important observation added later by Nekatcit was that no corn food was served at the feasting in the Bear Sacrifice Ceremony. What does this signify? Does it mean that the ceremony pertained to a period of Wapanachki culture[4]

---

4. Wapana'chkiwak, "Sunrise land people," a general term used to identify all Delawares and Munsees from Canada to Oklahoma (Speck and Moses 1945: 13).

when hunting was the dominant activity in the subsistence cycle, i.e., before agriculture prevailed? And does it represent the Wapanachki cognate ceremony to the Bear Feast of Algonkian hunting tribes of the northern Canadian forest zone (Cree, Montagnais-Naskapi)? I would venture an answer in the affirmative.

Procedures of the Fifth to the Eighth Night

Recitation of Dreams by the Spiritual Men

With the waxing of the moon to the stage of reaching its half phase, reckoned according to the tradition of the ritual to fall on or about on the fifth night, that portion of the program known as Recitation of Dreams was begun.

When the ceremony had advanced to this stage on the fifth night, it was considered to have gained in spiritual force. And note that its potency as such was increasing in proportion to the moon's waxing in fullness.

The ritual of this night was opened by the chief who gave a short sermon and address, lasting only about an hour. Among other admonitions similar in content to those of the preceding nights, he announced on this night that the Magical Men were ready to begin reciting their dreams, and he urged the audience to be quiet and respectful. He ceased at about the time when the moon in its half phase swung above the distant tree-tops.

In the meantime, the Sweeper at the east door had placed the two red benches just west of the center-post to be ready for the four Drummers, who were to repeat the chants of the Magical Men in reciting their dreams. He also took the folded hide drum from its sacred bag, together with the beating sticks and gave them to the Drummers. Then he turned around, and the chief handed him the sacred turtle shell rattle (fig. 14). This symbolical instrument he carried across to the south side of the house, where the Reciters of Visions were seated, and laid it on the floor in front of the one sitting there on the east end of the row. As each Reciter of Dreams repeated his chant, he laid the rattle again on the floor and pushed it to the man nearest him on his left to use as he did. The turtle had to go all the way around the Big House from east to west in this manner until it came back to the first Reciter. The turtle shell is not supposed to be picked up by any of the Reciters unless he would sing his dream recitation. When it had gone its round, the east Sweeper or Doorkeeper picked it up and placed it in its place near the center-post. These were the words of Nekatcit.

The ritual of the Recitation of Dreams was known as alo'man, for which word no analysis of syllables was given by Nekatcit. To him it denoted the formal chanting of individual dream or vision performed by a Spiritual Man accompanied by the Drummers, who repeated the song stanza by stanza.

The Recitation of Dreams or Visions, therefore, deserves particular notice at this point. The Spiritual Men who had received visitations from spiritual sources at some time in their lives, as outlined in a previous section of the study [not

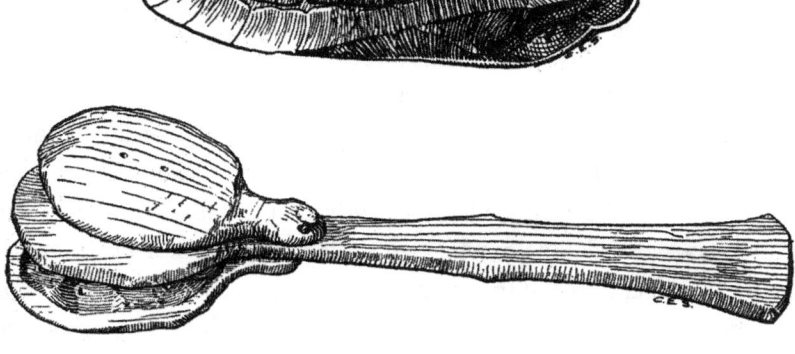

Fig. 14. (*Above*) turtle-shell rattle used by reciters of visions; (*below*) replica of wooden hand rattle used by vision reciters, made by Jesse Moses (figs. 4 and 5, Speck and Moses 1945: 47). Courtesy Reading Public Museum.

printed here] acquired varying degrees of supernatural power for preserving strength, health, and control over adverse circumstances affecting their own or community interests. Deep wisdom and ability to prophesy and to detect deception were among their endowments. The possession of such experience also gave them prestige and authority in the community to a degree unequaled by other means of obtaining station and control in tribal society. (Impostors are said to have tried to invent dream experiences to establish claims to right of admission to the company of Spiritual Men. The latter were especially keen in sensing their deceit, and impostors were socially disgraced after being exposed.)

The Spiritual Men were the elect or holy men in all ceremonial activities. They officiated at each of the recurrent religious festivals by repeating before the audience the song recitations acquired through their spirit-contact experiences. These chants were delivered as deeply significant rituals in the program of worship of the Bear Sacrifice Ceremony and others celebrated during the year. Fortunately they have left a profound impression upon the cultural memory of the band even after almost a century of Christianization. A few examples, necessarily fragmentary, were transmitted by tradition among aged members of the Munsee-Mahican band, whose fathers had chanted them in the Big House almost a century ago. I only could wish that we had more to offer on the subject, for they form one of the main props upon which the social and religious structure of Wapanachki culture rests.

It seems advisable at this point to repeat some of the observations previously made concerning the formalities of handling the turtle-shell rattle used by the Spiritual Men in chanting. There was only one rattle of this type employed in the rituals of the Big House. It was the privilege of the Sweeper or Doorkeeper of the east side of the house to have custody of the instrument. When ready to be used by the Reciters in their part of the exercises, the said Sweeper carried it to its formal resting place on the floor in front of the Singers' bench laying it at the feet of the first Spiritual Man expected to chant his vision. If moved to chant he took it up and proceeded to sing while advancing from his seat to the center-post, going once around it counter-clockwise, then returning to his seat. He danced shuffling his feet in short steps, body erect in stately bearing, and sang his verses in repetition. If, however, he did not feel moved to chant, he did not pick up the rattle but pushed it across the floor to the Reciter next to him on his left. That moved the rattle in a westward direction, coincident with the life course of the symbolical turtle—always westward. Finally, when the rattle had been passed to each Reciter, who had used or declined it in the formal manner, it was taken by the Sweeper in charge of the west door and placed on the floor in front of the chief, between his bench and the center-post. Lying there, it somehow represented the tiny star Alcor close to Mizar[5] in the analogue between the floor plan of the Big House and the Great Bear constellation.

In using the turtle-shell rattle each chanter held the shell, carapace up, in his right hand and shook it with an up and down and sidewise motion to give tempo to his song version. At the end of the chant he made a sharp downward motion of the rattle and ceased. The Drummers then repeated his verses accompanying themselves by beating their time on the folded skin drum with the sacred beating sticks (fig. 15). The four Drummers sat on their two benches west of the center-post, one pair facing the other, all holding the ends of the drum with their free hands. The sacred hide drum and the beating sticks remained in the custody of the Sweeper at the west door. At the termination of the Dream Recitations and the two succeeding dances, the Man's Dance and the Mixed Dance, he took the drum and beaters in charge and restored them to the bag consecrated to contain these objects. Note that the folded hide drum and its beaters were only used to accompany the singing of these three dances. Their function was of a high ceremonial nature and correspondingly limited to the three most holy dance events.

We now leave this stage of the performance to proceed with an account of the events that followed in order on the programs from the fifth night on, after the recitation of visions had ended each night. From this point on, the moon was in the half full and approaching the full phase.

The Man's Dance

On the fifth night, after the dream recitations were concluded, the performance of the Man's Dance, known as li'nka.n, literally "man's dance," was called for.

---

5. Mizar and Alcor comprise a distinctive binary star in the middle of the tail of the constellation Ursa Majoris, "The Great Bear," also known as the "Big Dipper."

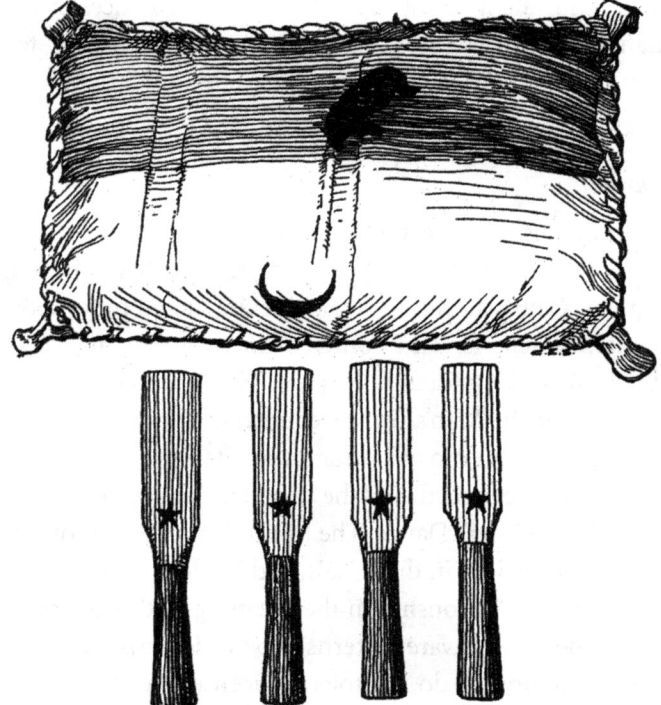

Fig. 15. Folded hide drum and beaters. Sky-Bear and New Moon are painted black; upper field representing the west, is painted red; lower field, representing the east is painted white. Stars are painted on red- and white-painted beaters. Length of drum, 18 inches; width of drum, 11 inches; length of beaters, 11.2 inches (fig. 3, Speck and Moses 1945: 44). Courtesy Reading Public Museum.

The dancers were all men of vigorous body and in their prime of life; they were referred to as "warriors" by Nekatcit. In breech-cloths and naked bodies, or in full native habiliments in accordance with their station and rank, they performed motions, which seem from some descriptions to have been something of a *tour de vigeur*, each performer displaying his agility and energy in body movements. Further particulars are lacking as to the nature of their actions, except that they followed the leader in single file counter-clockwise. The dancing path, or track, in the Big House for the Man's Dance was an oval course starting in front of the men's seats, going around the center-post, and between it and the two fires.[6]

Several passages in the now barely remembered wording of the song reveal the masculine qualities of the Man's Dance. There is a fragment of the dance leader's part which says, "We are going away, all of us!" It has reference to the myth, "The Boys Who Became Stars." The other men of the company uttered the

---

6. Speck wrote, "The Cayuga perform a social dance called by them, gane'hwai, "beating skin," in which a folded skin drum of the Delaware type was used. It is popularly known as the Delaware Dance and is evidently derived from the Delaware Man's Dance" (Speck and Moses 1945: 72, n. 70).

syllables Hau Ha', equivalent to "all right." One of the sentences of the song burden of this dance ran Ki.lu'na ki'nt'ka.na, "We are all dancing," to which the dancers cried in chorus Yo Ha' Yo Ha', also equivalent to "all right."

The Mixed Dance

In the order of performance, the second dance to be given, immediately following the Man's Dance, was the Mixed Dance, known as Kik'li'k.a.n, of which the proper name is a translation. It was one of the sacred processional types of dance movement in which men and women formed the dancing column and was accented by the beat of the folded hide drum. The movement was described as being similar to that of the Man's Dance, counter-clockwise around the center-post, except that the column moved around the interior of the Big House, passing outside the fires (between them and the doors) instead of between the fires and the center-post as in the Man's Dance. The Mixed Dance was another allegory of the functions of sex in society, in the rituals, and in life at large. I tried to discern elements of physical sex relationship in the meaning of this dance exercise, but there seemed to be none. Delaware patterns of behavior, especially those governing symbolism in ceremonies, do not tolerate license in expressions of physical sex relationship. There is an aversion to frankness in sex matters as compared with the Wabanaki groups farther east.

Distinctive traits of this dance were not noted, the leader of which was a "selected man." No songs of this unit were offered by the informants.

THE WOMAN'S DANCE

The third dance of the sacred series of three in which the folded hide drum was employed was know as Oxkwe'o ki'nt'ka.n, "Woman's Dance." Only women took part in the counter-clockwise march around the center post, although a male singer led the column. The brief notice of this dance given by Nekatcit stated that it was similar to the Man's Dance in other respects.

Conclusion of the Consecrated Performances on the Eighth Night

It is important for emphasis to repeat here that the three dances just listed constitute a group of events in the ceremony which possessed sacramental qualities. They were that part of the program in which fulfillment of the wishes of the Creator, as revealed to an ancestral priesthood in a time of religious revival following a crisis long ago, was the objective purpose. The subsequent exercises, we are given to understand, were carried out as a part of the festival intended to afford social relaxation to the people. This was also part of the Creator's design to combine pleasure and enjoyment with religious observances as will shortly be shown. Both Iroquois and Delawares emphasize this aspect as an essential feature of religious thought and activity, often to a degree that evokes censure by Christians who hail the "beatitudes of pagan creeds" as frivolity and sacrilege. Briefly stated, the Man's, the Mixed, and the Woman's dances formed a triad of sanctified demonstrations associated in religious rating with the rites and procedures that came before them.

From the fifth to the eighth night the ceremonial procedure was conducted as outlined to this point. On these nights other dances of a symbolical or social character could be brought in, if, in the opinion of the chief, the volunteers to sing the dream recitations were too few to fill the night's performance. For it was expected that dancing would take place as long as the moon shone before dawn. Dawn terminated all night celebrations. The change in tone of the festivities at this point was marked by the removal of the sacred instruments. At the conclusion of these dances the hide drum and symbolical painted drum beaters, prayer-sticks, and the turtle shell rattle were taken by the Sweepers and put away in the skin receptacle until the next seasonal ceremony required them again.

Secular, Symbolical, and Social Dances

With the removal from use of the sacred folded-hide drum and the beaters on this night, it being the fifth one of the convention, the religious tone of the ceremony was relaxed. The festival had entered its second period. The moon was waxing through the half phase to the full and would continue so until the end of the ceremony on the tenth night. The preaching period had terminated, the recitation of dreams and visions by the Magical Men had entered its first stage and would form the early night's part of the service to its termination. Now the late night's program of symbolical animal dances, the mask performances, the ceremonial games and some purely social dances were in the order of service. Some of the dance events came in a formal sequence after the recitations of dreams, others were optionally introduced toward the end of the night to provide relaxation and pleasure to those in attendance. From what Nekatcit stated, it would seem that the chief had the decision as to which dances would be performed in the latter series.

That pleasure, relaxation, and amusement were expected by the Creator as part of the period of worship is evident in the attitude expressed by the religious leaders. The combination of reverence and innocent indulgence in the pleasure of social interaction among the people was an element of ceremonial festivals among all the local groups constituting the Delaware Nation. In the words of the chief, as Nekatcit remembered hearing them quoted by the ancients, a call was given forth to the dancers, "Dance hard, folks, so our Maker will rejoice that he sees you dancing."[7] Such cries by the leaders of dances are customary in other Algonkian societies. And equivalent sentiments are expressed in Iroquois statements, showing

---

7. Quoted from a description of the Robin Dance (see note 8).

that the spirit of beatification is still alive in the religious tradition of peoples who regard happiness and joyfulness in ritual festivals, not as a sacrilege, but as a form of compliance with the wishes of the Being-to-Whom-They-Pray.

Among the animal symbolical dances which were listed as following the session of the Recitation of Dreams, the Robin Dance, the Raccoon Dance, and the Night Hawk Dance, were specifically mentioned by Nekatcit. For these the small water drum and the cow-horn rattle were brought forth by the custodian of properties and placed at the disposal of the dance leaders. The False Face performance and the War Dance were also in the same category.

That some dances with animal names were taken over directly from the Iroquois Long House festivals was also stated by Nekatcit. The songs were translated into Wapanachki approximate equivalents. One of the most popular and oft-repeated of this series was the Round Dance, known among the Iroquois as Kada'trot, the only one specifically noted by the informant. A Wapanachki version of part of the song is given under the heading of the dance below. It was a purely social dance, the purpose of which was to afford the pleasure of social intermingling among those attending the festivities. Their performance, however, came toward morning when the semi-reverential spirit of the night celebration had become relaxed.

Short descriptions of these initiative dances now follow as the usual order of their sequence from the fifth and sixth to the tenth and last night of the ceremony requires.

The Robin Dance

Under the native name, Tcicko''koc keo, literally "robin dance," a dance step and pantomime of the movements of a flock of robins was performed by a mixed group of participants. The song was given by the four Singers clustered on their bench west of the center-post, furnishing the accompaniment with the water drum and horn rattle. The dancers hopped and moved counter-clockwise in close formation around the Singers; further details and the syllables of the appropriate song are lacking.[8]

The Raccoon Dance

A dance in which everyone present was expected to take part—men, women, and children commingled—as one known as E'span keo, "Raccoon Dance." The manner in which it was performed reveals that it was an act of supplication on the part of the community to the Creator. All those present crowded up to the center-post and danced in an up-and-down motion in a compact group as close to the center-post as they could get. The song leader used the large snapping-turtle

---

8. Speck wrote, "The Cayuga also do a Robin Dance (called Dji.ckogo'kye) primarily as a social dance, though it may be requested by someone to 'do his health good'" (Speck and Moses 1945: 74, n. 71).

rattle, standing nearest of all to the feet of the post. Part of the leader's song as remembered was Atco' tanahe atc nehe', which meant "I am warm, I am really warm." At the conclusion of the song and action, he shouted, Ca', at which signal of dismissal the company went back to their places and sat down. The informant had nothing more to add to this description.[9]

THE FALSE FACE DANCE PERFORMANCE

Among other functions which it filled in the religious life of the band as expellers of disease, the company of False Faces also made its appearance in the Bear Sacrifice Ceremony in the series of rituals on this and the succeeding nights of the celebration.[10] The ritual they enacted was called Mes.i'nk keo, "Face Dance," the pattern of which was as follows: The False Face company consisted of twelve men of which one or two were Spiritual Men (Mani'towi'lnowak). Six of them wore white masks representing the Unami moiety group and came into the Big House, creeping on the floor and entering by the west door. As they reached the interior, they split into two parties of three each, going down the north and south sides of the building toward the center. By the east door, the other six entered, wearing red masks representing the Wapanachki moiety group, and crept in two similar parties of three down the north and south sides of the house. The twelve False Faces met at the center-post, stood up, and began the False Face Dance. Each of them carried a large Snapping-Turtle rattle and used it with vehemence.

The musical accompaniment for their act was furnished by the Singers using the little round water drum painted red.[11] The function of the False Faces in their performance was to clear away evil spirits from the proximity of the Big House and its occupants.

The chief then stood before his bench and addressed them, saying something like the following: "Take this in good part and dance the War Dance." By this announcement he made [it] known that the False Faces were to change from their usual role into the actions of the dance participated in by men enlisting for a war expedition.

While the chief was speaking, the Drummers took their seats on the two red benches west of the center-post as they had done for the Spiritual Men who recited their dreams. They were then prepared to chant the songs of the War Dance for

---

9. Among the Cayugas the Raccoon Dance (called sanuge'ha) is a social dance (Speck and Moses 1945: 74, n. 72).
10. Speck wrote, "False-face performances are characteristic of Iroquois ceremonies to an exceptional degree. They also function as agencies whose service is to expel disease from the community. The extensive writings of Fenton on the subject of Iroquois masking rites present a degree of detail which makes comparative discussion at the moment too complicated to introduce [cf. Speck 1949]. The close association for over a century between Cayuga and Delaware ritualists may account for some of the reputed resemblances between their dances" (Speck and Moses 1945: 75, n. 73). See Fenton (1987) for the definitive study of False Faces.
11. Speck wrote, "'Remember,' said the informant, 'that this water drum was used for all dances except for the three sacred dances, the Man's, the Mixed, and the Woman's Dance, which required the folded skin drum'" (Speck and Moses 1945: 75).

the False Faces. In this capacity, as before, the Drummers were referred to as Seli'mwak, "cranes," and continued to use the water drum.

The War Dance

There seems to have been little to differentiate the movements of the War Dance, so-called, from those of the False Face Dance. The War Dance was called Mata'kewin keo, a literal equivalent. The twelve False Faces performed this dramatic dance three times, at the conclusion of each performance giving the war-whoop. When the third dance of this series was finished and the whoop uttered, the False Faces suddenly ran out of the building through their respective east and west doors.

If the audience desired further entertainment after the rituals of the night, social dances were then in order. The Round Dance, or even others learned among the Iroquois, could be introduced.

The Round Dance

Among practically all tribes of the Atlantic Slope area between the St. Lawrence and the Gulf of Mexico, a purely social dance was, and still is, known under the name of Round Dance, Friendship Dance, and even Stomp Dance in some parts of Oklahoma where the dance figure has become diffused by the migration of tribes from east of the Mississippi. Its pattern is much the same wherever it is encountered. Using a hand rattle to accompany his song, the leader proceeds in a shuffling step at the head of a column of men, women, and children, who follow him in a counter-clockwise course around the dancing plot. The song is characterized by an introduction consisting of repeated meaningless syllables. When the actual song is begun the leader intones a lively series of verses in which he may indulge in some joking, often interspersed with double-meaning phrases risqué in nature. Irrespective of the tongues in which the participants and leaders have been brought up, the Round Dance has retained its almost universal southeastern woodland character.

The Munsee-Mahican, like all the Wapanachki, had their version of this figure; it was called Kowi.'ka't, "Round dance." Nekatcit recalled that Jacob Simonds, whose native name was Ka'zko, "Great Blue Heron," and a man of Tutelo-Delaware descent, called Wi'cti.l, were favorite leaders in this dance. They conducted social meetings in which they led the dance long after the Big House ceremonies were given up by the band. Part of the song contained the words Ko'yewa, Ko'yewa, meaning "Beef, Beef," to which the dancers in the line answered Wi'ngewa'nkaya, "It is good to eat," *ad libitum*. He recalled how certain boys in the company would add "Six cents a pound" to these phrases in a spirit of hilarity.[12]

---

12. Speck wrote, "Since writing the above, it has been learned that Jesse Noah, Gwuteme'k, 'One Fish,' is competent to sing some of these songs. He is now seventy-nine years of age [in 1945], and learned them in his youth" (Speck and Moses 1945: 76, n. 74).

After the dancing of the night was over, the Sweepers produced their brooms and swept the dance area of the Big House, each sweeping away evil sources of influence from the center of the building to his own door. The same was done at the conclusion of each night of activity to the end of the tenth night when all was finished.

The Nighthawk Dance

Known as Pi.ckwelane' o ka.n, "Nighthawk Dance," the performance to be now described and discussed was one of outstanding importance in the two major ceremonial complexes of the Wapanachki. It formed an element in the pattern of the Bear Sacrifice Ceremony, opening the native new year in late January and early February, and in the Green Corn Feast and its ritual of September.

In the ceremony of the bear sacrifice and the ritual connected with the celestial bear, the Nighthawk Dance was the concluding performance of the celebration, taking place customarily on the tenth or last night of the festival. It consumed nearly the whole night as a ritual prolonged by members of the audience, who presented gifts to the dancers as a means of obtaining through their offices certain blessings from the spirits. And at the same time, it provided occasion for the people to express their thankfulness to the Creator for past blessings. The pattern of the Nighthawk Dance was given by Nekatcit as follows:

The performing group consisted of two or four men who were good, experienced dancers. Stripped of clothing, wearing only the breech-cloth, they danced side by side near the center of the Big House. In their right hands they held rattles, originally of turtle-shell similar to those used by the Spirit Men in the Recitation of Dreams. In later times, however, the cow-horn rattle used in secular dances came to be substituted. In their left hands they originally held the wings of Nighthawks, but these were replaced in later times by the feather wands previously described, being made of any kinds of feathers attached in a row upon a string fastened to the end of a stick about a foot in length. The substitution of the horn rattle for the turtle-shell and the feather wands for the actual wings of the nighthawk, was possibly brought about through conformity with the Iroquois pattern of the Eagle Dance, to which the Wapanachki performance is strikingly similar in pattern.

The position of the song leader during the ritual was in front of the row of dancers. When the singer began his chant, the dancers assumed a squatting position of the body, keeping on their feet, and holding their rattles behind their backs. Their hands holding the feathers were extended. In this crouching posture, they proceeded by jumps toward the singer, shaking their muscles and upper parts of their bodies in imitation of the nighthawk diving downward through the air when emitting its "booming" sound.

Anyone in the audience was privileged to make a gift donation to the dancers. Such gifts were specifically corn-meal cakes previously prepared and brought to the Big House in baskets. With the donation went an appeal by the giver to the

Creator and lesser spiritual forces to grant the people a "good and healthful season," and a rendering of thanks to the Creator for the blessings of the past summer's growth, the blessings of life and health, and whatever other blessings had been enjoyed, individually or collectively. This occasion was open, in fact, to all persons who wished to make requests of the spirits for blessings of any nature and to express gratitude for such received.

The procedure for a supplicant to follow in making the donation was to strike upon the floor of the Big House with a staff. This was a formal signal for the dancers to stop suddenly, as though "freezing" in their motions. The song also ceased abruptly. Then the invocation was made by the giver of the alms. When the donation had been deposited with the rest and the prayer or beatitude concluded, the singing and dancing was resumed, continuing until it was stopped again in the same way by the next donation.

The Nighthawk Dance is the Munsee-Mahican cognate of the Eagle Dance widely known among eastern tribes of North America. The Cayuga Iroquois perform it, under the name Kanruga''e, in a slightly different manner as a curing ritual of a restricted society of doctors. [William N.] Fenton has devoted attention to the widespread Eagle Dance which he regarded in 1937 as associated with the historic Indian Calumet Ceremony (cf. Fenton 1953). This ritual was a reverential medium of man's communication with the spiritual forces. It formed the concluding event of the entire ceremony.

At the termination of the Nighthawk Dance, the Sweepers purged the Big House of lurking evil influences for the last time by sweeping the premises with their brooms, proceeding from the center-post to their respective doors as before. Then, before the dawn had appeared, the chief announced that the remainder of the sacrificial bear meat was to be shared among those in attendance. When the portions had been distributed and each had a helping, the chief bid the people go home. The ceremony was ended. In the words of Nekatcit, Na'lene Iowi.'le, "Thereupon it is all finished."

CHAPTER ELEVEN

Lula Mae Gibson Gilliland's Account, 1947

The following chapter contains Lula Mae Gibson Gilliland's unpublished account of Delaware religion. Gilliland was an Eastern Oklahoma Delaware woman born near the village of Bowring in 1905. A fluent speaker of Unami, she was dedicated to preserving the traditions of her people. Several pages of manuscript material written by her are on file in the Smithsonian Institution's National Anthropological Archives in Washington, D.C. These include the account reprinted here as well as a charming letter to Eleanor Roosevelt dated August 14, 1942, that was written in response to a radio announcement calling for information on Indian languages needed to help train "code-talkers" who were able to communicate in ways not understandable by the enemy.

THIS IS THE TRUE RELIGION OF THE DELAWARE INDIANS TRIBE

But I am sorry to say we don't carry out our Church any more, as so few of our older generation is living, and for twenty-five years we have not held services in our church. But the Church still stands at this date, about five miles from a little town, Copan, Oklahoma. I believe my tribe is the only tribe in the United States that has always had a Church house, only we call it a prayer house. It is built of native logs. It is a large building. There are large entrances, [one] at each end, but for some reason the rear entrance was all boarded up. The front entrance facing the east was hung over with skins of animals sewed together.

At the Center and the four corners of the building are [posts] square in shape, and the image of the evil spirit[1] is carved upon it. The one in the center is very large and the face of the evil spirit is on all four sides of it.

Two large fire places on each side of the Center Post. And a large square opening is in the roof of the building to prevent fire or sparks to catch the building afire.

---

1. I.e., Mesingw.

Each year fresh hay is placed all around the Church leaving a hard beaten pathway around each fire place as well as the Center Post.

At the front of the entrance another camp fire is built on the outside. And during the ceremony a slow fire is kept and a large pot is hung there. In it is corn that has been pounded to a powder and water is added to make a gruel. And it is served at the end of each meeting in small earthen bowls.

In the month of November, when the moon is full, the Chief sends word to all the tribe at what date the meeting will start. Long before this date people start arriving from all over the country and pick out the best camp site.

The chief then picks out three women and three men of good standing in the tribe to be the workers of the Church, and also he picks out a man to play the part of the evil spirit.[2]

The workers of the Church are camped out in front of the Church. On one side the women, and on the other the men. Each member has a partner camped opposite. And they eat all their meals together, each partner sharing what they have to eat. And one partner can not eat what the other doesn't eat. And if one partner decides on a snack between meals, he must first go and find his or her partner and share in what they eat.

They eat on a table made of a small tree that is made into a table with tree trunks made into suitable stools. Also a shelter is built over their heads with bushes to protect them from rain.

The evil spirit Man wears a robe made of bear skin and a horrible head dress. He wears turtle shells that have been sewed together and small pebbles put inside to make them rattle. He ties this on his ankles so when he runs or stomps they make a rattling noise.

After nightfall, no child is seen outside of his camp, he[3] prowls the outskirts of the camps. The children feared him so badly that when they heard him stomping they would run into their tents and hide under anything that was available. Nobody but the Chief knew who this man was. He stayed in the woods near the Church and there his food was taken secretly after dark. The children dare not venture very far into the woods to play during the day, as he was often seen roaming around the woods. But he did not come to the camps, only after dark.

The night of the opening meeting the Chiefs start to Church as soon as the moon starts to rise and then every one is given only a few minutes to get inside. These meetings last for twelve days. On the twelfth day the last meeting is held at Midday. All other meetings are at night.

During the whole time we are camped here no White Man's food is to be eaten. The braves will kill all the meat for every one in camp. They would leave early morning and return late in the evening. The brave that killed the most game

---

2. I.e., Mesinghoalikan.
3. The Mesinghoalikan.

would be quite a hero in the old days. Deer meat was the main game. During the day the women of the camps, not the workers, but women that were camped there, would dry this meat and cure it by cutting it in strips.

On the opening night the workers stand on each side of the doors, men on one side the women on the other. Everyone is to give his or her name upon entering, and no one leaves or enters the Church; only between dances. No other tribe ever enters our Church, and no White Man was ever allowed inside during our meetings. After every one is inside, as every one must go to Church—man, women, and children; even the babies. You have your own place to sit in the fresh hay, and under no condition are you to fall asleep. If you do one of the workers will shake you awake. If the babies go to sleep or the children, the workers will take them out and put them to bed. Sometimes these meetings would last till three or four o'clock in the morning according to how many men took part in the ceremonies.

Each family had a center place to sit, and if you were a Gibson and marry into the Curlyheads, your children could either sit with the mother's family or the father's at the beginning of each meeting except the last day. The chief would start his ceremony with a prayer so moving that it would cause many a woman to cry silently.

Then he would start on with his story of a vision he had of some miracle that God had placed for him. Now we believe we only have one God. We believe he controls everything; some other tribes have a sun God or a rain God and so forth. But we believe in one almighty God.

The Chief then goes on with his story telling until he breaks into a song he has composed himself and with a turtle shell in his hand that rattles he starts dancing and singing and the men follow him echoing his song. Then all at once he stops singing and only dances. Now this dance is not like our war and stomp dances. It is a slow and more laborious dance. He stomps very slow rattling his turtle shell all the time.

Whenever he stops singing the drummers take up where he left off. Now these drummers sit across the Church from the Chief and they sit cross-legged with the drum in front of them. This drum is made of deer skin and it is stuffed with hay and clapboards are placed across it, to make a pounding noise. These drummers have an art all their own, as they must pick up the Chief's song where he left off and while one sings one verse the other sings the other verse all at the same time. They sing and beat the drum until the Chief dances a few yards then he stops and he starts his story all over again. Then this is repeated until he has made it around both fire places. Another thing, whenever he gets even with the drummers, [they] stop too. Then everyone that dances has to shake hands with the drummers. Now the men can dance behind the chief or whomever happens to take the lead, and only the older women are allowed to dance at the end of the line. After the chief gets back to his place every one stands and his left hand is raised to his shoulder palm out. And the word oh——— is echoed through out the Church. That is when you are supposed to do your own personal praying.

LULA MAE GIBSON GILLILAND'S ACCOUNT, 1947

After that everyone sits down. Then any member can get up and tell his story and dance and sing.

After each ceremony the workers will build up the fires then sweep the entire path with the wings from a wild turkey.

At the end of the meeting the workers serve everyone a small bowl of broth. Then they all go by the Chief's place and shake his hand. Then they go off to bed.

Now the workers are allowed to serve refreshments and food at their camps before and after the meeting and they are paid with beads unlike [any] I ever saw before. They are a long white and black bead, and these they save until after the meetings are all over, then they present them to the Chief, and he repays them for their work with handsome gifts. In later years he gives them money. As my mother was often chosen as a worker and my father as a drummer, although my father was a college graduate, he never fails his Church.

After twelve days of these meetings the last day the service was held at high noon and the women, mostly old ladies, took part in the ceremonies and dances. They were allowed to tell of their visions. This was the day the drummers dreaded because they were unfamiliar with their songs. As the men told the same story and sang the same song night after night and year after year until the drummers memorize them.

But the women always looked so beautiful in their bright colored costumes and beads. And everyone wears a large spot of rouge, that is all the paint that is used. The workers paint your cheeks as you enter the Church each night.

On this last day the ceremonies start early at eight o'clock so everyone can get through by noon. That day the Chief gives his ceremony last and when he reaches the entrance the skins are removed from the entrance and he dances right on out of the Church. Everyone rises and follows him; that is the only time the children dance. The Chief dances to the end of the last workers camp. And there is a long line formed facing the east. and the chief starts this oh———— and it goes right on down the line only to begin again at the head. They re-echo this for twelve times, the Chief prays again and thanks God for the nice weather during the meeting as so often the Indian summer is here at that time of year. But should the weather be bad and stormy the Chief would pray all the harder as he says the God is angry for his people as some are sinners. After this the people broke up camp, happy to return to their homes.

CHAPTER TWELVE

Eastern Oklahoma Delaware Reminiscences, 1972–1994

This chapter presents a group of Eastern Oklahoma Delaware reminiscences recorded between 1972 and 1994. The first eight accounts represent the most extensive of the many unpublished interviews of Delaware elders conducted as a graduate project between 1972 and 1973 by Native American artist Ruthe Blalock Jones, Chun-Lun-Dit. Born in 1939 in Claremore, Oklahoma, to parents of Delaware, Shawnee, and Peoria ancestry, Blalock is currently head of the Art Department of Bacone College in Muskogee, Oklahoma. Blalock is a distinguished artist whose paintings on Native American themes in gouache, oil, and acrylic have been exhibited in several shows and have won numerous awards.

The final account is a brief memoir penned by Nancy Falleaf Sumpter, published in the Bulletin of the Archaeological Society of New Jersey *in 1994 (Sumpter 1994). In the memoir she emotionally recalls her childhood visit to the ruins of the last Big House in Copan, Oklahoma, in 1930 in the company of her family and some Big House elders.*

OLLIE BEAVER ANDERSON

I[1] used to attend all of those old Delaware meetings and especially after I married Tom Anderson. They always had him to be head Ush-kos, so I was always there doing the work for him. I don't know how many times I've camped there with those people and done all the cooking for my husband, Tom. I always try to help and I think I know all of the rules.

---

1. Ollie Beaver Anderson, whose Delaware name was Ala-pan-aqua, "Same As Other Women," was a Wolf clan woman born on May 10, 1888, near Bartlesville, Oklahoma. She was the daughter of Tung-shu-mu-tat, "Little Horn," and a granddaughter of the prominent nineteenth-century Oklahoma Delaware leader Black Beaver. Her husband, Tom Anderson, worked with Frank Speck. Mrs. Anderson reported that Speck placed all of her husband's Big House regalia, a number of specially commissioned reproductions of Big House ritual objects, and her Tuk-wem-tet, "blouse," in the collections of the University of Pennsylvania in Philadelphia. Her recollections are in Ruthe Jones (1973: 7–14).

They had six attendants, or Ush-kos, two from each clan (a man and a woman). They camped on each side in front of the Big House. Some I can remember who were Ush-kos: my sister, John Anderson, and Tom Anderson. They always got him because he's the man, we're same clan so they couldn't get both of us.

I'm probably the only one living who knows about the center post. They look for a big tree and that's where they will make the house. They use that tree where it is growing and cut it and work it down, take all the bark off, and smooth it and square it off. That is where they carve the two Mising faces on the side and the building is built around it. There are three smaller faces on the two side walls and none on the north. There are twelve in all and no faces on the outside of the structure.

I was there cooking for those workers when they built the new house, this last meeting house. They made all of the shingles for that house by hand. The men were John Anderson, Sam and Tom Buffalo, and my husband, Tom Anderson. I believe John Falleaf, Sam Anderson, and one other helped each other to carve the faces on the posts. They were painted black and red when they were all carved. They worked together and probably not just one person made a post.

They used to not allow children under ten years old inside the Big House and they're not supposed to sleep. I've seen a lot of them sent out, even old people if they go to sleep. The Ush- kos will punch them with a long stick because they're not supposed to do that.

The main one, Wen-ge-kun-a, he sits a little while and talks and pretty soon he begins to sing and then everyone gets up. The three men who get up and follow him repeat all the songs and the women who are related to him get in line and follow and they all go around the center post. They go east to north and they all pray Oh-Ah eleven times, they say Oh-Ho-Ho-Ho and sit down. Then the next one begins to sing twelve times and they all do that, those who can sing. You have to have power to sing, there can't just anyone get up and go over there and start singing, oh no! That power is gone a long time ago, there's no one living now[2] who goes by the power.

They talk about things they had to do when they were children, what they went through. Back in those days, they had to fit for something, that's why they're living. Their parents send them out when they're little, they want them to fit for something when they grow up.

Charlie Elkhair's vision: When he was small about three or four years old their fathers took him and two other little boys way out where no one could get to them. They found a place and put the three little boys in a hole and put a big rock over it so they couldn't get out. They left them there and told them, "Now you stay here and we'll come after you in four days." Well, they stayed there four days with no food or water.

---

2. I.e., in the Delaware community of 1972.

On the fourth day, Elkhair managed to dig a little hole there beside the rock and got out. The other two boys had already died and were lying there. When he crawled out he thought, "Well, I guess I'll die too!"

Somebody leaned over and told him, "Don't think you're going to die, you'll live to be an old man. Whatever you wish for from now on you're going to get it," and he said something began hitting him all over, it was sprinkling. He said he was laying there with his eyes open and the thing that spoke to him was a big black cloud leaning over him from the west. That cloud said, "Don't think you're going to die, I'm going to take care of you." It was the lightning that brought him up and that is the song he used in the Big House. The song tells all about what he went through. After he recovered he thought, "What am I going to do now, I have to do something. I'm going to help my people when they get sick. I'll do something so they can get well." So, that is the reason when he grew up he was a sweat doctor.[3]

My father had a power from three little frogs. When he died, Mary White came and got them, Uncle Julius Fouts wanted them but she wouldn't let him have them. She and my father were in the same clan so she had the right to get those things. She took them home with her and one time she sent for me. I went over there and she said, "I want you to stay two nights with me, I've got a lot of things to tell you. I want to talk about those Me-koo-she-kuna.[4] I'm going to tell you about them" So, we sat up late at night and she told me about the little frogs.

She would go and get them, they were in a little container all sealed up and nothing can get in there, she keeps it outside somewhere. "I'll always smoke and talk to them," she said. "I take them way out in the country where no one can find them. I leave them there four days. When I first take them out they look like old dried up leaves and in four days when I go and get them, they'll be alive. They come alive and jump around."

She takes them and smokes and talks to them, she tells them she will do that again in four years and then she would put them away again. She did that several times. Feed them they call that.[5]

When she died, no one took it on so it[6] stopped there. The heirs did not know anything about them so that the power was gone right there. It hurt me when I knew this power was gone, and even now I hate it but it's not my fault, it's theirs.[7]

---

3. A sweat doctor is a type of medicine man. Ruthe Jones also wrote that "Mrs. Anderson says one time after telling this story to a student she could not sleep all night for thinking of the two little boys who died. 'Every time I shut my eyes, I saw those two little boys,' she said."
4. Ruthe Jones wrote, "The Me-koo-she-kuna is something of a good luck charm. It is a gift and comes to a person and cannot be obtained consciously. My mother, Lucy Parks Blalock, said that it is something everyone knows about but very few people ever acquire. She said if a person is down and out, poor, sickly, etc., that is the person who will 'find one.' Some search all their lives for one."
5. Traditional Delawares believe it is important, periodically, to ritually feed oil, paint, or tobacco to spirits thought to reside within spiritually charged objects such as amulets and masks.
6. That is, the power within the frogs.
7. That is, the heirs.

In the Big House, she, Mary White, talks about the Tung-sho-mu-tat, the power she got from the deer. She said one time in there when they were passing the meat around they just threw a little piece in her pan and she should have had a big piece or maybe even the whole head because of her power from that animal.

When my father was living he got the name Tung-shu-mu-tat from the hunters. This same old lady Mary White, Rosie White's mother, and he were the same clan.[8] My father was the head or main hunter when they go eat. They were always in line and he was first. She gave him that name because he had a power from the deer.

One time my father ran into a big buck when they were out hunting. This buck knows everything that way.[9] It took after my father and my father said, "Well, this is it, no telling who will get ahead right here him or me." So, this deer came to where he was by the tree and they began fighting. "I would throw him on the ground, he'd jump up and throw me on the ground." They hustled there for a long time. Pretty soon, he said he was so tired he didn't know what to do. He went toward the tree where he had left his gun and ran around the tree and shot that deer, and that's where he got his name.

Some of the singers, Ta-la-kaw, I remember are: Sam Anderson, Tom Buffalo, and Jim Gibson. The drum is hay tied inside a deer hide with the hair left on and folded to the inside. It was tied with buckskin. There were two little paddles with Mising carved on them. Also in there they used little prayer sticks. They pass those around but not everyone can handle them.

On the tenth night, they clean everything out. They take out all the hay and clean the house on the inside, open the door and take those nails out of the boards. We'd help, everyone willing could help take that hay out. Then on the eleventh night it breaks up, that is the last meeting. Ta-mah-mon, means the last day or twelfth day, ending of the ceremony, when we all go out there and pray toward the east.

On the eleventh night the women go around, sing and pray; Ah-tay-home-ok they call it. Also, Tom used to help them.

Certain ones from different clans put that Mising suit on everyday. John Falleaf was light on his feet and could jump over bushes; he was the one who wore it. Oh! I want to tell you people were scared of that! In those days people had more of the feeling to be afraid and not just children—even women fell down and fainted.

Now, that thing must have had power. When he goes around the camps, they know about the time he comes down from the hill and they all look up there. All at once, here he comes running and jumping over bushes. He'd go all over the

---

8. Ruthe Jones identified the clan as Tuk-seet-ta-mee-mas.
9. Ruthe Jones noted that this meant the deer's power made him aware of the hunters.

camp and whoever gets close to him they had to hand him tobacco, but oh! We'd scream and cry. We'd be so afraid of him, but we managed to hand that tobacco to him.

It's just funny, the way he does, even the older women fall down and faint. Charley Webber wore it and also Grandma Spybuck's son, Sam White. I tell you that's something, it's nothing to play with.

For the paint, they dig a root to make that. Grandma Spybuck always went to get that. I don't know what kind it was, but they got it over by the Delaware cemetery. They brought it back and washed it, pounded it and mixed it with tallow and that's what those women use on the eleventh night. They do that every year. The only time they used it was the last night when the women sing. Pe-con is what they call it.

At the last meeting all the old people had died and there was hardly anyone left who could sing. Only Charley Webber, Ben Hill, and Tom Buffalo. Frank Wilson was "taking it up." When they died, why that was the end of it. There was no one living who could carry on.

So that house just sat there and finally they said they ought to tear it down before someone sets fire to it or something. Joe Bartles, Fred Woodward, John Falleaf, and Joe Washington did this and Joe Bartles began to take the things to the museum.

During the war[10] they had it at Fout's in a tent. We went nearly every night.

Charley Webber started that. They began to say, "We could have those meetings," so they began to fix a little house made of bark and a tent the best way they could fix it. They had a fire in the middle. It's pitiful, but I don't complain; whenever an Indian is trying to do right it's alright with me—it's good. They didn't have any faces, no center pole. We just all sat down and talked and sang those songs.

Charley Webber was always the one that started it; He began to sing. There were three of them—the other two were Reuben Wilson and Joe Washington. Also, Ben Hill.

They talked about everything, what to do to keep well and that they were unable to do some of the things they were supposed to do. The main thing they talked about was the war, so the boys could come home safe. No women talked; we just sat and listened.

I think they had it six nights; that's half of the old Big House meeting. They said, "Even if we could have six days that would help," so that was what they did. There were not very many there, everyone was down and out. A lot of boys were gone to the service, but we tried to have it the best we could.

---

10. World War II.

LUCY PARKS BLALOCK

Big[11] House, Hi'ngwikan, lasted twelve days, was held in the fall, October. The people camped; we never did. During the day it was like any camp, I guess—People got wood, etc.—children played.

I saw the Delawares carry out their rites; I did not pay close attention. It was not like nowadays, children did not question their elders. We went every night, got back home at two or three o'clock in the morning. We'd go to school during the day, then get ready and go back after supper. We tried to go as many nights as we could, but we did not always go every night.

There was a reason for all those things they did, they didn't just do them. I really don't know, and the old ones who would or could tell are gone.

Now the visions, not just everyone had them, only certain ones. They were the ones who recited. The visions "came to them" also in songs. I remember the songs a little, but could not sing without some thought. I've forgotten. We heard them so much every night. I don't remember; wouldn't dare try to sing one, [they're] that sacred and powerful. After all, they're relating their vision, what they saw, when they got it,[12] and when the song was given to them.

The leader would tell the Oshkosh, "Go out and holler." He[13] says Tum-meet-kat, Tum-meet-kat! When they hear that, why they go in, everyone knows too.

Everyone sits according to their clan, the children sit with their parents. On the west end, on north and south. For twelve nights it is the same, whatever your clan you're going to sit there. Whoever the leader is determines where others sit. His clan will be on the north.

If a person sits in the wrong place, the leader will tell them—make them move. We knew where to sit. White people were not allowed. They were seated according to clan and if different, then nearest to their clan. Bear, for instance, would be wolf, and so on.[14]

You could wear Indian clothes if you had them—shawl, head cloth, moccasins. Most wore everyday clothes. The folks told us to behave, be quiet, sit quietly, reverently when you're in there, because it was church. Inside there was hay all around. We sat on this. You could lean back on the wall and be more comfortable. It was comfortable in there. With the two fires it was warm. It was comfortable.

There were three men and three women Oshkosh. The men poked the fire, brought wood in, woke people up if they're asleep. If a child was asleep, they would

---

11. Lucy Parks Blalock, whose Delaware name was Ah-kqa-ah-pon-aqua, "Early Dawn Woman," was a Wolf clan woman born on June 14, 1906. A fluent speaker of Delaware, she was the daughter of Nancy Wilson Parks and George Parks. Her recollections appear in Ruthe Jones (1973: 15–20).
12. I.e., spirit power.
13. I.e., the Oshkosh.
14. This statement is unclear. It may refer to the seating of members of lineages or clans belonging to one of the three Delaware phratries, Turtle, Turkey, and Wolf; to visiting clan members of from other tribes; or to non-Indian relatives.

carry it out and put it to bed. They used a long stick to poke the fire. With this poker they would kind of nudge people to wake them up.

The reason for the six attendants, or Oshkosh, was the three clans—Tukseet, Pelee, Puku-wungu. A man and woman was chosen from each clan. Some from my time were Jim Jackson, Tom Halfmoon, and Silas White. The women were Orie Spybuck, named Ole-lung-un or something like that, and Rosie Parks.

A long time ago everybody had a Delaware name. Not just anybody could give a name; it had to be a gifted person. These names were used in Hi'ngwikan, in some way you had to have an Indian name. I don't really know about this, but on certain nights they had a ceremony. Names were called and that person was supposed to answer if he's there. They might call two or three times, and if they're not in there the leader tells the Oshkosh to go outside and holler loud until that person is located and the person answers. The Oshkosh comes back in and reports that the person answered. So the names had meaning. When the names were called, each one was paid so many K'aks. The K'ak was small beads, bugle shape, white, and made of shells. Some were long and some short. The Oshkosh had chili, pie, etc., you could buy from them. You pay with K'ak instead of money, in those days it was one dollar a yard.

At the beginning of the ceremony they did not start the fire with a match. They had some kind of apparatus they used; I don't know how it was made. After so many nights, I don't remember which, sixth or ninth, they start a new fire.

Some singers I remember are George Falleaf, Frank Wilson, Ben Hill, George Bullet, and Charlie Elkhair. The songs did not all sound alike. There were two drummers who sat across from the man conducting the meeting. Willie Longbone and William Easy, I remember.

The turtle shell. The leader has all those turtles in his care. At intervals they pass that turtle, like it is actually walking, you move it along in front of you, handle it carefully so it won't rattle, it goes all around.

The drum was long, covered with deer hide. They[15] used long flat sticks. On the last night they used special sticks. These had little Misings carved on them, painted black and white.

The hand game sticks they have nowadays remind me of prayer sticks. If you held one in your hand you could keep time; they danced slow.

The Oshkosh used a big turkey wing to sweep clean the path. The first woman sweeps half and the first man sweeps the other half at certain intervals. When they are getting ready to sweep, you can go out; just be sure and come back in before they finish. You go around the fire—don't just go any way.

It is hard to explain—there is so much to remember. I can only tell my version, but it doesn't explain why they did these things.

---

15. The drummers.

You can smoke in there—it is permissible. After all tobacco was strictly Indian, it belonged to them at one time.

About the hunt—I was a young child, and don't know how they did it. I heard about it but I did not see it. I don't know who was picked or how. They had certain songs they sang before the hunters left. When they came back with the game I guess they had more ceremony that went with it. They had a game pole—can't think of the Delaware word for it, it was also a part of the ceremony hunt. I couldn't name one and say, "He went." I heard the songs at our house. William Wilson used to sing them and tell us about it; I thought they were pretty. I never was actually there for that part; I don't know if I would know them now if I heard them.

A long time ago for the food they had deer meat and dried, pounded corn.

The Mising, or mask figure, was before my time. They had already gotten rid of the costume. I've only seen pictures and heard tell of it, but I never actually saw one. He was a powerful being. And whoever wore it, when they had it on it gave them power, could run five miles without effort. The mask had tiny holes for eyes—you wonder how or if they could see out. It was so powerful—when they had it on, they didn't notice the tiny openings and said they could see real good, run fast, and jump over fences, etc.

My father said he wore it when he was younger—said it gave him power, speed, etc. Most of those Delawares my father's age probably wore it—John Falleaf probably was one. It was not the same one all the time. I think people knew who was wearing it. The purpose on the camp ground was to see that children were on good behavior and did not get into mischief.

There were women who had visions. They recited them and danced. At-ta-Home-mwe—Telling about your vision in song form. At first, they go slow, kind of walk, the leader with the turtle shell. The other part they go faster, almost like stomp.[16]

On the last night when they paint people was a special night—They really clean up, burn cedar, and smoke themselves. That's when the women take part. Another thing, women menstruating were not supposed to be in there; neither was anyone who was intoxicated.

On the last night they had some kind of red paint in a container. The Oshkosh put a dab on each person's cheek and on the hair part, and also on the Mising. It was all a part of the ceremony—there was no laughing, it was all strictly ceremony. Even the tiniest infant was painted. On the center pole, up high, I've seen the ones who had to paint the Mising have to jump up in order to put that paint on. Pekon, Olu-mun was what they call the paint. They made it—it was some kind of a dye Indians used to dye things.

The last day in there seemed strange after being in there every night and then to be in there in broad daylight. Everyone in their best clothes—shawls, etc.

---

16. Meaning that dancing during the second part of the circuit was done as fast as the Stomp Dance.

They line up and go outside single file, way out there. The prayer call as they say it, raise hand up and say Hooo. Not everyone says it, but when you hear them, you put your hand up. "We're going to pray now," the leader says. That say that Hooo twelve times and the ceremony is concluded. After that they break camp.

ANNA ANDERSON DAVIS

I[17] was seven or eight years old, and there hadn't been a meeting for quite a while when my grandfather William Brown had a council at our house. Quite a few people came, and they decided to try and have the meetings again. They would have to go and clean and repair the Big House; They said the roof was bad. We went and camped when they had this renovating. And, when it was finished, they just went right into the meeting.

That was my first time to attend, and it was during rainy weather, which made it kind of bad for the campers. Grandmother had made me a pallet on the ground inside the tent, and when the rain got so bad, she woke me up. They had made their bed from saw horses, so they were above ground.

Grandfather was one of the Oshkosh-suk.

It always seemed to me that the Big House faced north, but I know it faced east. The men sat on the north. It lasted twelve days and twelve nights. From there on, the next time I remember going, I was about ten years old. Grandfather again was an Oshkosh.

For several years I was away at school.

Some I remember who were Oshkosh besides grandfather are John Falleaf and John Jackson. Tum-meet-kat, or leader, I remember, was Jane Hill's father—he had an Indian name. Charlie Elkhair was his helper. The singers, Ta-lak-caw, were my father, Sam Anderson, and William Easy. Women I remember are Aunt Ora Spybuck, Caroline Longbone, and, I think, Aunt Minnie Fouts.

I was probably about fourteen years old the next time, and I know one time I was away at school. Grandfather went over there where they were getting ready for the meeting. When he was coming home his horse's leg was caught in a fence brace and grandfather was thrown off and his leg was broken. Then, I guess, that's the time they came after me,[18] so after that I went to country school.

The last time, I remember, my brother Buck was one of the Oshkosh and grandmother camped with him to do the cooking. It was bad that time too—it turned cold. Once before, when my daughter Annette was about three months old, it was so bad we only went for one evening or one night. The next time, she

---

17. The daughter of Sam Anderson and Josie Bullet Anderson, Anna, An-heh-now-quah, "All Woman," was born into the Turtle clan in Dewey, Oklahoma. Her narrative appears in Ruthe Jones (1973: 21–26).
18. At boarding school.

was about a year old, about 1919, I think, we went several nights. After that, my children were ill, etc., and really the last time I went was when Buck was Oshkosh.

Yes, I remember seeing Mising. In a way, when I think of it now, he was east of a side of a hill. That was probably where they kept his "dress;" the headgear, face, etc. One time we children were out playing on one side of this hill. He has a big gourd, and when he makes it rattle, it just sounded like it was right there! All at once we heard that rattle, and, of course, we all jumped and ran for camp just as hard as we could go! And, of course, the more he'd shake that rattle. And one time I fell down! Oh, I was so afraid, I could hardly get up.

I guess probably one reason for Mising, we thought, was to keep the children close to camp so we wouldn't wander off. Everybody was frightened. About every afternoon, probably just guessing, it was about three or four o'clock, he would come out in the camp area. We never could see where he went. It seemed like he'd just disappear. And of course they'd tell us, "You'd better watch," because we never knew where he was going to come from. Yes, I was afraid! He's alright when he's at camp, but I don't know what I'd do if I ever saw him away from camp. Everybody always had tobacco, bite size, you know, and he'd come and take it. I gave it to him lots of times. They always said you had to, so he wouldn't get mad at you.

It was fun going there, especially to see some of the kids. A lot of times that would be the only time we would see some for the whole year. And, if you missed, why then it would be two years. A lot of them came from Bartlesville, and we lived around Post Oak.[19] Unless we accidently met in Bartlesville, that was the only time we saw some of them.

We finally decided the Mising was someone who dressed up. In the later years we all called John Falleaf Uncle John. He always wore boots, and I recognized those boots. But, at the same time, when they got that bearskin shirt on and that face and that head covering—I never did notice how that was made, but it covered him up, and the hands were covered, the bearskin hung way down; you never could tell much about him. But, when he shook that rattle, it would just make you have shivers. I don't know of anyone else who wore it, but I do know he did.

I was there last summer,[20] but it just doesn't seem like the same place. I know it is because everyone says so, but it just doesn't look like it to me. We used to ford a stream in the old days to get there. Mr. Endicott bought that area for his home. He has recovered two of those faces and had them built into his house around the fireplace.

In the evenings the women and children would gather, make a line, and carry wood. The sticks were two and three feet long; some of us could only carry one at a time. One of the most beautiful sounds was when the women pounded corn—three or four of them together. The rhythm seemed like four-four time,

---

19. North of Dewey, Oklahoma.
20. In 1972.

and the longer they'd go the faster they'd go, until someone gave out. They all seemed to enjoy it, and liked to do it.

Grandmother and I made us a Ko-ha-kun. When I was younger I wasn't big enough to help, and when I got big enough to do it, why she quit making pounded corn. So, I never really learned how to do it—there's an art to it; you don't just start right in.

One time I remember Tom Halfmoon was an Oshkosh. He was hollering "Tum-meeka," and said "Ta-meek-quak," "Cut off you head," instead of "Come in." He sat on the northeast corner. Grandmother used to participate, but I never did. The leader and assistant would be first—sing the songs twelve times. Then the Oshkosh man and woman brush off that ground. The reason I heard for this was that these tracks made by that one who's just finished his song must not be stepped on by anyone.

[They] take the turtle shell rattle and pass it around until it got to someone who wanted to recite. "The spirit moved him." He would then go through this again, sing twelve times and sweep off again. The services last until the turtle got back to the leader, then the Oshkosh bring in the hominy and serve the two leaders first, then everyone who had stayed in.

You were not supposed to sleep or the Oshkosh will poke you with a stick and wake you up.

The women's night follows the same procedure. The services begin by the speaker coming in to announce, "This is the night for the women." I think they chose beforehand who would be first. Some I remember are Sari Thompson, Sally Falleaf, Rosie Frenchman, and, I think, Aunt Minnie Fouts and Mary Drum. There were some others I can't remember.

Sometimes the men would have a "prelude," tell how the song came to them. But, I don't think the women did—just sang. When dancing, just the one reciting and the two singers sang. He would sing once and then they would join in. The others were dancing but not singing. Aunt Rosie Frenchman told me when she decided to try it, her father told her to be sure and say her words plain, so the singers could catch them. The women wore the Delaware blouses, shawls, and moccasins on this night. Other times they might wear their ordinary clothes. Ray Gunn has a painting of this in the History Room of the Bartlesville Public Library, given by Mr. Endicott. Where they cook the meat at night, a cupboard-like, goes lengthwise with the door in front of the entrance and not crosswise.

The Spybuck painting is very accurate. Lula Gibson[21] wrote a very accurate day-to-day account of the Big House one time. She lived in Wichita at the time, so it may have been in the Kansas City paper, but it was quite a long time ago.

It used to make me mad to hear people say, "We're going to Christianize the Indians," or, "We need to Christianize the Indians." Well, we worshiped God. What

---

21. The Lula Mae Gibson Gilliland account appears in chapter 11.

would you do if someone came over and made you change over to the Indian way of life? How would you like it? Of course, some didn't want to change and retaliated, but still ...

ELIZABETH LONGBONE

The[22] most precious and sweetest memories of my life are of the Delaware Church. Our old people would sit around the wood fire and tell us of the days and the beginning of the Church located five miles west and two and one half miles northwest of Copan, Oklahoma.

When the Delawares were moved here from Kansas in 1866 they were about as poor, weary, and heartsick as any people could be. Many were dying. God sent a spirit to help them. They called him the Mesing. He appeared and began to tell them what they must do. His face was half red and half black. He wore clothes made from animal skins. He disappeared after he had accomplished his mission. Then the Delawares built the Church building and held services for about six months at the beginning. The Delawares made a false-face and clothes as much like the spirit as they could, and these were worn by one of the Delaware men who went about keeping order in the camp.

My father, Willie Longbone, was born a year after the Delawares came from Kansas, in 1867. The Church was held here until the Delawares began to scatter out. Then it was held in October each year for twelve days and twelve nights. The big log house always seemed to need repairs. I remember when new shingles were put on the roof. These were made by the Delawares, very large, nothing like shingles these days. And fresh mud was mixed to fill in the cracks between the logs. The dirt floor was packed firmly so that it could be swept more easily. The floor in the Church was always swept with a big turkey wing, so you can imagine much stooping-over was done in sweeping the Church.

I always like to be around old people and I listened when they told of many things. One time I heard one of my rich cousins say in a prayer meeting he was very sorry that he did not listen when his old people would try to tell him things. I was very sorry for my cousin, because I knew that he truly missed so much. It seems now children are always asking questions and want to know "why" about everything that one says.

To me, the Church was beautiful, and I just couldn't wait to serve in the Church. There were always things the children could do to help, like carrying hay in a blanket into the Church which was used to sit on. This was one of the happy times for the children. The workers would line up and we each would gather the hay from a big pile, each as much as we could carry in our blankets. We marched

---

22. The daughter of Anna and Willie Longbone and the sister of Jack Longbone (see note 24), Elizabeth, Weh-me-quah, was born in 1909. Her narrative appears in Ruthe Jones (1973: 37–44).

behind the workers in single file into the Church, placed our bundles just so far apart around the Church near the walls. The hay was scattered and patted down across the west door, which was never opened until the last days of the service.

Then there was the wood for the fires at night in the Church. We were more than glad to gather the wood from the wood pile at the east end of the Church yard. The children carried the wood each evening, which we did with joy in our hearts. The wood was cut in three foot lengths and stacked neatly by the door on the right side. The door was a "wagon sheet," [what] we called them in those days, and the men workers always helped the people to get through the door.

Our people always made the children feel that we were very much a part of the Church. The preparations lasted nearly two weeks; after this the Church grounds were a very busy place with people moving in every day making their camps comfortable for themselves. The camps were made to combat any kind of weather. I always thought my grandmother had the best camp. She always had two tents with the fire-place between the two where she cooked. My grandmother was Susan Elkhair, a very fine lady. She always told me to always remember that I was a lady no matter what because we came from a very fine family. My father always told me to learn with the white man because he is smart. I think he told me this because I had heard so many of our old people say, "The white man does not like us." My father did not want me to believe that. The white people were good to my father; he seemed to understand them and their ways. My father told me many good things, and I did listen and today I am glad that I did listen.

Sometimes it rained a lot, and camp-fires had to be protected so a fire could be started quickly to cook the morning meal. Each camp built a large cupboard high off the ground to keep pots and pans and things that were needed around the camp. Oh, how good everything tasted! Dutch-oven bread and pies were baked in Dutch-ovens, too. Our mother was a very good manager; she always canned vegetables and fruit, dried corn, and we always butchered our own hogs. Mother popped corn for us and always seemed to have apples to give us to eat around the camp-fire at night. We children always helped dry corn. The whole family had a part in this way of life.

Just before sun-down after the wood was carried for the Church, the children all gathered in a field north of the camps and there we played games. Oh, we had such fun! We were never allowed to play in the dark. Our people said a child would always get hurt if we disobeyed. My father told how once they had disobeyed and all of a sudden he noticed there was an extra child playing with them, and they could not recognize it. That scared them so much they never played in the dark again.

After the Church was put in order the services or ceremonies were ready to begin. The Osh-kosh-shuk, or workers, were three men and three women. Their camps[23] on the north side of the Church yard and the women were camped on the

---

23. Meaning the men's camps.

south side of the Church yard. They ate their meals on two small tables out in the Church yard to the south of the Church yard fire-place, perhaps to have fellowship and talk of their work. Each took their own plates from their own camps to these tables to eat.

The meat pole, which looked like a tree with limbs with all the bark peeled off, stood at the southeast corner of the Church yard. On the fourth day of the Church, the hunters would leave to go out for deer, wild turkey, rabbits, squirrel, or any game they could find. This seemed to be a sad day. My mother would cry, and I asked why. She said many times the hunters ran into other tribes that were unfriendly, and sometimes our hunters never returned. My father told me the Sioux were very unfriendly toward the Delawares at that time.

The corn pounder, Co-hawk-cun, stood at the northeast corner of the Church building where the women would go early on mornings to pound corn that was needed for the day. The pounders were very heavy, and you had to be alert and strong to do this or you would get hit on the head or hands. It took two pounders to get corn ready faster. Mother said, "You should have seen six or eight women pound corn at once." She said they sounded wonderful, and you could hear them from a long way off.

I never attended many services when I was about four years old because I would be asleep at ten o'clock at night when one of the men Oshkosh called out over the camp, Toe-me-keck, for the people to go in the Church. The singers would wake me up, and I would just drop off to sleep again. Many a night I would awake in my fine ruffled dress with the pretty sash on it so disappointed.

When I grew older I could stay up and go into the Church. We were never allowed to sleep in the Church, the workers would watch and come over and poke us with the long pole they used to stir the fire with. The leader or preacher would talk a long time about the conditions around us, and how God wanted us to help and be good to one another. And about the crops and how thankful we should be for all these good things God gave us.

The two singers and drummers sat across from the preacher on the south side near the center. After the sermon, the men that had visions and times when God helped them through; many times it was sickness or when God gave them great power to do something they wanted very much to do. These things they told about as they held a turtle shell which they shook after a sentence or two. He walks around the east fire as he talks of his visions or help from God. Several other men follow, and the women follow the men around the fire.

There were two fire-places, one on the west end. I remember Joe Washington telling his vision. Then they start dancing and the singers beat on the drum and sing with the man, Joe or whoever it may be. This is called Ah-the-hom-mee. When Joe finished, another would start—in the early days there were many, and the services lasted until two a.m. or later. The singers were Willie Longbone, Jake Parks, Sam Anderson, and William Easy. These served as they were needed. My step-grandfather was the leader or preacher. Then later my uncle Frank Wilson led the Church. Willie Longbone and Frank Wilson served as the preachers for the Delawares for many years. They preached at funerals and served where they were needed.

We had to sit in places where our clan sat in the Church. If our mother was of one clan and our father another, we could sit in two different areas in the Church. The clans were Wolf, Took-seet, Turtle, Puk-kah-wung-ah-me, and Bird, Pleah. The drum was made out of a deer hide, just dried with the fur still on it, hay, small rope, four beautifully carved sticks about thirty-six inches long, three inches wide, sanded down smooth and shiny. The drum sticks were about eighteen inches long, with half red and half black faces carved on the ends. The middle posts in the Church were very large, carved square-like, with the half red and half black faces carved on the east side up high and on the west side. Each log that braced the building on the sides had smaller faces carved on them, too.

One of the women, Ora Spybuck, became ill one night, and I asked to serve in her place—she was one of the Oshkosh. It was decided that it would be all right, even though I was very young, only fourteen years old. No one, only God, knows the joy I felt in my heart as I served in this good woman's place. She had served twelve years in this place, which was considered the time one must serve in the Church to be assured of a place in heaven.

The workers were allowed to make soup, chili, pies, and coffee to sell at their camps to make money for the Church. It was such fun to go to these camps at night and buy this food to enjoy and know we were helping the Church, too.

The last time the Church was held in the Big House was in 1924. The old people decided young men must be chosen to be the workers so the Church could go on. My brother Emmett Longbone, Freddie Washington, son of Joe, and Buck Toney, three of our finest young men of the tribe, were chosen. One time since then, during the war in 1941, Minnie Fouts decided to have Church at her home in a tent to pray like we did in the days of the Big House. We attended this little service for twelve nights and God was with us. Conditions around the world became better. No matter where we are or how small we are, God hears us when we turn to him with all our hearts and soul. As Mrs. Fouts said, much was accomplished when we prayed and did the best we could with what we had. Bless her dear heart, she was so sweet and kind—everyone loved her.

The last day was carried out just the way it always was at the Big House. The women all worked together and cooked the meat, corn, and fried bread on an outside fire. Many brought food to help out so there was plenty of food for everybody. After the services and everyone had eaten, everybody lined up on the east side of the big yard. The leaders were on the south end, and the children on down toward the north end. The leader said the word *Oh*, and the people repeated it after him twelve times. Then the word *Ahh* was called out twelve times, each time repeated by the group on down the line. This word, *Ahh*, always seemed so funny to the children; it was hard to keep from laughing out loud.

The women always had a part in the visions and testimonies on the last night and the morning of the last day. Pow-lee-now Blackwing was one of the women I remembered. Eliza Peterson was one that took part, and Sarah Thompson was very good in this way, too.

The ceremonies were over by one o'clock on the last day, and everyone was sad because now they must pack and get ready to leave to go to their home. It had been such a happy time at the Church, and the Delawares thought of the wonderful blessings God had bestowed upon us during these days here. We had to travel slow in our wagons trying to get home before dark. And once again, God was pleased with his poor people, the Delaware.

JACK LONGBONE

Big[24] House had two doors, one on the west was closed all the time, one on the east they use. Got a big post in the middle, on each side got the false faces, two of them. Call them Mising. Painted read and black. Three posts on each side.

They don't use nails. Last one used clap bards for shingles, got so they bought nails and used them. It's made of shingles—got long ridge poles. On inside, cut a Mising face on each one of the poles—be ten little ones and two big ones. Twelve was their main number—what they went by. Twelve nights, twelve everything.

I was around there when they built the second one. My dad, mother, and all went up there. Sam White was one who helped make that house—was a good carpenter. George Washington, Jim McCartlin, Jake Parks, Ben Hill, William Easy, Julius Fouts. He never much directed lot of them; he just kind of stood by.

Three men guarded the place all the time. They slept inside that house at night—all the men and boys. I slept in there, had a good bed in there. Lot of the old people slept out in their tents. There were lots of old people in those days.

I remember the fire. They made that twice during the twelve nights. They make it with a bow—has buckskin strings on it—got a cross bow on it. Wrap the buckskin around there. They put a hard piece of wood down, and that long spear-looking thing, it goes real fast, but you have to work the bow. The Oshkosh does this. Then it starts smoking, they blow on that—makes fire. I remember Jim McCartlin was pretty good at that. Jim Parks was a helper. They used that fire eight nights.

It used to change hands every year. Tum-meet-kat, man that leads it, means he took it up. Uncle Frank Wilson, Joe Washington, Ben Hill, Charlie Elkhair. Sits there with the man who took it up, he was speaker there, done all the speaking, talking, praying. The old man who took it up, he would start. The meeting house sets east and west; they go around and start from south.

---

24. Jack Longbone, Pe-me-ah-queh, "Echo," was born in Dewey, Oklahoma, in 1905. A fluent Delaware speaker, he was the son of William Longbone and the brother of Elizabeth West, née Longbone. His narrative appears in Ruthe Jones (1973: 45–50).

Sometimes Joe Washington took it up, Tum-meet-kat. Where they start, man who took it up, he sings first, got his own song, you know; vision song. I used to know George Falleaf's and Ben Hill's songs. But you forget them when you don't hear them anymore. Ben Hill had two songs, Wen-ge-kuna.

Turtle shell goes, travels clear around. When the turtle shell gets back here[25] it's over then; they stop for the night.

Now those songs, sent out as a small boy by their parents to experience these things. When I was a small boy, my folks took me out, hills somewhere, left me. That's the way they start out. They believed they were all alone, but all the time someone from their family was near by, kind of watch out for them. They don't know this. They're afraid, animals out there, they get hungry. Nothing to eat but wild things, berries, etc. That's when they have a vision, something or someone might come to them, give them a message same time they give them that song.

My father, he went out like that. His what came to him and gave him the [power. The one] he talked about as the morning star. He told me about that. Told him not to be afraid, but he never did use it. He was always a singer, Ta-lak-caw. William Easy, he's a Ta-lak-caw, and my father he always sits there.

Tom Halfmoon, he was one Oshkosh. He sold chili and stuff, candy, like a store. They had a right to do that, you know. Got to calling him Chili Tom. They have three men and three women called Oshkosh. Do all the work. Men get the wood, the women do all the cooking. Have a place out there in front of the meeting house where they eat.

On the fourth day they went deer hunting. Towards the last, they never went; there was no deer. They'd be gone four days. Go out in the hills. They kill a deer they'd send somebody in with it. They had a pole east of the Big House, hang that deer meat on there. Had lots of hooks on it; a tree with limbs cut off sharp. I used to know the songs, but not now. If I could hear it just a little I could sing them, but right now I can't recall them. Can't remember the names of the hunters. My father used to go when he was younger. They sing those songs when they start off.

Toward the last every day was for something. On the eleventh night, women did their part; call it At-ta-home-mwe. There several women got that, vision they call it. Old Lady Spybuck, Sarah Thompson, and, towards the last, Jane Washington—several ladies. Had their own songs. They'd start out, lining up outside—you could hear them. Minnie Fouts was one. They'd say He- He-Ho-Way, or something like that, and they'd come in. They'd take that turtle. Seemed like Minnie Fouts was a leader among them, and William Easy's mother—had an Indian name, no English name, she that. Also Old Lady Pow-le-na Blackwing, grandmother to Rosie Shull, and Old Lady Peterson. I think Rosie Frenchman tried that one time.

---

25. To the leader.

On certain night they paint everybody. The old ladies, they get [paint] over in the hills. While they're singing the songs they go around and put some paint on everybody.

During the day those Oshkosh sing some songs, they cut these K'ak right in front of that center post, on the ground there. They cut the strings, the men on one side, the women Oshkosh on the other. While they sing some songs, they're supposed to cut beads. When they do that they put them in their mouth and make a noise, M-m-m-m—Delaware word means like you're picking up something. My beads, I got them from my folks. I've got about five yards. They were at the Woolaroc Museum,[26] but I keep them in the bank now. I go and take them out and look at them sometime. The drummers, they gave them a yard toward the end. They lay it there in front of them. White people call it wampum. Indians don't call it that; it's K'ak.

Mising, I've seen him. Had on that hide, bear I guess, and moccasins. Face was painted black and red. We were all afraid of him. They didn't allow noise around there, you know. He'd get after you. He sleeps out somewhere. If you see him you'd better have some tobacco, give it to him—he'll rough you up. He's a bad-looking old fellow. I was afraid of him. I gave him tobacco. He wanted Indian tobacco. He smokes quite a bit, I guess.

Towards the last, a U.S. Marshall came out to guard the place. Some drunks try to come around. They're supposed to stay away, don't come back for six days, but some tried to break the rules. They got pretty strict. John Brown was the U.S. Marshall they finally got. Us kids used to like to look at his gun. No one wore guns except the Marshall, [except] on the fourth day when they went hunting.

They wouldn't allow white people inside that Church. One night, I remember, my eldest brother Ray was an Oshkosh, the third one, I believe. He was married to a red-haired white woman. His wife wouldn't go. She knew they didn't want white people in there. One night toward the end she decided to go in. I was sitting by the drum; my dad was there. She came in, had a shawl on, and sat over on the northeast corner with the men. The clans had certain places to sit and they hardly ever let them mix up. Old Lady Falleaf had good eyes. She saw that hair. She stood up and grabbed her shawl and blankets. She talked Delaware and said, "This place is going to be taken over by white people. I see one white woman sitting right over there." She was mad and got all her things and went out, stopping by the door to tell her husband George, "Come on, let's go—these white people are taking everything." They went out and pretty soon Old Lady Beaver got up and did the same thing, and some others.

These fellows began talking, Ben Hill, Joe Washington, George Washington, and the Old Man Beaver—he didn't go out. These old ladies went out and told their husbands, "Let's go." They had to obey, you know. After they went out, the men

---

26. The Woolaroc Museum is located just southwest of Bartlesville.

talked it over awhile. Finally went ahead and started. That was about the seventh night.

One thing, they just ran out of people, the old people passed on. There were just not enough to take it on. Young ones did not know what it's all about. They were awful strict. People just broke in there when they didn't have it anymore. I don't know what became of it; they just took it off log by log, I guess.

About 1945 [they had it] at Minnie Fouts in a tent. They [did] alright. Tried to do the same thing up there. All sat around, danced, Wen-ge-kune. Joe Washington sang—Jake Parks sang. They had it about twice out there. Tom Halfmoon was there. Didn't camp, but went back and forth. A few people stayed out there. Still had the K'ak hanging up there like they're supposed to. They used them, but they had to give them back. They had three Oshkosh.

FANNIE MCCARTLIN

My[27] mother died when I was three months old, and my father, George Bullet, took me to live with my aunt and uncle Minnie and Julius Fouts at Post Oak north of Dewey. At that time, I was given the Delaware name I have now. They say before that I had another name at Alluwe.[28]

We used to go and camp. They'd clean that house [of] spider webs and sweep. Then they'd put down new hay all around. I used to like to go camp there, and one thing, I tell you, you never caught a cold when you went there. The only thing; there was a lot of smoke. It got into your eye and in your clothes.

At one time I kept all the names of the Ush-kos down on paper and the dates, etc., but it was misplaced. They [had] six Ush-kos, three men and three women. The head one, the next, and the next. Each is a different clan. The head one would be in the head tent. Old Man Elkhair always camped on the south end of the house. Aunt Minnie was usually one of the Ush-kos. I remember one time she was head and the next time we were at the last tent. We camped next to Aunt Rosie Parks. Those Ush-kosh have to be on the job, especially if they had corn to pound. Three of the women could do that at once. In our family, we have three pestles or pounders, and one Kohokan that we used to take over there to use, but they had their own that belonged to the Church. There is an art to that. You have to hold it just right or you'll get blisters. At certain times they sprinkle a little water on the corn as they're pounding it.

Mising-a-sa-pon is something they made. After the flour was made, roast that corn and what comes off will be brown; boil and sweeten it.

---

27. Fannie McCartlin was born into the Wolf clan at Alluwe, Oklahoma, on April 18, 1903. She was given the name Willis-ta-quah, "Something Like A Whirlwind," after her father, George Bullet, took her to live with her Aunt Minnie and Uncle Julius Fouts in Post Oak when her mother died three months after giving birth to her. Mrs. McCartlin's narrative appears in Ruthe Jones (1973: 51–58).
28. Alluwe is a Delaware community located about thirty miles east of Bartlesville, Oklahoma.

At night they did not start until about nine o'clock. The head Ush-kos had pie, chili, etc., to sell. And that money helped buy the meat. You could pay with bead, and sometimes you have to donate beads.

At night they have to get wood. They have two fires to keep going. The head man Ush-kos had a long stick or poker. If someone sleeps, he punches them. If the drummer or someone sees you sleep, not just kids but grown-ups, too, he'll holler, "Ush-kos!" And he'll go over there and punch them. And you can't cross just anywhere; you have to go around the fire. They sit still so long some old people just drop off to sleep. You're not supposed to be talking in there either.

Also, you have to know what clan you are. Our clan sat on the first door as you come in near the drummers. A long time ago they used to be Sam Anderson and Willie Longbone. That drum was a folded hide with the hair still on it to the inside. Two sticks go across the top tied on and two underneath. That had two not exactly forked sticks to beat that; drumsticks, I guess. Everyone who sings has his own song.

Each dancer had his own song. They're not made up. They're gifted to them. A long time ago, they said you're not supposed to treat your kids nice; kind of be a little mean to them. White people would say you don't coddle your kids. Old Indians believed if you treat a child too good, think too much of it, something will happen to that child—he'll die. That's why people don't go all out for their child; don't try to dress them up, maybe get ahead of everyone else. My aunt used to say, "You know we have mean people in our tribe. Something will happen to that child—it'll die; they might do something to it."

A long time ago they used to take the kids out, boys, and turn them loose somewhere—maybe out in the timber. These kids out in the woods would be scared. Anyone would be afraid left out in the timber by themselves. Maybe something will come along and help them take care of them. And this is where the songs come from.

After each singer is finished, the Oshkosh man and woman sweep toward the fire. They use a turkey wing instead of a broom. I saw my aunt do that. I think the wings are part of the Church things; they belong there. They keep them above the door and get new ones every year.

They do not allow girls or women inside the house during their menstrual period. They say you ruin that.[29] On the outside of the house were carved the outline of faces with crosses for eyes. I've seen it, and my father fixed that house. Instead of boards, they cut them themselves—made them thin. And the poles, too—they tried to get them all the same width. My dad used to make miniatures of the Big House for sale. We don't call it long-house; that's from the east. Delawares don't have such a thing. It always was Big House, Hi-ngwikan.

---

29. Meaning that menstrual women ruin spirit power.

My father, George Bullet, was one who helped make the carvings. We don't go there when the men work, so I don't know.[30] They all worked together, and all the faces looked pretty much alike. They were carved and then painted red and black. I can't remember which side was which. They never let the meeting house go without someone in there. There had to be someone in there all the time and never let the fires die; sometimes it gets pretty warm in there. After the meeting, the men and boys can go in there and sleep.

Whoever was Mising put on a hide and a Mising face. When he comes in, a lot of kids are scared. If he comes to your tent you're supposed to give tobacco or beads. But oh, we were afraid of it! Nowadays, I guess kids would just knock him down and maybe pull his clothes off. I never gave him tobacco. I was usually by myself. He would holler and shake a turtle shell rattle. Some people add a little more; I don't think it's true. They said he had big pockets with snakes in them. "He'll put you in those big pockets," they'd say, I think, just to scare the kids. I never knew who was under there. No one would tell. Even horses would get scared. All they had to do was say "Mising," and that's it; everybody would quiet down and beat it home. In later years they didn't have Mising. I never did know who put that suit on, but you had to give him something.

They used to pick so many men to go hunting. In those days you could get deer. Later on, deer got scarce, but they got what they could; squirrel, rabbit, etc., anything wild. I've heard of wild turkey, but I've never seen one. If they got a deer, they cleaned it out front by the tree with sharpened branches to hang things on.[31] They also had what nowadays they'd call a little arbor, where they kept the cooked food. They put things in there the day they cook, maybe a big pot of corn and meat if they have it. They may have had to buy beef, or back then everyone had hogs, and it wouldn't be anything to kill one and take it up there.

I used to know everyone's Delaware name. They call those names at night, and you've got to answer. Makes no difference if you're outside in the tent. You have to answer, come in, and get those beads.[32] If the person isn't inside, the Oshkosh goes outside and hollers until they find him. They might have to go to the tent and wake him.

Those beads or K'ak were worth at that time one dollar a yard. Every night they break one of those [strings] and put it on the ground. And, at a certain time, all those Oshkosh go up there. They pick up those beads and put them in their mouth. While they're doing this they make a funny sound. As much as you can get in your mouth, why that's yours to keep. You can do anything you want with it; sell it or trade it or whatever. When they get a yard they can string it up. Oh, some of them just shove each others hands away; they have fun out of it!

---

30. Meaning that women did not visit men at work at the Big House and therefore did not know who did what.
31. I.e., the meat or game pole.
32. I.e., K'ak, or wampum beads.

That's our religion, you know, those beads. You can't get them anymore. Some are white and some are blue. I've got a few beads, some baskets that my aunt made, and some moccasins she made. You had to know how to use those baskets. They get out where the wind is blowing and get all the hulls off the corn with a kind of throwing motion.[33]

When they made that fire they didn't use matches. My uncle had that thing; fire drill they call it. They put down some little twigs and run so fast that pretty soon there'll be smoke. They blow on that, and when it makes sparks they put twigs or dry grass on there and you'll have fire. Nowadays they call it friction, I guess. I've seen him do it many times. Just the men do that.

On a certain day they take all the old hay out in back and lay it there. They don't burn it. They clean everything out. On the last night they won't have a fire. They take everything out and leave only bare ground and put new hay all over that. Also, the last night when they use that drum, they take it all apart; take that hay out. That's when they take the hay and fire outside, and that's the only time they use that west door. A long time ago it was made of wood shingles. They had to use wood and make a door. Before that they didn't use nails either. The poles were notched and fit together.

My aunt and two Oshkosh go out and look for roots to make that red paint. It's a little plant, and she said they would look and look maybe half a day and pretty soon there it is. When they go out they don't eat. They put it in a Kohokan and they had two little bark dishes that looked like canoes. They put that in there with a little grease, I think. I don't really know, because we're not supposed to watch them. They paint everyone in there and those faces. And when you get that on I mean it stays on. They paint where your hair is parted and your cheeks. Someone would have to help them when they paint that big one on the center pole. The men would cup their hands to step up there it's so high.

We went from here.[34] I used to see Mary Big John and Nannie Ellis. Us three were in the same clan and sit together. Sometimes Nannie's grandmother might bring something like grapes for us to keep awake. I saw your grandmother, my Aunt Nancy Parks, and your mother, and Ruth and Edith [Parks]. Also Roy and Jesse Longbone and their mother Caroline and others. Sometimes I didn't go in, but my aunt always went in.

You can't make noise at the camps either. They used to tell us kids not to play outside at night even at home. Something will happen to you; your mouth might go to one side.[35]

The hardest thing the women Oshkosh had to do was find the root to make that paint and pounding corn. They have to find that paint. They pray before they go out and they don't eat until they come back. Those are hard jobs to do.

---

33. A flat winnowing basket.
34. I.e., Post Oak.
35. Perhaps a reference to palsy or paralysis caused by an encounter with a spirit.

Some that sang were Frank Wilson, Tom Anderson, Charley Elkhair, and Joe Washington. They were gifted for that. There were others that I can't think of. Everyone wore their regular clothes and the women wore shawls. On the last day everyone dressed up. Even women who didn't wear shawls all the time would put them on. The men who had them wore blankets and ones who had moccasins wore them.

Long years ago the men wore shawls around their bodies when they war-danced. Delaware women shouldn't carry a shawl over the arm with the costume. They carry a fan or tulip bag,[36] but not the shawl over the arm. On the last day, I think, some eat inside the house. Everyone goes outside and they line up and someone starts the prayer and it goes down the line.

They had it here just south of the yard a couple of times in the 1940's. I don't remember exactly when it was. I stayed here in the house most of the time. It was more like a common Church service; not exactly like the Big House. There were not enough of us to have Oshkosh, etc. There were a few dancers; Frank Wilson, I think, and Ben Hill and Old Man Elkhair—he was the leader.

Ben Hill was living then, and Charley Webber stayed here. He fixed up an arbor-like thing out of poles and canvas. They had one fire. There was hay on the ground and they brought blankets. One thing; they never used stools or benches. We furnished the wood, and it kept it warm in there. Seems like it was always lucky, even up there, in Copan, it didn't rain.

A few would have supper here, but most ate before they came. On the last day seems like they would try to have deer. One time I think they did have it. Everyone brought something [to eat] and put it all together, not like long time ago. Minnie Taxton and kids, Sally Falleaf and kids were there. John Falleaf, Ollie Anderson and some of her kids, John Anderson and his boys, Andrew and Kurt are the Longbones, especially Willie and his family, and Frank Wilson's family. Some folks stayed with us, but most went home and came back the next evening. Anna Davis was another one who came. They tried to carry on the songs and they danced.

WILLIAM (BILL) SHAWNEE

Went[37] to a few meetings of the Delaware Big House with my folks. They have it every fall. I began learning those songs, and grandmother heard me singing them around the house. "You ought not do that," she said. "It's our ceremony, Delaware

---

36. A deerhide purse carried by women, usually made of six segments which, when the purse is open, give the appearance of a tulip. It is decorated with beadwork and has long fringes with glass beads on them (James Rementer 2001: personal communication).
37. Born on January 6, 1902, William Shawnee, Ah-khe-no, "Measure or Measurement; Something Like An Equal Amount," was of mixed Delaware and Shawnee ancestry. He was a member of the Delaware Wolf clan. A highly regarded speaker at funerals, feasts, and dances held by both tribes, he was also an accomplished singer. His narrative appears in Ruthe Jones (1973: 59–62).

ceremonial way. It's not to be made fun of; we highly respect it." She said I might learn those songs and then, "First thing you know, people will be talking about you. Whether you are or not.[38] They might think you're making a mockery out of it—making fun. So best thing, just don't do it at all." So right then I quit. That discouraged me, but I figured she knows what she's talking about. I went a few times after that.

Ones I remember are George Falleaf, Ben Hill, Charlie Elkhair, Joe Washington, Old Man Fouts, Jake Parks. My grandmother was one of the main ones. La-tai-ah-quah, or Nancy Cedar, was her name. She was one of the Oshkosh; helped with the cooking and sweeping inside the Big House with turkey wing. Mother just went along.

We wore our regular clothes. As a kid I don't remember them telling me anything. Grandmother always wore moccasins and handkerchief. They had it every fall, but at the end it seems like they skipped a year or so. There was a lot of talking, praying, is about all I could say. The leader uses a turtle shell. It has a buckskin string and you put two fingers through it. They rattle that when they dance. They only use one turtle. There was one "set". Turtle, sticks, etc.—they use all that. When one gets through with the turtle they pass it on.

The clans sit at certain places. My clan sat on the north side near the singers. Every time they got through dancing the people shake hands with them. Then another begins, and they do the same thing. They do a lot of praying in there. Indian people believe in prayer. Also we're noted for being "psychic." We can "see things."

Inside there we sat on the ground on hay. Put a blanket down, same way as in teepee. The drum they use is different from others. They use a whole deer hide, shape it, and about twelve to fourteen inches wide. It is folded with the hair on the inside, filled with hay and sticks laid on top and all tied together. During the first part of the meeting they use "common sticks." Toward the last they use special forked sticks, about one and one-half inches wide with a little Mising carved on them. The drum has a keen sound to it, pretty loud and flat. One time I tried to make one of those drumsticks. Grandma caught me and made me cut it up.

The word for the singers is Ta-lak-caw. Some people say it means crane and they call them "cranes." It means brants; the word for crane is Chun-ques.

About the hunt; they cut down a tree for the game pole. This is where they hang deer meat when the hunters [return]. There was a certain way they used to come in, but I've forgotten. During the time the hunters are gone, during the day, they used to sing. They were practicing, I guess.

We used to have wampum. Don't know what happened to it; misplaced it, I guess. They scatter those beads on there loose; they call that "killing fleas." The Oshkosh get down on their knees making a mumbling noise, pick them up, and

---

38. An actual vision singer.

put them in their mouths. Also during the ceremony they have a rest period. They stop awhile, and you can smoke. They had a pouch of tobacco and a certain kind of long pipe. When they get through with that they start again.

I remember seeing Mising. I was afraid of that. It was a scary-looking thing. Scared the dogs and even the horses. Everyone would run in the tents and [children] under the beds. Grandma gave me a piece of tobacco. I was supposed to keep it with me and give it to him, but I was afraid of it. I used to run to her lap and put my head down in her apron. One time, when I was older, he came and a kid always notices things. As I looked down at that Mising, he was wearing cowboy boots. After he left, I said, "Grandma." "What?" "Grandpa must be a cowboy." "Ahhh," she said. We always call that thing Grandpa. We're talking Delaware all the time.

I knew it was somebody dressed up, one of the guys around here. But we didn't ask questions. We were not to be too nosy. We respect that. They kept it away from us and we knew better than to ask questions. That's one way [children] are different nowadays. I kind of differ from the old people there. We could have learned more, maybe have more left today.

There was a certain day for Mising. He danced and they all danced with him. In a way the Seneca things remind me of the Big House, but not too much. They have the false face.

I do know a few of the songs yet.

IRENE ANDERSON TIGER

I[39] was born and raised in Dewey, Oklahoma, and as a child I always attended the meetings of the Delaware Big House with my parents. They were held regularly in the fall of the year. I remember because I always had to be absent from school for approximately two weeks every year. I hated to miss that much school because I knew it would be hard to make up the work. But we always took the excuse and since it was for Church, sacred to us and we had to go and camp. I never got the feeling of being made fun of by the teacher. But of the attitude of the others I don't know because we never talked about it.

We went and camped there with the rest of the Delawares. We always went in a wagon or horse and buggy. We took all of our camping equipment, dishes, bedding, and supplies. There were two rows of camps facing each other in front of the Big House where the Oshkosh stayed. My father always helped in the meeting house, or all the way around. He was an Oshkosh, and my mother did the cooking.

At the last meeting we camped on the north row on the side of the meeting house. It was very cold and beginning to turn fall. Some nights my mother would

---

39. Irene Tiger, Ala-mah-liquah, "Going Away Woman," was the daughter of Ollie and Tom Anderson. A member of the Wolf clan, she was a fluent Delaware speaker. Her narrative appears in Ruthe Jones (1973: 63–67).

put coals from the fire in a bucket and bring them into the tent for us children. I remember getting up early in the mornings and having to wash my face in cold water.

My father and the other Oshkosh ate inside the Big House. My mother helped cook the food and we helped take it in. A typical meal might be potatoes, coffee, beans, bread, and corn. The bread was Dutch-oven bread baked by placing coals on the lid. Sometimes fry bread, but usually Dutch-oven bread was served. Large bowls and not cups were used for coffee, and the plates were soup plates, what we call Indian plates.

The Longbones always camped. Frank Wilson camped right down the row from us about three camps down. Across the way on the south side and down on the end I remember the camp of Jake Parks because it was always so neat and cozy. They made it snug by putting a tarp or wagon sheet around the front of the camp to keep out the wind and it was always very neat. Some families camped year after year in the same place. If a person was an Oshkosh they camped there in the rows in front of the Big House. I do remember several times camping in the back when my parents were attending and did not have special jobs.

The grounds were always cleaned off bare around the Big House. We used to help carry wood in the evenings, and we were never permitted to play around the Big House. We had to go out away from the grounds to play. Our parents never allowed us to play there because it was a place where we prayed in our ceremony. It was sacred, so we never played there.

Our parents always cautioned us at night if we went inside we had to stay awake, be quiet, and sit up. Also, you couldn't come out anytime you want. There were certain times when you could come out. We always had to think about these things and make up our minds if we were going to go in there, to sit still and stay up regardless if we got sleepy.

Inside they had hay for us to sit on. We wore our everyday clothes and never dressed up or had a particular costume. The ones who danced, I remember seeing them wearing moccasins. I remember the inside very well. On each pole inside were the carved Mising faces painted black and red. The ones on the side were smaller. The center pole was large with two faces carved on it. Also, the little drumsticks had the Mising face carved on them. We never got to look at them because they were kept on the drum when not in use.

The men prayed in Delaware; they did not talk English. Frank Wilson, Ben Hill, and Old Man Elkhair always did the singing and probably others, but I remember those men. They always sang with the turtle shell rattle. They had their own songs. Each one was different. They led the dance.

A song I remember was Mr. Elkhair's! This is the interpretation as it was in Delaware. Apparently from his experiences when he was younger, as a boy he was in a storm, maybe a tornado. He could hear things, the wind and all. Also Frank Wilson's song. One part of the song he said he saw a person out in the woods. These were visions. When they were small they were taken out and they would see these things. So the things they sang about were what they had seen; something or someone came to them and gave them a message. The way it was explained to me was that these things gave them "power."

The drum I will never forget. It was different from any you see today. It was hide with hay in it, with sticks across it to hold it in place and a rope around it. They would beat on it and then go right into the beat of the songs.

The dancing was single file around the fire. Of the women who sang I remember Minnie Fouts and some older ones I can't recall by name. They all wore long dresses, handkerchiefs, and moccasins when they danced. The only dance which is similar, but never did remind me of the Delaware ceremony, are the ones at White Oak.[40] They dance in single file and use the turtle. I think the same family or the man who is singing owned these turtles. Probably each man who sang had his own turtle.

The wampum beads were used as compensation. When my mother brought the dishes back from the Big House after each meal there were always three or four beads in the bottom of the coffee cups. That was the way we got the beads, and we would clean them and string them. Eventually we would have quite a lot. We ended up with very few. Usually you would have to give them back in payment to someone else. Right now in our family we have a string of beads that my dad fixed. There are a few odd beads and some wampum. Our daughter wears them with her costume.

After each dance the women Oshkosh sweep the dance area with a turkey wing. They had doormen who stood by the door, took care of the door. I remember they had to stand up all during the ceremony. The paint was made from herbs. My father had a dish. It was a little container five or six inches long, made of bark tied on either end. It almost resembled a little canoe. They put the paint in there. I never saw them make the paint, but I remember it was pretty red. I think different ones probably made it, and not the same ones.

There was probably not one certain reason the Big House Ceremony was stopped. It wasn't an easy thing to do every year. I was small at the time and didn't understand a lot of things. Some things which stand out in my mind about the Big House were how clean the grounds always were, and the men who sat on the north side, those who prayed and sang. I can see them now standing in single file, the leader with the turtle shell, shakes it as he sings and begins to dance. And the faces all around. Those are the things that stand out in my mind.

I never saw the Mising. It was before my time. Our mother used to tell us about it. It was a masked figure in a costume. It carried a stick and looked like a bear. She said people were really frightened, and that all they had to do was just mention it and the children would go into their camps they were so frightened. He would go around and they'd see him coming and everyone would run and be quiet then. She said even the dogs were afraid. I've seen the pictures, but I never saw one.

---

40. A Shawnee community in Craig County near Vinita, Oklahoma.

All through this, Hi'ngwikan is what we always called it whenever we spoke of it. It is only recently that it has come to be called Big House.

NANCY FALLEAF SUMPTER

A Visit to the Meeting House, 1930

The[41] Meeting House, sometimes called the "Big House," was a big log structure located northwest of Copan, Oklahoma. It was used years ago as a ceremonial house for the Delaware tribe. I wanted to put this story together while I can still recall how I felt on seeing it for the first and last time.

One warm Sunday afternoon in the fall of 1930, the family and our "company" decided to drive to the old Meeting House. Rumors were that the roof was falling in and the interior posts were being defaced and ruined. The reports were getting worse, the blame being put on Boy Scouts who would camp there on weekends, leaving their debris, hacking on the corner and center posts, and carving their initials. Fires were built and the remnants scattered throughout the area inside.

This kind of news was distressing to our folks, so with Aunt Rosa [Frenchman], Uncle Dennis Frenchman, Joe, Fred, and Jane Washington, Mom, Dad, Mona, and myself, we traveled in three cars to the wooded site. There in a cleared section sat the long log house, roof sagging, but the sides appeared fairly strong. Entering through the eastern door (Mona and I followed last) we were all stricken by the damage within the large sacred room. Now that I am older I realize how sick at heart my people must have felt.

They spoke softly to each other in Delaware. Neither Mona or I could understand, but the hushed tones and inflections of the conversation conveyed to us how shocked and hurt they were. They walked all around the inside area. I don't remember anyone touching anything, they just slowly walked and looked upon all the damage to all that they once held in reverence. This was once their strength, their healing, their hold on nature and spirit. They were probably remembering the times they gathered here to pray, to sing and dance—mentally going through each step of the ceremony, seeing faces of those long departed, remembering songs no longer sung and the sound of the drum and the turtle rattles. They must have known in their hearts that this was all leaving them and it would be final when the old logs fell, crumbled, and decayed. The littered floor, once swept clean with turkey wings, the dancers, the elders speaking of visions and spiritual messages, were now like distant echoes—lonely echoes.

---

41. In the prefatory note to her publication of this account (Sumpter 1994: 60), Mrs. Sumpter wrote: "I've written this story from notes I had jotted down after seeing a picture of the Meeting House painted by Geneva Howard and given to my brother Numerous Falleaf in the 1960's. It reminded me of the time I saw this house in disrepair, and even as a young girl I felt sad for the older ones. I knew the purpose for the House, that it was a spiritual place, but I was much too young to see and know about the ceremonies that had been held there."

They walked outside and over the old campgrounds, now overgrown with weeds, probably recalling the happy faces and friendly handshakes. What good times they must have had. It was Delaware meeting Delaware in joyous reunion.

It was a quiet ride home in our car. Mom and Dad were deep in their own thoughts of what they had seen. The sight was sad for Mona and me, and we were then unaware of the ceremonial rites performed there. Now I can almost feel the impact of the terrible wounding, in knowing they never again would travel that old road back to the Meeting House. (None of our family ever returned.)

Years later we asked why the Delaware people did not remove the posts and faces while they were still standing. Why didn't they save what they could before all was burned, either intentionally or by accident. They told us the Meeting House must stand intact until it fell and decayed. Since it was not used as a ceremonial house any longer it would crumble and decay in its time; nothing must be removed. The old people were gone, the songs unsung, the prayer sticks and rattles put away, and the drum silenced. No spirals of smoke rise from the roof now, no aroma of cooked meat, and no stories of visions and good dreams.

The Delawares stayed away, but the ever-reaching hand of the white man removed the carved red and black faces, the posts, and even the old logs that could be salvaged. The supporting posts were removed and the walls crumbled and fell—and the Delaware people grew weaker.

Stories among Delaware elders are that the Meeting House must never be rebuilt. There is to be no revival of the songs, they are gone. Neither the posts with carved faces painted red and black, nor copies of any of the ceremonial pieces are to be duplicated ever again. This is the way it should be, and the way it must be.

No trace of the Meeting House remains, no one can truthfully say or point to where it once stood, it has returned to its beginnings. The ground is covered now, all is gone, so let it lie where it has fallen.

CHAPTER THIRTEEN

Nora Thompson Dean's Accounts of the Eastern Oklahoma Unami Delaware Big House, 1973–1984

This chapter presents three accounts by Eastern Oklahoma Delaware traditionalist Nora Thompson Dean that were published between 1973 and 1984. Like her ancestors before her, Nora Thompson Dean, "Touching Leaves Woman" (1902–84), maintained a lifelong commitment to preserving the traditions of her people. As a young woman she attended the last complete Big House ceremonies at the Copan Xingwikaon from around 1909 to 1924. From that time on she devoted herself to learning as much as the elders would teach her about Delaware religion. One of the last fluent Unami Delaware speakers, she passed this knowledge on to younger Delaware people and several generations of scholars. The following accounts were recorded in conversations with Ruthe Blalock Jones (1973: 29–34) and during field interviews with Jay Miller during the 1970s and early 1980s (Dean 1984; Miller and Dean 1978: 39–43).

THE JONES INTERVIEW, 1973

I with my family attended the Big House Church from the time I can remember until the last one which was held in October, 1924 (fig. 16). I graduated from high school the following spring, and have a ring with the date on it, and that is how I remember the date of the last meeting.

Outside, the Hi'ngwikan was eight or nine logs high and about twenty-seven feet wide by fifty feet long. This is an approximate guess, as I never did measure. We all went up and camped twelve days or maybe longer, according to the weather. Ta-ma-ha-mon, Delaware word for it. If the weather was bad, we went home early.

Years ago there was Mising, "Spirit of the Game Animals," who rode around with a group of men to notify and pick out the Oshkosh-suk. Sometimes he would create a commotion, dressed in bearskin and mask, etc. People rode in

Fig. 16. Nora Thompson Dean. Courtesy James Rementer.

buggies in those days, and they say their horses would be scared and maybe even cause a run-away.

Three women and three men Oshkosh were picked. The women Oshkosh camped in a row on the south-side, and the men were in a row across from them on the north side. Two men I recall as Tum-meet-kat are Ben Hill and Frank Wilson. I believe Frank Wilson was the last one, in 1924. At that time all his relatives could eat in the Big House if they so desired. The Oshkosh-suk would have to furnish this food to be brought into the Big House three times a day. So they always tried to select people fairly well fixed financially. Some writers called them janitors. I never did. I prefer to call them workers. They sweep around, keep the fires going, cut beads, etc.

There were certain nights during the Big House called Wil-teem, when they call different men of each clan to come up and get a portion of beads after one was called to cut these beads. This bead cutting was done in front of the center pole. This was holy ground. No one was ever permitted to cross between the east fire and the center pole because of that. The center pole had two faces, one on the east and one on the west side. Those faces were carved in relief in white man's way. There were three on the north side, three on the south, and two on the west and east sides, making a total of twelve faces on the inside. These faces on the sides were smaller and were intaglio. There were positively no faces on the outside.

The top was clapboards; hand-made shingles on the side. We all went up there one time when the old one burned down, and remade the Hi'ngwikan. That was long years back.

I believe on the tenth night they remade the fires. The east door was always used. The west door was never used except when they took out the ashes of the old fire. The new fires were done for the lady's night. We call that At-ta-home-mwe. The ladies I remember are Mrs. Liza Falleaf, my aunt Lucy Willits, Pow-len-now, who was deaf, and my mother, Sara Wilson Thompson. In my mother's day, she said this ceremony lasted nearly all night. But in my time it was usually over around midnight because the men who sing the vision songs were getting few and far between.

Pil-hicks-soo-teen: Also on the night they burned cedar, when everyone was cleansed and the cedar smoke would be so dense you could hardly see across.

We also had Ma-ta-he-kuna, prayer sticks, which we used on certain nights. There was a ceremony attached to this. The Oshkosh-suk had to pass while the drum beat at a very fast time, and these Ma-ta-he-kuna had to be passed on each side by the Oshkosh-suk while the drum was being beaten. And during the time the men Wen-ge-kuna'ed [recited their vision songs], these were held up, and they prayed, Hooo-Haaa. That was the time you were supposed to lift up your prayer stick in prayer to the Creator inside of this Church.

A PERSONAL ACCOUNT OF THE UNAMI DELAWARE BIG HOUSE RITE, 1978

My parents, brothers, and I attended the Big House (Xingikaon) every year. I don't think we missed a year from the time when the new Big House building was built, around what I believe to be 1909 or 1910, on up until 1924 when they had the last full rite.

Before they started the services, some men were usually sent around on horses to notify people when the exact camping day would be.[1] The Mes.i'ngheli.'k.an (the impersonator of the being called Masing dressed in mask and bearskin suit) would travel with these men. Sometimes he rode in a buggy. (Once the train that used to run out to the rock quarry scared the horses and they ran away with Masing in the buggy. Another time a new White settler couple had their team bolt and run away when they met Masing's buggy on the road. Generally, the team of the

---

1. Miller wrote, "The building where the services were held was built in the timber, near water, and had a level cleared area for camping."

buggy that carried the Masing was kept from running because of the blinders the horses wore.) They tried to ask people who were "empty" (without a supernatural vision). They once asked my father, but he couldn't find anyone to tend the stock on the farm, so he had to refuse. My father was sent away to boarding school when he was young so he didn't have a vision. My mother did have one, so these men always asked her to recite on the last day with the other women visionaries. They picked three men and three women to be the assistants or helpers. The Tëmikèt (Enterer or Leader) had already been chosen. They tried to get someone who could afford to get food for the women assistants, who would cook it and feed it to his clanspeople (members of the matriclan of the Enterer) during the rite.

The assistants went to the Big House site several days before the camping day to prepare the area for the rite. They cleaned out the building and put hay on the floor for the people to sit upon. The hay forms a strip about four feet wide from the walls out to the center.

There were twelve faces carved on the support posts and center post inside the Big House. There were three faces on the north side, three on the south, two on the west door, two on the east door, and two facing east and west on the center post. There were absolutely no faces on the outside of the Big House whatsoever, despite the fact that some people think there were. The Wolf clan women sit on the north east corner, then the Tëmikèt, the Wolf clan men at the north west corner, the Turtle women along the west end, the Turtle men at the south west corner, then the two drummers, the Fowl or Turkey men at their right, and finally the Fowl women at the south east corner. So that the men and women were seated separately. On the south side of the east door, the three men assistants were stationed and the three women were stationed on the north side. The men assistants took care of things on the south side, and the women were responsible for the north side. On the wall above the drummers on the south side hung a bucket filled with Wisahkakw (boiled and stained red oak bark infusion). From time to time, the drummers would get up and drink some of this to clear and soothe their voices and throats. In my day the two drummers were Willie Longbone on the east side and Jake Parks on the west. On the north wall behind the Enterer we hung a piece of white cloth, about four feet square, where the strings of wampum (Kèkok) hung the whole time until they were paid out on the thirteenth morning to the assistants.

I want to describe the drum that was used in the Big House. It was rolled up into a sort of long shape. I would say at least three feet long or longer. It was a whole deerhide stuffed with deer hair, and over the top there were two slats, very thin pieces of board. Sometimes during the daytime during the rite men and boys would go inside the Big House and have what they call a trial sing (Ahkwètalamwin), a sort of try-out singing of special Long-Winged Creature songs which refer to the thunders.

On the first night and on all other nights of the service, the men assistants were around the church house and shouted "Tëmikèkw!, Tëmikèkw!" at about dusky dark. They continued the shout, which means "all come in," "all enter." So we all went into the Big House and took our proper seats. We brought in shawls and blankets to put on the hay. When we were all seated, a male assistant pulled closed the flap on the east door. It was canvas attached to a pole at the bottom to keep it tight. In the old days, my mother said that it was a deerhide. When everyone was seated why the Tëmikèt arose and addressed the people. He told us what we were there for, to worship the Creator. He gave thanks for our brothers and sisters, all of our relatives, grandchildren, the vegetation, the trees, the water, the rain, the stars, the moon, everything. He gave thanks that we would all live to meet again in the next rite. After his opening speech, he sat down. Meanwhile, the turtle shell rattle with the leather thong handle (Shuhënikàn) was placed in front of him, so he picked it up and started to sing his vision song. When he moved out into the center, well, anyone could follow him that wanted to. While he recited, all the men must answer him, that is, repeat the words of his vision song. He started out his dance, moving counterclockwise, and anyone could follow him except for children. They were not permitted to dance in the Big House. The women joined in too, but they formed a separate line of their own. From time to time he stopped at different intervals during his recitation and he recited some more of the experience by which he acquired his vision. The men answered him, that is, they said whatever he said. Finally, he finished and went back to where he was originally seated. Whenever someone recited his vision song and experience (Wendji.kane$^{e'}$i), everyone in the Big House stood until he was through. You were not permitted to sleep or even doze in there. Because if you did, the assistants would come over and nudge your foot with their firesticks, which were long thin poles for tending the fire. They were warm from this use. After the man finished, the turtle shell was shoved toward the east until it reached another visionary. (I recall very well how afraid I was to make that turtle rattle because if you do why the drummers on the south side would beat the drum twice in answer to your shake on this turtle. So when I handled it, I was very careful.) It continued on around, an assistant took it across the east doorway. When it reached a vision song man (Wenjikaneit), he shook the rattle and was answered by the singer-drummers. Then he began his vision recitation. So this went on, in my day, until about 11:30 or midnight. My mother said that in the old days, there were so many vision song men that it lasted until almost daylight.

So that was the first of the ceremony. The second night was the same and the third night. There was not too much variation in those first three nights.

On the fourth day, the hunters were called in, though I can't say too much about the hunters because they discontinued the hunters in my day. I will repeat what my mother, father, and older brother told me took place long ago. The hunters were called in during the daytime and the drummers would sing a hunting song for them. They would pray for them. They would burn tobacco. The hunters were advised what to do, and the women assistants gave each of them a sort of lunch (Nimëwakàn), consisting of cooked meat and ordinary corn bread

(Lenahpön) in a little parcel. The hunters were gone two or three days and just before they came back to camp they shot a rifle once for deer, two shots for two deer, etc. The campers would notify each other that the hunters were back. The hunters went into the Big House to be prayed for and blessed again. Then they were released from this hunting. When the deer were dressed and butchered, some members of the older generation would receive the hides. But I cannot elaborate too much on this hunting, because, in my day, they got beef from the butcher. Sometimes young men also hunted squirrels for the campers.

The fourth, fifth, sixth, and seventh nights were much the same as the previous nights.

On the ninth morning, the assistants opened the back or west door to carry out and dump the ashes from the two fires. They cleaned the Big House very well and called in some (clean) [chaste] person to come and use the fire drill (Sànghikàn) to kindle a new fire. I never saw this because women were never permitted to see this, only men and boys. The new fire was built in preparation for the service on the ninth night.

There were special events on the ninth night. On the tenth night they had a general cleansing called the PilhIksutin. The assistants burned cedar in the fire before the services and fanned the smoke around the Big House. Sometimes the smoke was so dense that you could hardly see across the room. The assistants brought out the paint dish, during, what I guess you would call now, an intermission, and the women assistants would paint us on the north side. The men assistants would paint the ones on the south side and also the two carved faces on the center post (Mësingòkw). I can recall that the faces were so high up that these men would have to jump two or three times to put the red on the left cheek. The old women made the red paint (Pekawn) from bloodroot. Men and women were painted on the red cheek, but only women were painted down the part of the hair. After this was done, visionaries continued to recite. Later there would be another short intermission and maybe some of the old men would say "Hayuhpu, Hayuhpu" which means "Let's all have a smoke." Other old men would respond "Wehe." Then they would all light their pipes and smoke. For smoking they mixed sumac leaves with commercial Velvet and Prince Albert tobacco. For offerings, they used commercial Bull Durham. This was sort of a rest period. Later they would bring out the twelve prayersticks (Mahtehikena) and change the drumsticks. They substituted the drumsticks with the faces on them from now until it was over. The men assistants distributed prayersticks on the south side and the women assistants did the same on the north side. These were distributed to a fast beat on the drum. They had to be evenly distributed, six on one side and six on the other. There were times I remember that the assistants had to re-gather and re-distribute the prayersticks. After all this, visionaries recited again. The ones who were given these sticks, held them in their right hands, and kept time with the beat. Whenever the reciter paused to give prayer to the Creator, they said "Hoo Heee" and you were supposed to hold the prayersticks up in the air. I recall that one time I was given one of these prayersticks by Mrs. Minnie Fouts. I was rather young and I just stuck it in the logs behind me. So, she came up to me and said, "Here, you're supposed to use one of these." I got it down again, kept time, and held it up each time they gave the prayer to the Creator.

On the tenth night, there was a wooden bowl inside the door on the right hand side. Everyone who entered the church door had to drop at least one or two wampum beads into it. The beads were gathered by the assistants and taken to the Enterer. The bowl was like a flat serving bowl a little under twelve inches wide at the top, about four and one-half inches deep, and had a round bottom. Later in the night, the beads were scattered in the sacred area, between the center post and the east fire. No one was ever permitted to walk on that area. The assistants were called up to kneel, pick up the beads quickly in their hands, and put them into their mouths while they made a humming sound like "mmmm." Sometimes they would drop some out of their mouths which caused a little quiet chuckle in them. This was called the Mawesi.

The eleventh night was a continuation of the usual pattern except that they had what was called the Wiltin. It was actually held about three times during the twelve day service. They would call out the men's Delaware names. If you were not inside the church house, the men were sent outside to call out the name. The man was supposed to say She wàn, "I am here," and the assistants would return into the Big House and say Meči Kenaxkumkuwa, "Now he has answered all of you." Then they would call out another name. Sometimes they would name seven or eight men. These named men gathered in the Big House and one of them was selected to cut a small string of wampum placed again in the sacred area. He cut the string into so many sections as there were men named. Each man would take his share, file outside, line up facing east, and pray. Everyone was very quiet inside while the men outside were praying. Things would resume much as before.

On the twelfth night it was time for the women visionaries to Ahtehumwi. This is the time that they wear their finery; beautiful clothing, ribbon work, moccasins. The women would line up by the door, and each lady would select a male visionary to dance by her side and join in her song as she recited her vision. My mother usually selected a man call Nehëneyuxwe, "One Seen As He Walks," whose English name was William Wilson. He danced inside and my mother danced outside next to the hay. She usually made only one full circuit, pausing from time to time until she finished her recitation. Then the next lady would recite. In my day there were only about five women left: my mother, Sarah Wilson Thompson, of the Wolf clan; Lucy Wilson Willets of the Wolf clan; Lisa Fallingleaf of the Fowl clan; a woman called Pawlinaw, I think her English name was Mrs. Blackwing, of the Turtle clan, and another woman whose name I forgot. That night the services are much as before.

In the morning after the twelfth night, we had the Temahema, which means "the end" or "the conclusion." Something like that. In the morning we all went into the church dressed in our fine Indian clothes, moccasins, ribbon work, pretty

Indian skirts, blouses, paint. Again the Enterer would stand and give thanks to the Creator that we had gone thus far with the services and he would call upon the Creator that we may meet again next year to pray together again. He prayed for the children, the grandchildren, continuing much the same for the rain, the vegetation, game animals, the crops, all wild things, and so forth. A Delaware's prayer is rather lengthy because we try to give thanks for everything we receive in our daily life. After he finished the prayer, the man took the rattle and recited his vision. As he did so, we all danced in toward the center post. Men, women, and children each arose from wherever they were sitting and individually danced to the center post. This was called the Lentkan, "Common Dance." Sometimes you would not get to dance very far because there would be quite a crowd in there. I remember that once the old women were crying and wiping their tears away with their aprons because they sensed the end of the Big House Rite. That was in 1924, the year I graduated from High School. When the man sang his last vision song, everyone raised their hands and said again Hooo, Heee. Then the assistants were given wampum. Not a yard length as they did in the old days because the wampum was becoming scarce then. Everyone filed out of the east door and we all went a goodly distance from the building, lined up north and south facing east, and the men shouted the prayer words. The old people would stand in the line, but the young knelt if they were agile. The men on the north side shouted Hooo, then a man shouted Natanukw, "Watch out," and the men on the south side would immediately respond Heee. This was done twelve times with the left hand raised to the Creator. After twelve times it was all over. Everyone in the camp, even the campers who did not attend the services, was supposed to get in the line.

Then the services were over and everyone packed up and went home.

REMEMBRANCES OF THE BIG HOUSE CHURCH, 1984

The sun felt warm on that beautiful autumn day as my dad and I rode along the dirt road in a Studebaker wagon drawn by two bay horses named Maude and Topsy. The wagon was heavily loaded with a tent, cooking utensils, and other camping equipment. The horses were large so the load was no strain on them. My dad and I sat on a spring seat so we were comfortable as well.

A great surge of happiness welled up inside me, because we were on our way to the Xingwikaon. My mother and brother would also be along but in an old Model-T Ford. We felt that my mother would be more comfortable riding in the car. It was a journey of about twenty miles from our home to the Big House Church.

Long before we turned off the main road we could smell the smoke from the campfires. The trees were all dressed in their scarlet and gold leaves. The area was sandy so the wagon didn't make much noise as we drove into the campgrounds, but the dogs heard us and ran out in groups barking at us. As we stopped at our campsite my cousins and others ran over to greet us.

We soon had our tent set up, and a few things unloaded when my mother arrived in the old car driven by my brother. She too seemed glad and had a smile on her face.

My father dug eight deep holes inside the tent, and then went out with his axe to cut eight forked poles and four straight poles. The forked poles were driven into the holes in the earth to form a bedstead, and the strong straight poles were put across the head and foot of the bed. In our wagon we had boards brought from home and these were placed on the poles, and on the boards we placed ticking stuffed with hay or straw which served as our mattresses, and then blankets and pillows. My father and brother would sleep in one of these beds and my mother and I in the other.

My father then dug a hole about one-and-a-half feet deep inside the tent, almost in the middle. He filled this hole with hot coals from our cookfire which was outside in front of the tent. The heat from these coals would keep us comfortable and warm, even during the coldest days of fall.

At dusk, one of the men, Àshkasàk (attendants), began his usual nightly call Tëmikèkw!, "Everyone come in!" Tëmikèkw! This year one of the male attendants was a distant relative named Pèmuxwe, "He Who Walks By;" he was about twenty-four years of age. As my mother and I started toward the meeting house we met him and I jokingly said to him, "What kind of cake, chocolate or cherry?" I was referring to his not saying the final sound of the word. He gave me a glowering look because he thought I was trying to correct him. Even then, some of the younger people were losing out on their native language.

After we went into the Big House Church my mother and I sat down on the blanket she had brought in to spread on the soft hay. We sat in our usual space in the northeast corner of Church, just east of the Tëmikèt, who, that year, was my uncle, Pèmataekàmën (Frank Wilson). This was the place where the women of the Tùkwsit (or Wolf) clan sat.

The men and women do not sit together in the Xingwikaon. The Tùkwsit men sat west of the Tëmikèt (the Tëmikèt being the man who ran the meeting) on the north side of the church.[2]

The Xingwikaon or Big House Church was a building about twenty feet wide and forty or fifty feet long. The main door was on the east, and on the inside of the doorposts was carved the face of Mësingw, the guardian spirit of the game animals. His face was also carved on the three wall-posts located on each of the north and south sides, and two additional faces were carved on the posts of the west opening. In addition to these ten faces, the big center post, which had been carved from a huge Burr Oak, had two Mësingw faces carved on it; one looking east and the other looking west. Some people have the mistaken idea that we

---

2. Dean wrote, "It should be noted that women were not permitted in the Xingwikaon during the time of their menstruation. Also, the campers and people who planned to attend the Church practices sexual continence, as the Church House was to be kept pure."

worshiped these faces or prayed to them, but we did not. The Mësingw was one of the Manëtuwàk (Lesser Spirits) and like the Lenape people he too was created by Kishelëmukòng (The Creator).

Our old people cautioned the younger ones not to carve the Mësingw faces unless they themselves were members of the Big House Church. One of the last men in the tribe who carved these faces was Reuben Wilson, Wikpèkixing, "He Who Is Like Receding Water," and he told, in his vision song, that he had received his power from the Mësingw.

My mother and I were already seated when my father and the youngest of my brothers entered. My brother took his seat with the Tùkwsit men, but my father went around the two fires which had been built east and west of the Mësingòkw (the center post) to go and sit with the members of his clan, the Pële (Turkey) people.

Among my Lenape people, one always belongs to the clan of his or her mother, and that is why my brother could not sit with my father; they belonged to different clans. At such meetings the seating arrangements never changed, regardless of the clan of the Tëmikèt who ran the meeting.

As I sat by my mother, Sarah Wilson Thompson, Ehèlinaoxkwe, "Woman Who Looks Like Someone Else," in the Xingwikaon I felt happy and content. I could hear the crackling of the burning wood in the two fires, and smell the fragrant aroma of the fresh hay and the wood smoke.

When all were assembled inside the church the man Ashkas who was nearest the door pulled the canvas, closing it tighter at the bottom where a pole was attached. This held down the canvas and helped to better keep out the cold. There were three men and three women Ashkasàk (ceremonial attendants); the men sat on the south of the door and the women sat on the north side. They remained inside the church unless they had to go out to bring in wood or other things.

The quietness inside the church was soft and soon the Sakima (or chief) rose to his feet while the people sat with bowed heads. He began his address by saying: "Elàngundiàng (My Kinspeople), now the time is here to worship Kishelëmukòng, and we must all live in a way that He will pity us, His children. Be friendly with each other. Be thankful to have lived another year." His prayers and advice continued for some time. Then he said, "Now I shall pray and ask Kishelëmukòng for His mercy and to bless us with rain, but I will ask Him also to have the Manëtuwàk who walk upon our mother, the earth, to go on roads that will not destroy or hurt us. I will ask Him to bless our elders, parents, grandparents, grandchildren, the vegetation, trees." And then he would begin the prayer which was usually rather lengthy.

After his advice and prayer, he sat down again. Then the Tëmikèt picked up the turtle rattle which was on the ground in front of him and placed his fingers under the two buckskin thongs on the back of the rattle and he shook it strongly. The two Talekaok, (Singers), who were sitting across from him in the church, answered by two hard beats upon the long deerhide drum. He began to

Wěnjikanei (recite and sing his vision song) beginning by reciting short lines [each repeated by the Talekaok]. At this point the Těmikèt rose to his feet, shaking the turtle rattle, and continued with his vision words [repeated by the Talekaok] as he stepped slowly to the swept area. Then he began dancing still shaking the turtle rattle and taking short quick steps counter-clock-wise around the inside of the church house, as he began to sing [and was echoed by the Talekaok].

All this time the Talekaok kept the same rhythm as his song. They were called Talekaok because they sounded like Canada Geese on their long flights north and south, as they kept repeating the visionary's words and song. The visionary danced about ten feet, and then said "Kwih!" There was never any whooping; things were not boisterous but gentle and dignified. During the dance any adult could join the dance.

Finally, the visionary, still standing, stopped to recite more of the vision words, and then the remainder of the song. He continued on in this manner, reciting and dancing, until he had made the entire round of the two fires. He then raised his hand saying "Hooo! Hooo! Hooo!" and took his seat.

No one is permitted to leave or enter while the vision song is going on. Also, from time to time between the songs of the different visionaries the Talekaok (the singers) will take a drink from a small bucket which hangs behind them, and which is filled with Wisahkakw, an infusion of red oak bark.

After the visionary sits, he passes the turtle shell rattle eastward. Almost everyone helps pass it. I was always afraid that I would drop it, because to the least sound of the rattle the drummers respond with the beat.

When the first visionary finished, the man and woman Ashkas sweep both sides—the man sweeps the south path, and the woman sweeps the north. If there is an intermission, some elder usually says: "Haiyuhpu! Haiyuhpu!" He is answered by the people saying "Wehe! Wehe!" Then it is proper to smoke their pipes.

The Ashkas replenishes the fire using the Tahkwěndalès (a stick used as a fire poker) to stir the coals. By then, the smokers are finished so the turtle shell rattle is passed around giving the other visionaries a chance to recite and sing their songs. I was told that before my time, when the rattle had made the round, Sapan (corn gruel) was brought in by the women Ashkasàk and passed to all. My father even had a Shěmuwèmhòn, or horn spoon which he took in to eat with.

Towards the end of the evening everyone prays twelve times with uplifted hands and the Těmikèt dismisses the assembly for the night saying that we will all meet and pray again tomorrow night. We all filed out and headed for our camps and bed. Sometimes some of the men would sleep inside the church.

I awakened the next morning and it seemed very bright inside the tent, and I could smell coffee and the aroma of cooking food wafting in the air. Soon I heard the soft and gentle voice of my mother conversing with my father in the Lenape language. She said, Kitel kun! Chikha në hèmpsikaon, "What a lot of snow! Sweep it off the tent," and he swept it off the roof of the tent.

I stepped out to wash my face and hands. The fire was burning good and the coffee pot, cast-iron kettle and fry pan were all on to cook. My mother was cooking Kahahpon and meat and I set the drop-leaf table using our enamel plates and cups.

The meeting went on about the same each night until the night when the Wiltin took place. This is a calling of the names of the men, their Lenape names. This took place on several other nights as well.

One Wiltin that I remember well was when the Tëmikèt said, Ashka, dum nata Ohëlëmitakwsi, "Ashkas, call that Ohëlëmitakwsi." This was my father's Lenape name and it meant "One Who Can be Heard From Afar." He had not yet come into the Xingwikaon as there was something he had to do at our camp some distance away. The Ashkas went out and called his name, and my father answered She wan! "This one is here!" Everyone in the church chuckled as his answer so well fit his name, the "One Who Can be Heard From Afar." Then the Ashkas came back in and gave the regular reply, Mèchi kënaxkumkuwa, "Now he has answered you all." Then my father came to the Xingwikaon.

On the same night one man was called to cut the wampum. He placed the beads on the holy ground—a space between the center posts and the east fire. He then announced Natëmukw kèkëwo, "Come and pick up your wampum." He called two other men, one from each clan. If one of these men was not inside the church, the Ashkas was instructed by the Tëmikèt to call him. The Ashkas went outside shouting his Lenape name. The one being called shouted back She wan, "This one is here!" After they were all assembled the men picked up their portions of wampum and went out and faced the east and prayed.

Because this practice had been discontinued by my time, I will repeat what my parents told me. According to their account, the hunters were called in on the morning of the fourth day. They would line up and tobacco would be sprinkled into the Grandpa fire. Then cedar was burned for the hunters and prayers were offered so that they could kill a deer. The women Ashkasàk would tie Nimëwakàn (a lunch) on their saddles.

The leader of the hunt was told that if a deer was killed to bring it into the camp, but before approaching the camp he was to fire his rifle to announce his arrival. The Mësinghòlikàn, or impersonator of the Mësingw, comes in before the hunters leave and he dances rapidly and then sees the hunters off. Several men were also sent to the meat pole east of the Big House to pray twelve times with wampum in their hands. This was to be paid to the hunters on their return.

In my day, I used to see the elderly women cry and wipe the tears from their eyes with their aprons because there were no deer anymore. Every place the hunter went there were "No trespassing" signs. Nevertheless, the hunting songs were still sung.

During intermissions my cousins and I would go outside to buy things from the Ashkasàk, as there was always someone at their camps. Candy cost two wampum beads, chili with crackers was four beads, and pie was five or six beads. My mother was known for her culinary arts, so she made the pies in a Dutch oven for the Ashkasàk.³

Throughout the day the young men got wood in wagons, cut it to assorted lengths and stacked it outside near the door of the Big House. They could then help the older women pound corn, and they would climb the long ladder to the top of the Textakan or cupboard where the staples were stored. Throughout the day the men would also Ahkwetalamwi (sing practice songs) inside the church.⁴

My uncle, George Tom Anderson, Kwëchkwipahkikàmën, "He Who Causes Leaves To Move As He Steps," would often come by our camp with his axe on his shoulder on his way to get wood. He would take some of us girls along to pick wild grapes. Some of the women would use these to make Shëwahsapan (grape dumplings).

On one of the nights a wooden bowl was placed inside the door of the Big House on the north side, and as the people entered they would drop in as many Kèkok (wampum beads) as they could spare. My mother always gave me three or four beads to drop into the bowl. These were used to pay the Ashkasàk and others at the Xingwikaon.

Throughout the meeting everything was done in perfect order and calmness; gentleness reigned in all things. No feathers of any kind were used by anyone except the two turkey wings used by the Ashkasàk to sweep the area after each visionary's song.

When the time came for the wampum beads to be given out, some were scattered between the center post and the fire on the east. The Ashkasàk were told to go get them, and they had to kneel and pick up the beads and put them in their mouths as fast as they could, all the while making a humming noise like "Hmmmmm." At times some would be dropped, and the sight of this would cause amusement to everyone. This gathering of the wampum beads was called Mawënsin, "Gathering berries."

The other nights in the Big House were much the same as the first few nights, but on the evening of the ninth night a new fire was made with the Sànghikàn (fire drill), and the ashes from the old fire were carried out through the west door which

---

3. Dean noted, "There were no ice boxes used at the Big House, and the food was stored on the Tèxtakàn or on the cupboards at the camps. If there was any cooked food left, charcoal was placed in it to keep it fresh, and it was kept in a cool place."
4. Dean noted, "No drunks or drinking of alcoholic beverages were allowed anywhere around the Xingwikaon or the camps. The Àshkasàk would make anyone leave who came there drunk. The Àshkasàk were forced to make some of the Christian Delawares leave the camps as well. Some of these people fancied themselves preachers, and they tried to convert the traditional Lenape people. I have heard them preaching to us, telling us how we would all go to Hell, and telling our older people how they were punishing their women and children by making them camp out in the cold. They said we were all heathens, and their talk became so strong they were asked to leave. Strangely, since the revival in the interest in traditional Indian ways, the descendants of some of these 'preachers' are now telling how their ancestor had preached at the Big House, apparently not knowing that they had been there preaching against it!"

was then opened for the only time during the Big House meeting. The drumsticks which had been used on earlier nights, the ones with X-like designs were put away and the one with the Mësingw faces were brought out.

Also on this night the twelve prayer sticks were brought in. When the night's services were begun, these were distributed quickly - very quickly, to the fast beat of the drum. The Ashkasàk had to pass them out so that the plain sticks corresponded to the striped ones. If they did not, the entire procedure had to be repeated.

The recipient of the prayer stick held it up while praying. One of the women Ashkasàk, Minnie Fouts, Wèmeehëlèxkwe, "Reverberates Everywhere Woman," gave one to me. Instead of holding it I put it on the log ledge behind me. She came to me very quickly and gave it to me again and instructed me that everything had to be in perfect order. I felt embarrassed because I had failed to follow rules.

All those who owned turtle shell rattles would bring them in and put them in a line in front of the Tëmikèt. The backs of the turtles were measured and wampum was given to the owner; the amount given was the same length as the turtle's back. The owner would pick up his rattle again during the service. One man, Julius Fouts, Pètanihing, "He Who Throws Something In This Direction," had a rattle so huge that when he shook it, to keep time during the service, it sounded so loud and harsh that the people there would give soft chuckles of amusement.

On another night there would be what is called Pilhìksutin or cedar burning. Cedar smoke was used to purify everything, and to carry the prayers of the people on up to where the Creator lives. I recall that my eyes were burning because the smoke was so thick and I could hardly see across the building. Meanwhile, the women Ashkasàk would prepare the Olàmàn or Indian paint. This was used to paint everyone in the Church. The men Ashkasàk would paint the Mësingw faces on the walls and centerpost. I remember seeing Tom Halfmoon, Ahkwelpinùnd "He Whose Head Is Covered Up," jump high to paint the Mësingòkw (the center post). The men also painted the drum, the drumsticks, and so on.

There were also women visionaries, and my mother was one of these. Almost every year when she sang her vision songs she would get William Wilson, Nehëneyuxwe, "He Who Can Be Seen As He Walks," as the man to dance beside her on the left side, as was the custom for the women visionaries to do.

In the morning on the final day everyone entered the Church, and one man was appointed to sing his vision song. All who wished to do so could join in, and the people stood up during the song and the dance as they had done each night. At the proper time, everyone would dance toward the center post. My cousins and I danced with them and as we danced toward the center post our hands would be raised from time to time as the prayer call Hoo! Hoo! was given twelve times.

At the end of the ceremony we took our seats, and wampum, which had been hanging by strings on the wall behind the Tëmikèt, was paid out to the Ashkasàk each of whom would get one yard.

Everyone would then file out the east door and would form a line north and south facing east. The younger ones would kneel while the south end said "Hoo!"

twelve times and the north end finished with "Heee!" like an echo. Everyone was now dismissed until the next year.

At the present time, in the afternoon of my life, when I think about the Big House Church and our annual meetings there, I can still remember the older women during those last years (1923 and 1924), with the tears streaming down their cheeks during the meeting. At the time I thought, "Why are they crying while I am so happy?" I enjoyed our meetings. The elders knew that these meetings could not endure much longer. The visionaries were getting older; some were now too old to sing their songs. The younger people could not be sent out to receive visions because our land was filling with strangers who put up fences and signs—strangers who made laws to tell us what we could or could not do with our children and ourselves.

In spite of this, in my meditations, I can still "see" my mother dressed in her ribbon-worked skirt, leggings and moccasins, with her tan little hand grasping the turtle shell rattle. My eyes still fill with unshed tears, as I remember these events. Each day that I attended the Big House Ceremony is like a shining bead in my rosary of life. Now there are only memories and a pain inside of me.

Appendix: Delaware and English Names of People Referred to in the Texts

Ah-khe-no, "Measure," "Measurement," "Something Like An Equal Amount." William Shawnee.
Ah-kqa-ah-pon-aqua, "Early Dawn Woman." Lucy Parks Blalock.
Ahkwelpinùnd, "He Whose Head Is Covered Up." Tom Half Moon. Also known as Axkwe'lpango'xwe, "Overturns Mountains When Walking."
Ala-mah-liquah, "Going Away Woman." Irene Tiger.
Ala-pan-aqua, "Same As Other Women." Ollie Beaver Anderson.
An-heh-now-quah, "All Woman." Anna Anderson Davis.
Buckongahelas, "One Whose Movements Are Certain." Also known as Pachgantschihillas.
Čəpəlʌntpas, "Curley-Headed One." Captain Curley-Head.
Chun-Lun-Dit, "Little Bird." Ruthe Blalock Jones.
Ehèlinaoxkwe, ehɛlináoxkwe, "Two Women That Look Alike Woman," "Woman Who Looks Like Someone Else." Sarah Wilson Thompson.
ɛma:, Frank Wilson's nickname.
ɛnxinau, "That's All You See Of Her." Anna Anderson Davis.
ɛnxinund, "You See A Bit Of Him." Fred Washington.
Gwuteme'k, "One Fish." Jesse Noah.
Kapyü'hüin, Isaac Montour.
Ka'zko, "Great Blue Heron." Jacob Simonds.
Kokwəlupuxwe, "He Walks Backwards." Charlie Elkhair. Also known as Koᵘkwəl.əpo'xwe, denoting someone who is walking along slowly then turns around in the opposite direction.
Kwəčkipahkíkʌmən, Kwëchkwipahkikàmën, Kwu'tepagi.'kamen, "He Makes The Leaves Move As He Steps," "He Who Causes Leaves To Move As He Steps," "Rustling Leaves (When Walking)." George Tom Anderson.
La-tai-ah-quah, Nancy Cedar.

Maxkok, "Red." One of the spiritually blessed Delaware men on the Six Nations Reserve.

Mekinges, daughter of Chief Anderson.

Mɛtɛxin, "Where He Landed When He Jumped," also known as "Jumper." Furgeson Longbone.

Mečipahkúxwe, "He Who Walks When The Leaves Are Worn Out." Jake Parks.

Na'nküma'oxa, Michael Anthony.

Nehëneyuxwe, "He Who Can Be Seen As He Walks." William Wilson.

Nekatcit, "Tame Little Fellow." Nicodemus Peters.

Nikanipahkúxwe, Ni.ka'ni.paxoxwe, "He Walks Ahead of Leaves," "Walking in Advance, Leader." Joe Washington.

Ohëlëmitakwsi, "One Who Can be Heard From Afar." James H. Thompson (father of Nora Thompson Dean).

Ole-lung-un, Orie Spybuck.

Pachgantschihillas. See Buckongahelas.

Pawlinaw, Pow-le-na, Pow-len-now, "Blackwing." Lucy Willits, also known as Mrs. Blackwing.

Pɛmataekʌmən, Pèmataekàmën, "Things Bloom Where He Steps." Frank Wilson.

Pe-me-ah-queh, "Echo." Jack Longbone.

Pèmuxwe, "He Who Walks By."

Pètanihing, "He Who Throws Something In This Direction." Julius Fouts.

PwɛthɛkkʌmƏn, "He Pushes, Moves, Kicks, Or Rolls Something This Way." Willie Longbone.

Sarcoxie, John Sarcoxie.

Schaponque. No further information available.

Tatkowínau, Liza Falleaf.

Tayeno'xwan, James Wolf.

Teo'kali, "Blackbird." Jesse Moses, Sr.

Tomapemihi'lat, Nellis F. Timothy.

Tung-shu-mu-tat, "Little Horn."

Twenyucis, a Delaware-Tutelo woman elder of the Six Nations Reserve.

Way-en-gee-pah-kee-huh-lex-kway, "Touching Leaves Woman." Nora Thompson Dean.

Weh-me-quah, Elizabeth Longbone.

Wèmeehëlèxkwe, Wɛmeehəlɛxkwe, "Reverberates Everywhere Woman." Minnie Fouts.

Wikpèkixing, "He Who Is Like Receding Water." Reuben Wilson.

Willis-ta-quah, "Something Like A Whirlwind." Fannie McCartlin.

Wítanahkúxwe, "He Walks With The Trees." John Anderson.

Wi.tapano'xwe, "He Walks In Daylight." Charlie Webber.

Xko'kwsis, "Little Snake." Josiah Montour.

Glossary

Delaware words and names are indicated in bold face. All are Unami unless otherwise noted in brackets. Spelling variations are listed as they appear in the texts. Names in parentheses identify text sources.

A'ckas (Harrington; Speck). See **Àshkas**.
Ahkwetalamwi; **Ahkwètalamwin** (Dean). The act of singing practice songs.
Ah-tay-home-ok (Anderson); **Ahtehumwi** (Prewitt; Dean); **Ah-the-hom-mee** (Elizabeth Longbone); **Ateho'mwi.n** (Speck); **At-ta-Home-mwe** (Blalock; Jack Longbone; Dean). Women's vision recitation on the last night.
Ahtehumwéitcik (Prewitt). Women's vision reciters.
Ala'ngwe (Speck). Delaware-Mahican Star Clan.
A-la-pa-cte (Morgan). Dreamers.
Alo'man (Speck). Munsee rite dream recitation.
Ane'i (Speck). Path.
Àshkas (sing.) **Ashkasàk** (pl.) (Dean). Ceremonial attendant; **ʌskásʌk** (Prewitt). Helpers.
Aⁿsipla'gün (Harrington). Bark dish.
Cantico (Denton; Kluge and Luckenbach; Penn). Dance.
Chun-ques (Shawnee). Cranes.
Co-hawk-cun (Elizabeth Longbone). Corn pounder; *see also* **Ko-ha-kun**.
Ees.e'm'h@n (Speck). Mussel-shell spoon.
Elàngundiàng (Dean). My kinspeople.
Èmsinutay (Prewitt). The bag.
Engōmeen (Captain Pipe). "Grand national worship of the Delawares"; *see also* **Gamwing**.
E'span keo (Speck). Munsee Raccoon Dance.
Gamwing (Speck); **Ga'mwing** (Harrington); **Gum-mween** (Morgan). Big House Ceremony; *see also* **Ngamwin**.
Gicelëmû"kaong (Harrington). Great Spirit; *see also* **Kishelëmukòng**.
Gitctla'kan (Harrington). Thanksgiving Ceremony [Munsee].
Haiyuhpu (Dean); **Hayuhpu** (Dean). "Let's all have a smoke"; **Hayupu** (Prewitt). Smoke Time.
Hi'ngwikan (Blalock; McCartlin; Tiger; Dean). Big House; *see also* **Xingwikaon**.
Hweisk-queem (Wampum). Indian corn.
Kahahpon (Dean). Corn meal and meat.
K'ak (sing.) (Jack Longbone; McCartlin); **K'aks** (pl.) (Blalock); **Kakw** (Prewitt); **Kèkok** (Dean). Wampum beads.

Kë'tanïto'wët (Harrington). Great Spirit [Munsee].
Kik'li'k.a.n (Speck). Mixed Dance [Munsee].
Ki.lu'na ki'nt'ka'na (Speck). We are all dancing [Munsee].
Kinnickinnick (Speck). Tobacco and sumac-leaf smoking mixture.
Kišelamukɔng (Prewitt). "He Who Created Everything With His Thoughts"; the Creator.
Kishelëmukòng (Dean). Our Creator.
Ko-ha-kun (Davis); Kohokan (McCartlin); Kohók∧n (Prewitt). Corn mortar.
Kowi.'ka't (Speck). Round Dance [Munsee].
Ko'yewa (Speck). Beef.
Kweᵉtci'peneᵉs (Speck). Evening star.
Kwi (Harrington); Kwia (Elkhair); Kwih (Dean); 'Kwi/ya (Speck). Stop!
Lenahpön (Dean). Corn bread.
Lentkan (Dean); Ləntkən (Prewitt). Common Dance.
Lin-I-'kan (Speck). "Man's built house"; ceremonial cook house [Munsee].
Machtuzin (Zeisberger). Sweating Ceremony.
Manito (Speck); Manï'to (Harrington); Manitou (Adams; Speck); Manitto (Kluge and Luckenbach); Man.i't.u (Speck). Spirit (sing.).
Manitous (Speck); Mani'towük (Harrington); Manittos (Zeisberger); Manitu-oo-ak (Wampum); Manëtuwàk (Dean). Spirits (pl.).
Mani'towi'lnowak (Speck). Spiritual men [Munsee].
Masing (Dean). Spirit Face; see also Mesing.
Ma-ta-he-kuna (Dean). Prayer sticks.
Mata'kewin keo (Speck). War Dance [Munsee].
Ma'tehi'gun (Harrington); Mahtehikena (Dean). Prayer sticks.
Mawesi (Dean); Mawêsi (Prewitt); Mawĕnsin (Dean). Gathering Berries; part of Big House Ceremony in which attendants gather wampum beads and place them in their mouths.
Me-koo-she-kuna (Anderson). Talisman.
Mələk (Prewitt). Goose.
Mesing (Elizabeth Longbone); Məsingw (Prewitt); Mesingw (Elkhair); Mësingw (Dean); Messingk (Speck); Messingq (Adams); Mising (Anderson; Blalock; Davis; Jack Longbone; McCartlin; Shawnee; Tiger; Dean); Mïsi'ngwe (Harrington); Misings (pl.) (Blalock); Mizi'nk (Harrington). Spirit Face.
Mësinghòlikàn (Dean); Mes.i'ngheli.'k.an (Dean); Mïsinghâli'kün (Harrington); Mizinkhâli'kün (Harrington). Mesing impersonator.
Mësingòkw (Dean). Center post in the Big House.
Mes.i'nk keo (Speck). Face Dance [Munsee].
Mising-a-sa-pon (McCartlin). Brown and sweetened boiled corn meal.
Mizinkï'nlïka (Harrington) Mask Society dance [Munsee].
Mkäähi'gün (Harrington). Prayer sticks [Munsee]; see also Ma-ta-he-kuna.
Muxhatol'zing (Harrington). Eight-day form of Big House Ceremony.
Nee-shaw-neechk-togho-quanoo-maun (Wampum). Twelve-Day Ceremony [Munsee?].
Ngamwin (Speck); 'ngammuin (Zeisberger). Big House Ceremony.
Nimëwakàn (Dean). A lunch.
Olàmàn (Dean); Olu-mun (Blalock). Red paint.
Oshkosh (Adams; Blalock; Jack Longbone; McCartlin; Shawnee; Tiger; Dean). Big House attendant (sing.); see also Àshkas.
Oshkosh-suk (Davis; Dean); Osh-kosh-shuk (Elizabeth Longbone). Big House attendants.
Oxkwe'o ki'nt'ka.n (Speck). Woman's Dance [Munsee].
Pa"tümawas (Harrington). Great Spirit [Munsee].

Pawaw (Denton); **Powow** (Brainerd). Medicine person.

Pe-con (Anderson); **Pekawn** (Dean); **Pe-kon** (Blalock); **Pe.kon** (Elkhair); **Puccoon** (Speck). "Crimson—Grows in Timber"; red pigment.

Pele (Prewitt); **Pële** (Dean); **Pelee** (Blalock); **Pleah** (Elizabeth Longbone). Turkey, fowl, or bird phratry or clan.

Pi.ckwelane' o ka.n (Speck). Nighthawk Dance [Munsee].

Pil-hicks-soo-teen (Dean); **Pilhìksutin** (Dean); **PilhIksutin** (Prewitt); **PilhIksutin** (Dean). Cleansing cedar burning.

Pi'lsuⁿ (Harrington). Pure.

Powüni'gün (Harrington). Deerskin drum.

Puk-kah-wung-ah-me (Elizabeth Longbone); **Pukuwungu** (Blalock); **Pukwango** (Prewitt). Turtle phratry or clan.

Pu küⁿdi'gün (Harrington). Drumsticks with human faces and features.

Pw'awahe'gün (Harrington). Drum [Munsee].

Pw'awahe'günük (Harrington). Drumsticks [Munsee].

Sakima (Dean). Chief.

Sʌŋghikʌn (Prewitt); **Sànghikàn** (Dean). Pump-drill used to start fires in the Big House.

Sapan (Prewitt; Dean); **Sä'pan** (Harrington). Corn-meal gruel or pudding.

Seli'mwak (Speck). "Cranes"; drummers [Munsee].

Sexi'kiminsi (Harrington). Soft maple.

Shëmuwèmhòn (Dean). Horn spoon.

Shëwahsapan (Dean). Grape dumplings.

Shuhënikàn (Dean). Turtle-shell rattle with leather handle; *see also* **Šuhənikʌn**.

Šuhənikʌn (Prewitt). Turtle-shell rattle.

Tahkwëndalès (Dean). Fire-poker stick.

Ta-la-caw (Jack Longbone; Shawnee); **Ta-la-Kaw** (Anderson; Davis); **Talekaok** (Dean); **Təléka** (Prewitt). Big House singer, often called a "Crane."

Ta-ma-ha-mon (Dean); **Ta-mah-mon** (Anderson). Last Day of the Ceremony; *see also* **Temahema**.

Tale'gunük (Harrington); **Təlekáok** (Prewitt). Singers.

Taxo'xi xowüni'gün (Harrington). Shaking the tortoise-shell rattle.

Tcicko' 'koc keo (Speck). Robin Dance [Munsee].

Təmahəma (Prewitt); **Temahema** (Dean). Concluding ceremony on the thirteenth morning.

Təmikɛkw (Prewitt). "Everyone enter"; **Tëmikèkw** (Dean). "All come in."

Təmikɛt (Prewitt); **Tëmikèt** (Dean); **Tum-meet-kat** (Blalock; Davis; Jack Longbone; Dean). "Enterer"—ceremonial leader.

Tɛxtakʌn (Prewitt); **Tèxtakan** (Dean). Cupboard storage platform used in Big House campsites.

Took-seet (Elizabeth Longbone); **Tuk-seet** (Blalock); **Tuk-seet-ta-mee-mas** (Anderson); **Tùkwsit** (Prewitt; Dean). Wolf phratry or clan.

Tuk-wem-tet (Anderson). Blouse.

Tuⁿda'i wäheⁿ'ji manïtowük (Harrington). "Fire drill of the Manï'tos."

Tung-sho-mu-tat (Anderson). Power from the deer spirit.

Ush-kos; **Ush-kosh** (Anderson; McCartlin). Attendant; *see also* **Ashkas**.

Wapana'chkiwak (Speck and Moses). "Sunrise land people."

W'a'tekan (Harrington). Munsee Big House.

Ween-da-much-teen (Wampum). Twelve-Day Ceremony [Munsee?].

Wendji·kaneᵉ'i (Dean); **Wen-ge-kun-a** (Anderson; Jack Longbone); **Wen-ge-kune** (Jack Longbone); **Wənjikanéi** (Prewitt); **Wënjikanei** (Dean); Vision recitation.

Wənjikanéit (Prewitt); **Wenjikaneit** (Dean). Vision-song reciter.
Wil-teem (Dean); **Wiltin** (Dean, Prewitt). Calling of names in the Big House.
Wisahkakw (Dean). Red-oak-bark tea.
Wito"pi (Harrington). Red-alder bark.
Wsinkhoalican (Zeisberger). Human-face image; *see also* **Mësinghòlikàn**.
Xingwikaon (Dean); **Xingwikáon** (Prewitt); **Xi'ngwikan** (Harrington). Big House.

Bibliography

Adams, Richard C.
1890 Notes on the Delaware Indians. In *Report of Indians Taxed and Not Taxed. United States Census for 1890*, vol. 10. Washington, D.C.: U.S. Government Printing Office.
1904 *Ancient Religion of the Delaware Indians: Observations and Reflections*. Washington, D.C.: Law Reporter.
Bierhorst, John
1995 *Mythology of the Lenape: Guide and Texts*. Tucson: University of Arizona Press.
Brickell, John
1842 Narrative of John Brickell's Captivity among the Delaware Indians. *American Pioneer* 1, 2d ed.: 43, 46, 48, 56.
Brinton, Daniel Garrison
1885 *The Lenape and Their Legends, with a Complete Text and Symbols of the Walam Olum*. Library of Aboriginal American Literature 5. Philadelphia: published by the author.
Callendar, Lee A., and Ruth Slivka
1984 *Shawnee Home Life: The Paintings of Earnest Spybuck*. New York: Museum of the American Indian, Heye Foundation.
Dean, Nora Thompson
1984 Remembrances of the Big House Church. In *The Lenape Indian: A Symposium*, ed. Herbert C. Kraft, 41–49. Archaeological Research Center, Publication No. 7. South Orange, N.J.: Seton Hall University.
Denton, Daniel
[1670] 1966 *A Brief Description of New-York*. March of America Facsimile Series 26. Ann Arbor: University Microfilms.
Dowd, Gregory Evans
1992 *A Spirited Resistance: The North American Indian Struggle for Unity, 1745–1815*. Baltimore: Johns Hopkins University Press.
Dwight, Sereno E., ed.
1822 *Memoirs of the Rev. David Brainerd, Missionary to the Indians on the Borders of New-York, New Jersey, and Pennsylvania: Chiefly Taken from His Own Diary*, ed. Jonathan Edwards. New Haven, Conn.: S. Converse.

Fenton, William N.
1953 *The Iroquois Eagle Dance: An Offshoot of the Calumet Dance; with An Analysis of the Iroquois Eagle Dance and Songs, by Gertrude P. Kurath.* Bureau of American Ethnology Bulletin 156. Washington, D.C.
1987 *The False Faces of the Iroquois.* Norman: University of Oklahoma Press.

Gehring, Charles T., and Robert S. Grumet, eds.
1987 Observations of the Indians from Jasper Danckaerts's Journal, 1679–1680. *William and Mary Quarterly* 44, no. 1: 104–20.

Gilliland, Lula Mae Gibson
1947 Notes on Delaware Religion, Ceremonies, and Dances. MS 3873. Manuscript on File, National Anthropological Archives, Smithsonian Institution, Washington, D.C.

Gipson, Lawrence Henry, ed.
1938 *The Moravian Indian Missions on White River: Diaries and Letters, May 5, 1799 to November 12, 1806.* Indianapolis: Indiana Historical Bureau.

Goddard, R. H. Ives, III
1979 Delaware Big House Ceremonial. In *Native North American Spirituality of the Eastern Woodlands: Sacred Myths, Dreams, Visions, Speeches, Healing Formulas, Rituals, and Ceremonials*, ed. Elisabeth Tooker, 104–24. New York: Paulist Press.

Goedhuys, Diederick, trans.
1996 Adriaen Cornelissen van der Donck: Description of New Netherland. In *Mohawk Country: Early Narratives about a Native People*, eds. Dean R. Snow, Charles T. Gehring, and William A. Starna, 104–30. Syracuse, N.Y.: Syracuse University Press.

Grumet, Robert S., ed.
1999 Journey on the Forbidden Path: Chronicles of a Diplomatic Mission to the Allegheny Country, March–September, 1760. *Transactions of the American Philosophical Society* 89, no. 2: 1–156.

Hallowell, A. Irving
1926 Bear Ceremonialism in the Northern Hemisphere. *American Anthropologist* 28, no. 1: 1–175.

Harrington, Mark Raymond
1908 Vestiges of Material Culture Among the Canadian Delawares. *American Anthropologist* 10, no. 4: 408–18.
1921 *Religion and Ceremonies of the Lenape.* Indian Notes and Monographs 19. New York: Museum of the American Indian, Heye Foundation.

Heckewelder, John
[1818] 1876 *History, Manners, and Customs of the Indian Nations Who Once Inhabited Pennsylvania and the Neighboring States.* Rev. ed. Memoirs of the Pennsylvania Historical Society 12. Philadelphia.

Hoffman, W. J.
1891 *The Midewiwin or "Grand Medicine Society" of the Ojibwa.* Bureau of American Ethnology Annual Report 7. Washington, D.C.

Hulbert, Archer Butler, and William Nathaniel Schwarze, eds.
[1779–80] 1910 *David Zeisberger's History of the North American Indians.* Ohio State Archaeological and Historical Quarterly 19: 1–189.

Hunter, William A., ed.
1954 John Hays' Diary and Journal of 1760. *Pennsylvania Archaeologist* 24, no. 2: 63–84.

James, Bartlett Burleigh, and J. Franklin Jameson, eds.
1913 *Journal of Jasper Danckaerts, 1679–1680.* New York: Charles Scribner's Sons.

Jameson, J. Franklin, ed.
1909 *Narratives of New Netherland, 1609–1664.* New York: Charles Scribner and Sons.

Johnson, Jeremiah, trans.
1841 *Adriaen van der Donck: Description of the New Netherlands. Collections of the New-York Historical Society*, Second Series 1, 125–242.

Jones, Peter
1860 *Life and Journals of Kah-ke-wa-quo-na-by (Rev. Peter Jones), Wesleyan Missionary.* Toronto: A. Green.

Jones, Ruthe Blalock, ed.
1973 Hi'ngwikan: Delaware Big House Ceremony. Manuscript in possession of James Rementer, Dewey, Okla.

Kent, Barry C., Janet Rice, and Kakuko Ota
1981 A Map of 18th Century Indian Towns in Pennsylvania. *Pennsylvania Archaeologist* 51, no. 4: 1–18.

Kinietz, W. Vernon
1940 European Civilization as a Determinant of Native Indian Customs. *American Anthropologist* 42, no. 1: 116–21.
1946 Delaware Culture Chronology. *Indiana Historical Society Prehistory Research Series* 3, no. 1: 1–143.

Kraft, Herbert C.
1986 *The Lenape: Archaeology, History, and Ethnography.* Newark: New Jersey Historical Society.

Landes, Ruth
1968 *Ojibwa Religion and the Midewiwin.* Madison: University of Wisconsin Press.

Michelson, Truman
1912 Ethnological and Linguistic Field Notes from the Munsee in Kansas and the Delaware in Oklahoma. MS 2776. Manuscript on File, National Anthropological Archives, Smithsonian Institution, Washington, D.C.

Miller, Jay
1976 The Delaware Doll Dance. *Man in the Northeast* 12: 80–84.
1980 A Structuralist Analysis of the Delaware Big House Rite. In *Ethnology in Oklahoma*, ed. John H. Moore, 107–33. University of Oklahoma Papers in Anthropology 21, no. 2.
1994 The 1806 Purge among the Indiana Delaware: Sorcery, Gender, Boundaries, and Legitimacy. *Ethnohistory* 41, no. 2: 245–66.
1997 Old Religion Among the Delawares: The Gamwing (Big House Rite). *Ethnohistory* 44, no. 1: 113–34.

Miller, Jay, and Nora Thompson Dean
1978 A Personal Account of the Delaware Big House Rite. *Pennsylvania Archaeologist* 48, nos. 1–2: 39–43.

Morgan, Lewis Henry
[1851] 1962 *League of the Iroquois.* With an Introduction by William N. Fenton. New York: Corinth.
[1877] 1976 *Ancient Society.* New York: Gordon Press.

Newcomb, William W., Jr.
1956a *The Culture and Acculturation of the Delaware Indians.* University of Michigan, Department of Anthropology, Anthropological Papers 10. Ann Arbor.
1956b The Peyote Cult of the Delaware Indians. *Texas Journal of Science* 8: 202–11.

Nichols, Deborah, ed.
1997 *Legends of the Delaware Indians and Picture Writing* by Richard C. Adams. Syracuse, N.Y.: Syracuse University Press.

O'Callaghan, Edmund B., and Berthold Fernow, eds.
1853–87 *Documents Relative to the Colonial History of the State of New York*. 15 vols. Albany: Weed, Parsons.

O'Donnell, Thomas F., ed.
[1655] 1968 *A Description of the New Netherlands, by Adriaen van der Donck*. Syracuse, N.Y.: Syracuse University Press.

Oestreicher, David M.
1994 Unmasking the Walam Olum: A 19th-Century Hoax. *Bulletin of the Archaeological Society of New Jersey* 49: 1–44.

Petrullo, Vincenzo
1934 *The Diabolic Root: A Study of Peyotism, the New Indian Religion among the Delawares*. Philadelphia: University of Pennsylvania Press.

Pomfret, John E., ed.
[1683] 1970 *William Penn's Own Account of the Lenni Lenape or Delaware Indians*. Republication of an edition published by Albert Cook Myers, 1937. Wallingford, Penna.: Middle Atlantic Press.

Prewitt, Terry J.
1981 *Tradition and Culture Change in the Oklahoma Delaware Big House Community: 1867–1924*. Laboratory of Archaeology, University of Tulsa, Contributions to Anthropology 9.

Roark-Calnek, Susan N.
1977 Indian Way in Oklahoma: Transactions in Honor and Legitimacy. Ph.D. diss., Bryn Mawr College.

Speck, Frank G.
1931 *A Study of the Delaware Big House Ceremony*. Publications of the Pennsylvania Historical Commission 2. Harrisburg.
1937 *Oklahoma Delaware Ceremonies, Feasts, and Dances*. Memoirs of the American Philosophical Society 7. Philadelphia.
[1949] 1995 *Midwinter Rites of the Cayuga Long House*. Reprint, Lincoln: University of Nebraska Press.

Speck, Frank G., and Jesse Moses
1945 *The Celestial Bear Comes Down to Earth*. Reading Public Museum and Art Gallery, Scientific Publication 7. Reading, Penna.

Sumpter, Nancy Falleaf
1994 A Visit to the Meeting House. *Bulletin of the Archaeological Society of New Jersey* 49: 60.

Tooker, Elizabeth
1970 *The Iroquois Ceremonial of Midwinter*. Syracuse, N.Y.: Syracuse University Press.
1979, ed. *Native North American Spirituality of the Eastern Woodlands: Sacred Myths, Dreams, Visions, Speeches, Healing Formulas, Rituals, and Ceremonies*. New York: Paulist Press.

Van Gastel, Ada
1990 Van der Donck's Description of the Indians: Additions and Corrections. *William and Mary Quarterly* 47, no. 3: 411–21.

Vogt, Fred W.
1975 *A History of Ethnology*. New York: Holt, Rinehart, and Winston.

Wallace, Anthony F. C.
1956 New Religions Among the Delaware Indians, 1600–1800. *Southwestern Journal of Anthropology* 12, no. 1: 1–21.
1969 *The Death and Rebirth of the Seneca*. New York: Alfred A. Knopf.

Wallace, Paul A. W.
1981 *Indians in Pennsylvania*. Rev. ed., William A. Hunter. Harrisburg: Pennsylvania Historical and Museum Commission.
Wampum, John [Chief Waubuno]
1845 *The Traditions of the Delawares*. London: Bowers Brothers.
Weslager, Clinton A.
1971 Name-Giving among the Delaware Indians. *Names* 19, no. 4: 268–83.
1972 *The Delaware Indians: A History*. New Brunswick, N.J.: Rutgers University Press.
1974 Delaware Name Giving and Modern Practice. In *A Delaware Indian Symposium*, ed. Herbert C. Kraft, 135–45. Harrisburg: Pennsylvania Historical and Museum Commission.
1978 *The Delaware Indian Westward Migration, With the Texts of Two Manuscripts (1821–22) Responding to General Lewis Cass's Inquiries about Lenape Culture and Language*. Wallingford, Penna.: The Middle Atlantic Press.
White, Leslie A., ed.
1959 *Lewis Henry Morgan: The Indian Journals, 1859–62*. Ann Arbor: University of Michigan Press.
Witthoft, John
1949 *Green Corn Ceremonialism in the Eastern Woodlands*. University of Michigan Museum of Anthropology, Occasional Contributions 13. Ann Arbor.

Index

Adams, Richard C., 55
Adams, William, 49, 52, 55
Alluwe (Okla.), 169
American Museum of Natural History (New York, N.Y.), 79
Anderson, George Thomas, 19, 121, 122, 192
Anderson, John, 18, 152, 173
Anderson, Josie Bullet, 159
Anderson, Ollie Beaver, 151–55, 173, 175
Anderson, Sam, 152, 154, 159, 164, 170
Anderson, Tom, 116, 151, 152, 154, 173, 175
Anthony, Michael, 79, 83, 84
Attendants (Askasak, helpers, workers), Big House repairs and preparation of ceremonial grounds, 62–63, 101, 166, 183; call people to services, 188; cedar burned by, 185; and children, 149, 156; fires, ceremonial, 8, 56, 60, 63, 81, 99, 112, 115, 150, 156, 181, 185, 190; firewood gathered by, 63, 97, 156; food, 8, 14, 16, 36, 37, 56, 60, 63, 66, 70, 81, 97, 98, 99, 108–109, 113, 115, 131, 135, 150, 151, 157, 161, 164, 165, 167, 169, 170, 174, 176, 181, 183, 190; game distributed by, 14, 16; guard Big House, 166; and hunters, 14, 51, 67, 90, 109, 184; maintain order, 8, 63, 99, 177, 192; Mawesi ritual (wampum-gathering), 13, 68, 110, 168, 171, 174, 186, 192; as messengers, 60, 62, 81; names of, 19; notified by men and Mesinghalikun, 180; number of, 156, 163, 167, 169, 180, 183, 189; paid with wampum, 70, 71, 90, 99, 115, 118, 150, 157, 171, 183, 191, 192; paint faces, 100, 113, 150, 158, 167, 172, 177, 185, 193; paint Mesingw carvings, 113, 158, 172, 177, 185, 193; phratry, two from each, 101, 152; prayer sticks distributed by, 185, 193; seating arrangement in Big House, 8, 189; selected by chief, 148; sleepers wakened by, 8, 99, 149, 152, 156, 161, 164, 170, 184; sweep visionary/dance path, 8, 10, 50–51, 56, 60, 63, 64, 70, 81, 92, 99, 101, 108, 112, 115, 118, 131, 145, 146, 150, 157, 161, 170, 174, 177, 178, 181, 185, 190; tents, location of, 62, 99, 148, 152, 163–64, 176, 181; Wiltin ritual (calling of names), 13, 110, 112, 171, 181, 186, 191; work, 62, 97, 148, 151
Atsingnetsing (Corning, N.Y.), 34

Bacone College (Muskogee, Okla.), 151
Bartles, Joe, 155
Bartlesville, Okla., 17, 151, 160, 169
Bartlesville Public Library, 161
Bear, 126–30; bones burned, 135; Circum-Boreal Bear Ceremonialism, 36, 128–30, 132, 135–36; hide, 127, 130–131, 135; sacrifice ceremony, 128–36, 143, 146; "Smooth" Bear, 127–28
Beate: baptized at Friedenshüetten. Pa., 42; as "the greatest lying prophet," 46–47; at Moncy Town, 42; as seer and teacher, 45–46; visions, 42–43, 44, 47; and the Wyandotte, 46
Bethlehem, Pa., 38
Big House: Boston Creek (Ontario, Can.), 128; built around living tree, 152; Christians preach against it, 17, 161–62; Copan (Okla.) Big House, 3–4, 18, 21, 147, 151, 162, 178–80; Dance

Path (Beautiful or Great White Path, Milky Way), 4, 8, 10, 60, 98, 101, 105, 108, 120–21, 139; Delawares and Cayuga Long House, 84; Lenape language, 17; nails, 98, 166, 172; rites unobserved, disaster due to, 35, 72, 74, 93–94, 121–22; tent campsite, 18, 40, 62, 81, 148, 159, 163, 175, 180, 187–88; uninvited Indians, 17; White River (Ind.) Longhouses, 38

Big House Ceremony: attempt to revive in 1940s, 17, 96, 155, 165, 169, 173; eighth night, 140; eleventh night, 186; fifth night, 136, 138, 185; first night, 10, 14, 103–108, 133, 183, 184; fourth day, 184, 191; fourth night, 13, 14, 110, 167, 184, 185; last full ceremony, 3, 17, 21, 165, 180, 187, 194; ninth morning, 185; ninth night, 13, 14, 68, 91, 111–13, 157, 192; second night, 108–109, 184; seventh night, 13, 111, 185; sixth night, 90, 131, 157, 185; tenth night, 154, 181, 185; third night, 56, 109, 184; Turkey group ceremonies, 117; twelfth night (and following morning), 5, 13, 14, 69, 91–92, 113–15, 150, 154, 158, 165, 166, 167, 172, 183, 186, 193–94; Wolf group ceremonies, 117

Big John, Mary, 172
Black Beaver, 151
Blalock, Lucy Parks, 18, 153, 156–159
Bowring, Okla., 147
Brainerd, David, 30–33, 76, 120
Brown, William, 61
Buffalo, Sam, 152
Buffalo, Tom, 142, 154, 155
Bullet, George, 157, 169, 171

Calumet ceremony, 146
Canestio River, N.Y., 34
Canfield, Ontario, Can., 128
Captain Curley-Head, 19
Captain Pipe, 49, 51–52
Captain Pipe's Town (near Sandusky, Ohio), 49
Cass, Lewis, 49
Cedar, 13, 53, 69, 91, 112, 113, 158, 182, 185, 191, 193
Cedar, Nancy, 174
Ceremony Leader (Tamiket, "Enterer"), 8, 10, 19, 54, 56, 61, 62, 65, 66, 82, 83, 87, 90, 94, 98, 100, 103, 109 110, 117, 133–34, 136, 146, 148, 150, 183, 184, 186, 187, 188, 189, 190, 191, 193

Chief Anderson, 55
Chief Anderson's Town (Anderson, Ind.), 38
Christian Delawares, 17, 35–36, 38, 50, 192
Claremore, Okla., 151
Code Talkers, 147
Color symbolism: black, 4, 58, 124; red, 4, 58, 124, 132, 135, 136, 143, 185; red and black, 3, 4, 28, 32, 56, 59, 62, 70, 74, 84, 87, 91, 97, 98, 113, 152, 165, 166, 170, 176, 185; red, black, and white, 139; white, 130, 132, 139
Conner, John, 40
Conner, William, 55
Cooweescoowee District, Okla., 95
Copan, Okla., 147, 173
Copan Lake Reservoir, 3
Councils, 24
Craig County, Okla., 177
Curing, 32, 41, 103

Dances, 25, 29, 31, 34–35, 36, 39, 43, 44, 85–86; Cantico, or Round Dances, 30, 144–45; Cantico Stomp, 55, 158; Common Dance, 16, 187; Doll Dance, 94; Eagle Dance (Iroquois), 146; Man's Dance, 138–40; Mesingw Dance, 32, 76–77, 94, 143–44; Mixed Dance, 140; Nighthawk Dance, 145–46; Otterskin Dance, 94; Raccoon Dance, 142–43; Robin Dance, 142; Thanksgiving Dance, 57–60, 84–85; Trance Dance, 24; War Dance, 144; Woman's Dance, 140
Danckaerts, Jasper, 24
Davis, Anna Anderson, 19, 159–62, 173
Davis, Buck, 159, 160
Dean, Nora Thompson, 5, 13, 20, 180–94
Deer, 4, 14, 16, 56, 62, 67, 70, 73, 92, 93, 185, 191; deer-hoof rattles, 39; disappearance of, 21, 171, 191; hunting of, 28, 51, 109–10, 149, 167, 185, 191; spirit power from, 154
Delaware River, 29, 58
Denton, Daniel, 28–29
Detroit Public Library, 49
Dewey, Okla., 62, 159, 166, 169, 175
Directional symbolism: east, 35, 36, 53, 54, 56–57, 59, 64, 70, 83, 93, 114, 115, 133, 154, 165, 182, 184, 186, 187, 188, 193, 194; east–west, 4, 54, 57, 59, 62, 70, 80, 91, 97, 98, 132, 166, 184, 188, 190; left, 4, 62, 70, 91,

99, 118, 124, 185; north, 4, 59, 64, 65, 94, 132, 185, 189, 190; north and south, 62, 93, 187, 193; northeast, 188; right, 4, 56, 59, 62, 65, 93, 118, 124, 184, 185, 190; south, 33, 57, 59, 60, 91, 185, 189, 190; southeast, 94; southwest, 95; west, 56, 59, 60, 64, 80, 83, 112, 121, 133, 138, 163, 172, 182, 185, 192

Dowd, Gregory Evans, 38

Drum: board drum, 30; dried deerskin drum, 8, 10, 39, 50, 52, 53, 54, 56, 59, 62, 65, 68, 70, 77, 80, 82, 83, 84, 90, 91, 92, 98, 103, 105, 107, 110, 136–38, 141, 149, 154, 157, 164, 165, 170, 172, 174, 177, 178, 183, 184, 189; drum sticks, 13, 39, 50, 53, 68, 70, 80, 83, 84, 90, 98, 112, 136–38, 141, 154, 157, 165, 170, 174, 176, 185, 193; water drum, 143

Drum, Mary, 161

Dunnville (Ontario, Can.), 128

Easy, William, 157, 159, 164, 166, 167

Elkhair, Charlie, 8, 10, 13, 14, 16, 61, 63, 72, 74, 87–94, 103–105, 152–53, 157, 159, 166, 169, 173, 174, 176

Elkhair, Susan, 163

Ellis, Nannie, 172

Erie, Lake, 49

Fairfield (Ontario, Can.), 38

Falleaf, George, 157, 167, 168, 174

Falleaf, John, 152, 154, 155, 158, 159, 160, 173

Falleaf, Liza (Lisa), 19, 186

Falleaf, Mona, 178

Falleaf, Numerous, 178

Falleaf, Sally, 161, 173

Feather wands, 145

Fenton, William N., 146

Fire: addressed as grandfather, 105, 107, 111, 113, 191; ashes removed, 56, 60, 112, 121, 182, 185, 192; cook fire, 188; fire making, 60, 63, 68, 80, 81, 90, 98, 112, 121, 157, 166, 172, 182, 185, 192; pure fire, 5, 50, 60, 63, 68, 81, 91, 98, 107, 112, 121, 157, 192

Food and cooking: apples, 163; bark tea, 183, 190; bark utensils, 80, 93, 172; baskets, 92, 93, 145, 172; beans, 53, 82, 176; bilberries, 37; bowls, 176; bread, dutch-oven baked, 163, 176; bread, fried, 165, 176; broth, 150; buckets, 99; candy, 167, 191; ceremonial meals and feasts, 8, 14, 16, 24, 25, 30, 31, 35–36, 37, 39, 40, 43, 44, 53, 54, 57, 60, 67, 68, 70, 83, 91, 135, 146, 165, 184–85; chili, 165, 167, 170, 191; coffee, 165, 176; coffee pot, 191; cookhouse, 131; cooking fire, 188; corn meal, porridge, bread, and cakes, 5, 8, 16, 30, 36, 39, 40, 53, 60, 63, 66, 67, 82, 83, 87, 89, 99, 108–109, 113, 145, 148, 157, 160, 163, 165, 169, 171, 172, 176, 190, 191, 192; corn meal addressed as mother, 109; cupboard, 163, 192; eggs, 37; enamel plates and cups, 191; fry pan, 191; grape dumplings, 192; grapes, wild, 192; Indian soup plates, 176; kettle, 36, 39; kettle, brass, 89, 91; kettle, cast-iron, 191; kettle, cooking pot, 148, 171; molasses, 37; mortar, pounder, 8, 99, 160–61, 169, 192; pies, 163, 165, 170, 192; potatoes, 53, 58, 176; pumpkins, 53; salt, not used, 135; soup, 54; spoons, 43; spoon, horn, 190; spoon, mussel-shell, 67, 109; squashes, 53, 82; strawberries, wild, 80; strawberry drink, 80, 82; sugar, 37; winnowing basket, 172. *See also* Meat

Fouts, Julius, 61, 72, 153, 166, 169, 174, 193

Fouts, Minnie, 19, 61, 159, 161, 165, 167, 169, 177, 186, 193

Frenchman, Dennis, 178

Frenchman, Rosa, 161, 167, 178

Gender roles and relations, 18, 65, 189

Gender symbolism, 122–25

Generational categories, roles, and activities, 14, 15–16, 20

Gibson, Jim, 154

Gift giving, 27, 36

Gilliland, Lula Mae Gibson, 147–50, 161

Gipson, Lawrence H., 38

Goddard, R. H. Ives, III, 95, 96

Goshen, Ind., 38

Grand River Reserve. *See* Six Nations Reserve

Great Awakening, 30

Great Fish River (Mississippi River), 58

Half Moon, Tom, 116, 118, 119, 120, 157, 160, 167, 169, 193

Harrington, Mark Raymond, 5, 13, 31, 50, 57, 61–86

Heaven, 64–65

Heckewelder, John, 35, 74

Hemlock bough, smoke, 54, 81

Heye, George Gustav, 61
Hill, Ben, 8, 155, 157, 159, 166, 167, 168, 173, 174, 176, 181
Hill, Jane, 159
Historical Society of Pennsylvania, 34
Horn Rattle, 145
Howard, Geneva, 178
Hudson River Valley, 21
Hulbert, Archer Butler, 35
Hunter, William A., 34

Jackson, Jim, 157
Jackson, John, 159
Jacob, 42
Johnson, G. H. M., 50
Johnston, John, 49
Jones, Peter, 50, 85
Jones, Ruthe Blalock, 151–77, 180
Joseph, 23
Joshua, 42
Juneauta (Juniata, Pa.), 30, 31, 120

Kinnickinnick, 98, 106–107
Kinship relations and obligations, 16–18, 51, 94
Kluge, John Peter, 38, 42–48

Little Caney River Valley (Okla.), 3, 62
Little Horn, 151
Longbone, Anna, 162
Longbone, Caroline, 159, 172
Longbone, Elizabeth, 162–66
Longbone, Emmet, 165
Longbone, Ferguson, 19
Longbone, Jack, 166–69
Longbone, Jesse, 172
Longbone, Roy, 172
Longbone, Willie, 8, 157, 162, 164, 165, 167, 170, 173, 176, 183
Long Island, N.Y., 28
Luckenbach, Abraham, 38–42

McCartlin, Fannie, 169–73
McCartlin, Jim, 166
Maryland, 30, 32
Mask Society, 85
Maxkok, 126–28, 130
Meat, 4, 16, 39, 54, 83, 99, 113, 164, 165, 170, 191; bear, 36, 40, 126–31, 135, 146; bear grease, 135; deer, 14, 16, 30, 36, 37, 40, 51, 53, 56, 57, 62, 70, 83, 89, 92, 149, 154, 157, 164, 167, 171, 185; deer liver, 135; moose, 135; pure animals and birds, 101, 105; rabbits, 164, 171; squirrels, 164, 171, 185; wild turkey, 164, 171
Mekinges, 55
Me-koo-she-kuna, 153
Mesinghalikan (Mesingw impersonator): acute vision of, 100, 158; addressed as grandfather, 100; capacity to do evil as well as cure and help, 119–20; celebrated in springtime dance, 76–77; controls deer, 89, 99; costume taken to museums in the east, 21; costume gone, 158; dances, 4, 13, 47–48, 57, 67, 76–77, 86, 110, 175, 191; dancer, 154; dancer selected by chief, 148; disease cured by, 85, 100; disease, protects children from, 37, 77; evil spirit man, 148; first appeared, 119–20; frightens unruly children, 77, 100, 158; Harrington identifies masked dancer at Juneauta Town as, 31, 32; helps hunters, 78, 89–90; hideous appearance, 40, 48, 51, 57, 168, 175, 177; hunters ask for success, 67, 89–90; polices meetings, 51, 78, 158, 168; rides buggy, 182–83; rides on horseback, 76, 182; separate rites among Munsee, 83; silent, 57; speaks, 85; terrifies children, 4, 57, 77, 148, 154, 160, 168, 171, 175; terrifies dogs, 175, 177; terrifies horses, 171, 175, 180; terrifies women, 154; tobacco given to, 4, 77, 86, 100, 155, 160, 158, 171, 175 travels with messengers announcing meeting, 180, 182; Turkey group has rights to costume and rituals, 94
Michelson, Truman, 13, 87
Michigan Territory, 49
Miller, Jay, 5, 96, 116, 180
Missionaries, 30, 34, 35, 38, 50, 85
Moncy Town, Ind., 42
Montour, Isaac, 79, 86
Montour, Joseph, 126
Montour, Josiah, 126, 134
Moravian Archives (Bethlehem, Pa.), 35, 38
Morgan, Lewis Henry, 49, 52–53, 55
Moses, Jesse, Sr., 126
Moses, Jesse, Jr., 126
Munceytown, Ontario, Can., 79, 83
Museum of the American Indian, Heye Foundation (New York, N.Y.), 61

Muskogee, Okla., 151
Myers, Albert Cook, 29

Naming customs and practices, 18–20, 157
New Jersey, 30
New Netherland, 23, 25
New York, 28, 30
Nowata County, Okla., 17

Oestreicher, David M., 58
Offerings: burnt cedar, 13, 53, 69, 91, 112, 113, 158, 182, 185, 191, 193; burnt deer-tail-hair, 4; burnt hemlock boughs, 54, 81; deer, 29, 31, 111; deer skin, 36, 40, 54, 71, 93, 121; first fruits, 29; tobacco, 4, 37, 67, 77, 86, 89–90, 100, 109–10, 154, 168, 171, 184, 191; wampum, 28, 54; water, 4
Ohio, 35

Parks, Edith, 172
Parks, George, 156
Parks, Jake, 8, 164, 166, 169, 174, 176, 183
Parks, Jim, 166
Parks, Nancy Wilson, 156, 172
Parks, Rosie, 157, 169
Parks, Ruth, 172
Penn, William, 29–30
Pennsylvania, 29, 30, 34, 35
Peters, Nicodemus, 126, 128–46
Peterson, Eliza, 166
Peyote Religion, 21
Pheasant, Monroe, 79
Philadelphia, Pa., 95
Piqua, Ohio, 49
Post, Christian Frederick, 34–35, 49
Post Oak (Okla.), 169, 172
Prayer Call, 28, 34, 35, 40, 45, 53, 54, 57, 58–59, 68, 69, 70, 71, 72, 83, 93, 112, 149, 150, 159, 165, 182, 185, 187, 190, 193, 194
Prayer sticks, 68, 70, 83, 84, 90, 98, 112, 154, 157, 174, 182, 185–86, 193

Raccoon Creek (Okla.), 107
Ranck, Anna Maria, 38
Revolutionary War, 49
Ritual: ceremonial fires, traditional methods, 60; chastity during, 51, 121; children, 152, 184; Christian Delaware preachers, 192; deer meat, 53; dogs, 56, 60; domesticated animals, 99; entering or leaving during, 65, 149, 190; help each other, 127; honesty, 40; hospitality, 40; intoxicated people, 158, 192; laughing, rude behavior during, 56, 60; liquor or strong drink, 40, 45, 54, 81, 99; love, 40; matches, 60, 63; Mawesi (Wampum gathering), 13, 14, 69, 90, 174, 186, 192; men avoiding company of women during, 56; men avoiding each other, 188; menstruating women, 81, 99, 158, 170, 188; mixing of sexes during, 184, 188; nails or iron, 98, 166, 172; people from other tribes, 149; purity and purification, 5, 50, 72, 81, 98, 101, 103, 105, 111–12, 115, 158, 182, 185, 188, 191, 193; ritual hunt, 8, 13, 14–15, 36, 51, 53, 62, 67–68, 81, 89, 109–10, 126–31, 148–49, 154, 158, 164, 167, 171, 184–85, 191; salt, 135; sleeping, 8, 99, 149, 152, 161, 164, 170, 184; sweating ritual (Machtuzin; Muxhatol'zing), 36–37, 73, 99, 121; tug-of-war, 133–34; unity, 40; "unlawful" pleasures, 52; walking, prescribed paths of during, 56, 170; white people, 17, 57, 149, 156, 168; white man's food, 148; white man's tools, 45, 63; Wiltin (Calling of Names), 13, 14, 157, 171, 181, 186, 191; women and children, 121, 185
Rochester, N.Y., 49–50
Rogers County, Okla., 17
Roosevelt, Eleanor, 147

Schmidt, Wilhem, 122
Schwarze, William Nathaniel, 35
Scioto River (Ohio), 120
Secaughcung (N.Y.), 34
Seven Years' War, 34
Sex, discussion of, 140
Shamanic possession, 24–25, 28–29, 31–32
Shamans, 99, 102–103
Shamokin (Pa.), 120
Shawnee, William, 173–75
Shawnee Prophet, 38
Sickness, 31
Silver brooches, 39
Simonds, Jacob, 144
Singers (Talekoak), 8, 10, 50–51, 52, 53, 54, 59, 62, 65, 68, 80, 82, 84, 90, 91, 98, 103, 105, 110, 136, 140, 143–44, 149, 150, 154, 155, 157, 161, 164, 168, 170, 174, 183, 184, 189, 190
Six Nations Reserve (Ontario, Can.), 79, 80, 83, 121, 126, 128

Smoothtown District (Ontario, Can.), 126
Speck, Frank G., 5, 95–146, 151
Spirits: animal, 24, 101; cloud, 102; directional, 4; Evening or Great Star, 102; evil, 103; Evil Manitou, 97; fire, 102, 105, 107, 111, 113, 191; Great Spirit (Creator, Great Manitou), 4, 25, 41–42, 45, 46–47, 53, 54, 59–60, 63, 64, 65, 79, 81, 83, 84, 97, 98, 99, 102, 105, 108, 111, 113, 114, 115, 118, 120, 134, 140, 145, 182, 184 186, 189; Great Spirit's wife, 26–27; Manitous, 24, 25, 37, 43–44, 100, 105, 113, 120, 189; in Me-koo-she-kuna, 153; Mesingw, 3, 4, 32, 37, 39–40, 45, 50, 56, 62, 67, 74–76, 85, 87, 89, 97, 100, 105, 113, 119–20, 127, 147, 152, 162, 165, 166, 171, 176, 183, 188, 189; moon, 111; Mother Earth, 64, 101–102, 189; Pleiades, 102; protecting deities, guardians, 41, 56, 60, 73; Sun, 102, 114; Sky-keepers, 4; Thunderers, 4, 64, 101, 183; Tortoise, 101–102; Turkey, 101; Water, 105, 111; Wind, 111; Winged people, 4
Spybuck, Orie, 157, 159, 165, 167
Star clan, 126
Sticks, 27, 28, 29, 81
Still, Isaac, 34
Sumpter, Nancy Falleaf, 151, 178–79
Susquehanna River, 30, 58, 76, 120
Sweat Doctor, 153
Sweathouse, 37, 73, 99, 121
Symbolism: Big House, 4, 138; duality, 122–25; earth, 64, 105, 101, 189; fire, 36, 105, 107, 111, 113; Great Spirit, 102, 105, 108; Mesingw, 4, 72, 100, 105, 158; Milky Way, 121; Moon, 111; prayer call, 72; Ritual Hunt, 13, 14; Thunderers, 101; Tobacco, 109–110; Tortoise, 101, 102; Turkey, 101; turtle-shell rattles, 103, 107; wampum, 118, 172; Water, 105, 111; Wind, 111. *See also* Color symbolism; Directional symbolism; Twelve, symbolism of

Tatamy, Moses Tunda, 34
Taxton, Minnie, 173
Teedyuscung, 34
Thanksgiving, 16, 24, 40, 45, 57, 59, 63, 64, 82, 84, 91, 101, 103, 105, 107–108, 111, 113, 127, 145, 146, 150, 164, 166, 184, 187, 189
Thompson, Sarah Wilson, 19, 161, 166, 167, 182, 186, 189
Tiger, Irene Anderson, 175–78

Timothy, Nellis F., 79, 85
Tobacco, addressed as grandfather, 109–10; chewing, 67; offering, 4, 37, 67, 77, 86, 89–90, 100, 155, 168, 171, 184, 185, 190, 191; smoking, 25, 37, 39, 52, 60, 65, 98, 106–107, 153, 158, 175
Toney, Buck, 165
Tooker, Elisabeth, 95
Traditions: Big House ceremony, 72, 101; Big House, origin of, 56, 57–59, 60, 74–76, 79, 87–89, 96–98, 118–19, 121–22; Cayuga False Faces, 86; creation of the world, 26–27; Creator, visit by, 41–42; end of the world, 102; Evil Spirit created beings, 103; Mesingw, origin of, 74–76, 119–20, 162; Munsee-Mahican, 134–35; races created separately, 42; tortoise, 102; vision quest, origin of, 103
Tribes: Cayugas, 86, 146; Cherokees, 17, 55, 95; Conoys, 30, 32; Eastern Oklahoma Delawares, 5, 17, 55, 61, 73, 87, 95, 96, 98, 134–35, 147, 151, 180; Iroquois, 146; Kansas Delawares, 3, 17, 18, 49, 55, 73, 87, 162; Mahicans, 23, 117, 126; Munsee-Mahican, 126–46; Munsees (Minsis), 23, 74, 79, 80, 83, 86, 96, 98, 117, 120, 126, 135; Nanticokes, 30, 74, 117; Peorias, 151; Shawnees, 17, 151, 177; Six Nations Reserve (Can.) community, 50, 86; White River (Ind.) Delawares, 38–48; Wiechquaeskecks, 23; Wyandottes, 46
Tulip bag, 173
Turkey or fowl group, 10, 18, 53, 56, 59, 62, 69, 71, 94, 97, 101, 117, 156, 165, 183, 186, 189
Turtle group, 10, 53, 56, 59, 62, 69, 71, 94, 95, 97, 101, 103, 117, 122, 156, 159, 165, 183, 186
Turtle-shell rattle, 10, 13, 32, 36, 39, 45, 50–51, 52, 53, 54, 56, 59–60, 65, 69, 70, 80, 82, 85, 90, 91, 92, 100, 101, 111, 112, 114, 115, 136–38, 141, 143, 145, 149, 157, 161, 164, 174, 176, 178, 184, 187, 189, 190, 193; addressed as grandfathers, 103, 107
Twelve, symbolism of: altar stones, 30; days and nights of ceremony, 4, 5, 13–16, 17, 50, 51, 53, 54, 56 59, 62, 63, 70, 80, 87, 97, 98, 101, 114, 148, 156, 159, 162, 165, 166; days of Turkey group rites, 117; deer eaten at ceremony feast, 53, 81; jumps by vision dancers, 51; levels of heaven, 4, 58–59, 70, 72, 87, 98, 101, 105, 115; of Machtuzin, 37;

masked dancers, 143–44; members of Mask Society, 85; Mesingw post carvings, 3, 59, 72, 87, 89, 105, 152, 166, 182, 183, 188; prayer calls, 51, 67, 69, 70, 71, 83, 92, 93, 112, 150, 152, 159, 165, 187, 193, 194; prayers, 51, 190, 191; prayers for hunters, 67; prayer sticks, 68, 79, 80, 90, 98, 185, 193; ritual hunters, 53, 126; songs, 70, 92, 93, 152, 161; things created by Great Spirit, 84; times for sweeping visionary path, 59, 64, 70, 118; tobacco offerings, 67; tug-of-war, 133
Twenyucis, 126–28

Unala'tko (Unalachtego), 74, 94
Unami, 73, 80, 82, 94, 96, 143, 147, 180
University of Pennsylvania, 151

van der Donck, Adriaen, 23
van Rensselaer, Kiliaen, 23
Vinita, Okla., 177
Visions: acquisition or quest, 5, 33, 34, 50, 59, 60, 84, 103, 107–108, 126–28, 149, 152–53, 154, 156, 167, 170; recitation, 5, 8, 10, 13, 34–35, 36, 39, 45, 50–51, 52, 53, 54, 56, 59–60, 65, 82, 84, 91, 101, 103, 104–105, 107–108, 136–38, 145, 149–50, 152, 156, 161, 164, 167, 170, 176, 178, 182, 184, 185, 187, 189, 190; visionaries, 5, 8, 10, 14, 19, 39, 50–51, 53, 54, 60, 65, 81, 82, 84, 91, 98, 101, 104, 107, 119, 126, 128, 136–38, 149, 152, 154, 156, 158, 161, 164, 176, 184, 185, 186, 187, 190, 194; visionary imposters, 137; women's recitation (Ahtehumwi), 5, 10, 13, 14, 69–70, 91–92, 113–14, 150, 154, 158, 161, 166, 167, 182, 186, 193

Walam Olum, 58
Wallace, Anthony F. C., 38
Wampum (shell beads), 13, 16, 27, 30, 36, 37, 46, 50, 51, 53, 57, 60, 67, 68, 69, 70, 71, 82, 84, 85, 90, 92, 93, 98, 99, 101, 110, 112, 113, 115, 118, 150, 157, 168, 169, 171–72, 174, 177, 183, 186, 187, 191, 192, 193; embodies Delaware religion, 172; symbolic heart of Delaware religion, 118
Wampum, John (Chief Waubuno), 50, 53–54
Wapanachki, 135–36, 142, 143
Washington, Fred, 19, 165, 178
Washington, George, 166, 168
Washington, Jane, 167, 178
Washington, Joe, 18, 116, 117, 118, 155, 164, 166, 167, 168, 169, 173, 174
Washington County, Okla., 3, 16–18, 21
Webber, Charlie, 13, 95–115, 117, 155, 173
White, Mary, 153–54
White Oak (Okla.), 177
White River (Ind.), 38
Whites: forbidden to enter Big House, 17, 57, 149, 156, 168; prohibitions against their tools, implements, and religion, 45; spirits will not come, 25, 29; whiskey, usury, and other evils brought by, 42
Willets, Lucy Wilson, 186
Willits, Lucy (Mrs. Blackwing), 166, 167, 182, 186
Wilson, Frank, 8, 18–19, 122, 155, 157, 164–65, 166, 173, 176, 181, 188
Wilson, John, 21
Wilson, Reuben, 155, 189
Wilson, William, 157, 186, 193
Witchcraft, fear of, 41, 46
Woapicamikunk (Muncie, Ind.), 38, 40, 42, 43, 44
Wolf, James, 79
Wolf group, 8, 18, 49, 53, 56, 59, 62, 65, 69, 71, 94, 97, 101, 117, 118, 121, 151, 154, 156, 165, 169, 173, 175, 183, 186, 189
Wooden bowl, 98, 106, 115, 186, 192
Woodward, Fred, 155
Woolaroc Museum (Okla.), 168

Yonkers, N.Y., 23

Zeisberger, David, 35–37, 74, 80

www.ingramcontent.com/pod-product-compliance
Lightning Source LLC
Chambersburg PA
CBHW080243170426
43192CB00014BA/2546